WILEY

iPad™ Fully Loaded

Published by
Wiley Publishing, Inc.
10475 Crosspoint Boulevard
Indianapolis, IN 46256
www.wiley.com

Copyright © 2011 by Wiley Publishing, Inc., Indianapolis, Indiana

Published simultaneously in Canada

ISBN: 978-0-470-87824-8

Manufactured in the United States of America

10 9 8 7 6 5 4 3 2 1

For general information on our other products and services or to obtain technical support, please contact our Customer Care Department within the U.S. at (800) 762-2974, outside the U.S. at (317) 572-3993 or fax (317) 572-4002.

Wiley also publishes its books in a variety of electronic formats. Some content that appears in print may not be available in electronic books.

Library of Congress Control Number: 2010937811

About the Author

ALAN HESS

Alan is a San Diego-based commercial photographer and author, specializing in concert and event photography. He has also photographed everything from portraits to products. He is the author of four Digital Field Guides: *The Composition Digital Field Guide, The Exposure Digital Field Guide, the Sony A200 Digital Field Guide* and the *Sony A700 Digital Field Guide*. His concert and backstage images appear in numerous online and print publications and they've been used for promotional purposes, including music packaging.

Alan has written for *Photoshop User Magazine* and teaches concert photography and workflow at Photoshop World.

He is a huge computer nut and tends to live on the bleeding edge of technology. A long-time Apple user, Alan eagerly awaits the announcement every year from Cupertino and has been an iPod, iPhone and iPad user from the day these devices were released.

Alan can be contacted through his Web site, **www.alanhessphotography.com**, where he publishes a regular blog. You can follow Alan on Twitter, where he goes by ShotLivePhoto.

Credits

Acquisitions Editor
Courtney Allen

Project Editor
Jenny Brown

Technical Editor
Chris Tome

Copy Editor
Jenny Brown

Editorial Manager
Robyn Siesky

Business Manager
Amy Knies

Senior Marketing Manager
Sandy Smith

Vice President and Executive Group Publisher
Richard Swadley

Vice President and Publisher
Barry Pruett

Book Designer
Erik Powers

Media Development Project Manager
Laura Moss

Media Development Assistant Project Manager
Jenny Swisher

Acknowledgments

To my family and friends, thanks for putting up with me as I walked around with my nose buried in the iPad, muttering to myself as I found another cool app or function—or became disgruntled by one. I wish I could tell you that now that the book is written I will put the iPad down… but that's really not that likely. It's just too cool.

Many many thanks to Courtney, Jenny, Chris and Erik for keeping this project on track, keeping me honest and making my words look great. This book really is the combined effort of a group of people and not just me. I really can't thank you all enough.

A special thanks goes to all my Twitter followers who jumped in with suggestions and answers whenever I asked. You are all the best. It's really amazing to get that instant feedback and was really helpful when dealing with this new technology.

As always, a special thanks to my wife Nadra for putting up with my long hours of writing and for her tolerance when I started to carry the iPad with me everywhere!

For Nadra

Contents

Chapter 8: News — 105

Chapter 9: Music — 123

Chapter 10: Photography — 137

PART 3: INTERNET CONTENT — 159

Chapter 11: E-mail — 161

Introduction

I love new technology.

Really, I do.

I was among the eager mass of people who tuned in on January 27, 2010, to see what new "must-have" gadget Steve Jobs had in store for us. That was the day he revealed the iPad.

I immediately knew I wanted one; I just didn't know why.

Then came that long wait for the UPS driver to … finally … arrive with my iPad on April 3, 2010. It was the longest 65 days ever!

Ok, So I'm exaggerating a little, but I really was excited for the new device, and I was not alone. The iPad is considered one of the biggest success stories in the world of consumer electronics. Indeed, it's been quite a year, and I've found that the only thing better than having a great new piece of technology is getting the most out of it. And that's what this book is all about—how to get the most out of your iPad by getting the most onto it.

This is a book about iPad content. Music, videos, books, PDFs, word documents, Internet radio, and even comic books can be part of your iPad experience. And there's even more …

BEFORE WE GET STARTED

The original iPad came in six different versions, but they can really be broken into two categories: those with Wi-Fi only and those with Wi-Fi and 3G. Each of these two models comes in three different memory sizes: 16GB, 32GB and 64GB.

All the first generation iPads came with a 9.7-inch diagonal touch screen display, weigh about 1.5 lbs and are half an inch thick. This book will cover both the Wi-Fi and the Wi-Fi / 3G models along with the pros and cons of each.

THE WI-FI VERSION

The Wi-Fi-only version of the iPad has a built-in 802.11a/b/g/n chip. This allows it to connect to the fastest Wi-Fi networks: the 802.11n networks. The thing is that the iPad can function great without being on a network at all, but certain features will not be available.

Functions that require an Internet connection include Mail, Web browsing, the iTunes Store, the App Store, the iBooks Store and many other apps. So using the Wi-Fi iPad, especially when you're away from your home or office can require a little planning. You need to make sure that you load your iPad with all the content you'll need until you find a Wi-Fi access point.

WI-FI / 3G VERSION

The Wi-Fi / 3G version of the iPad costs more than the Wi-Fi-only model. This makes sense, because the 3G version does more. Primarily, it connects to 3G networks, which offers much more functionality. But there is another cost, and this is the price of the data plan you have to buy to access the 3G network.

As I write this, there are only two options for data here in USA, and both are through AT&T. You can get either 250MB per month for $14.99 or a 2GB plan for $25 a month. So, if you have the cheapest data plan, it'll cost you $179.88 per year. If you go with the bigger data plan, that totals about $300 a year.

A 16GB iPad with Wi-Fi and 3G goes for $629.00. Add to that the big data plan, and you've spent more than $1200 in 24 months. Yeah, iPads aren't cheap.

One nice thing about the data plans is that they run for 30 days and not per the calendar month, so if you need a data plan and sign up for one, then you have 30 days for data. Each country has its own plans and providers, so check in your area. But do the math first, so you're prepared for the hidden costs and understand the true overall price you're paying for data.

It's also important to know that the data plans are set to automatically renew. So unless you travel frequently in areas without Wi-Fi service, you might want to turn off the auto renew. Check with your data provider on how to do this.

Another thing you need to know about using the 3G data plan: It has a limit. You can't download more than 20MB at a time over the 3G network. This means it's not possible to download movies or TV shows on your iPad unless you're connected to a Wi-Fi network. There are also some apps that are too big to be downloaded via the 3G network and require Wi-Fi.

ONE LAST THING

A term that's used over and over in this book is: *Tap*. Since the iPad is controlled with your fingers, all you do is tap on menu choices or icons to select them. There is no mouse, so there's no way to *click* on anything on your iPad.

Those are the basics. Now, let's get started …

PART 1

Content Basics

Content

The Skim

Images • PDFs • Business Files • Books
Audio • Videos • Moving Content

This book is all about getting, sharing and using various types of content on your iPad, so it seems to be a good idea to run through the basics of content. This chapter describes the different types of content available in this digital age and points out what can (and can't) be used on the iPad. Here we go …

IMAGE FILES

The iPad is great for viewing images. For details on this type of content, take a look at Chapter 10: Photography. It goes into more depth than we will here about what kinds of images can and can't be used on the iPad. Here's an overview:

JPEG

This image type was created and named for the Joint Photographic Experts Group and is a method of reducing an image file size via compression while keeping the quality high. The JPEG format is quite common on the Internet, because it doesn't require any special software. All Web browsers and most e-mail programs will allow users to view JPEG images right from the program; the iPad is no different.

TIFF

The Tagged Image File Format is also a tool for saving images with no loss of image quality. There's no compression here though, so TIFF files are rather

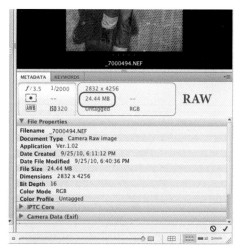

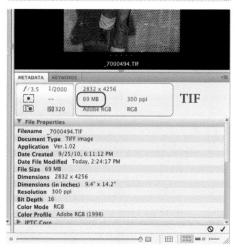

large. But because of its widespread acceptance, most TIFF files are supported natively on the iPad. Note that not all TIFF types are supported, so make sure to try them out.

GIF

The Graphics Interchange Format is a bit-map image format that was introduced way back in 1987. It has since become one of the default methods for graphics on the Internet. File quality of GIF images can be very low, because the method used to create the small file sizes throws away a lot of color info. GIF images are supported natively on the iPad.

RAW

This type of image is created by individual camera manufacturers, so support is hit or miss. As of right now, RAW files are only sup-ported on the iPad when they are imported through the Camera Connection Kit (covered in Chapters 10 and 19). And since RAW files are created by camera manufactures, it might take awhile for newer file types to be sup-ported by the iPad.

PDF FILES

PDFs are used everywhere, and this format is very useful. Created originally in 1993 by Adobe Systems, the Portable Document For-mat is independent of software and hardware and even operating systems. In 2008, Adobe officially released the PDF as an open stan-dard, meaning there would be no commercial software needed to create or read these files.

Figure 1-1
These three captures show the same file: the RAW image, the JPEG image and the TIFF image. It's important to see the difference in file size among
the three.

4

Throughout this book, you'll see that there are a lot of uses for PDF files. In fact, if there is one file type you should heed (even at the expense of others), it is the PDF. I say this because PDFs can be used in so many different apps.

For starters, PDFs can be read natively in the iBooks application and mail programs. And the business iWork applications on the iPad uses PDF files, and many of the document reader apps have PDF support built in, too.

BUSINESS FILES

This group of file types is traditionally used in business, but they also apply to anyone in school or who just likes to write or play with numbers or do presentations.

Word

There are actually two different types of Microsoft Word documents. The first are files with the .doc extension. This covers older documents … going back to Word for DOS and up to Word 97, 2000, 2003 and 2004 for Windows as well as Word 98, 2001x and 2004 for Mac.

The second type of Word file ends in the .docx extension, which is used by Word 2007 for the PC and Word 2008 for the Mac. This extension will be used by Microsoft going forward.

The iPad supports both types of Word files natively and can view these file types without any extra apps. See Chapter 15 for more on the iPad's word processing capabilities.

Excel

There are two Excel spreadsheet file types that the iPad can read and view without extra help. These are files that use the .xls and the .xlsx extensions. The older Binary Interchange File Format (BIFF) file types must be translated

in Excel before they can be used on the iPad. Fortunately, these file types are becoming increasingly rare. See Chapter 16 to learn more about working with spreadsheets on the iPad.

PowerPoint

As with Word and Excel, there are two different PowerPoint file types that can be seen on the iPad. These are .ppt and the .pptx files. Chapter 17 covers iPad tools for creating fantastic presentations.

Pages

The iWork Pages application is Apple's version of a word processor. Since there is a Pages app for the iPad, it makes sense that all Pages documents can be viewed natively on the iPad, even if a user doesn't have the app installed. To open *and edit* Pages files, you do need the Pages app. This is covered in Chapter 15.

Numbers

Numbers is the Apple iWork spreadsheet program, and all Numbers spreadsheets are viewable on the iPad. There is a Numbers app available for the iPad that allows editing of Numbers documents. Chapter 16 provides

Figure 1-2

Send multiple attachments that can be downloaded on the iPad.

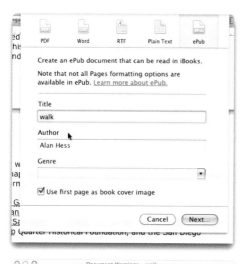

Figure 1-3

The export menu in Pages allows you to create an ePub from your Pages file.

TIP

Using Pages to create an ePub is really easy. Instead of saving a file, click file> export and then pick "ePub" from your options. You can now import and read your document in the iBooks app.

great information on the capabilities of the Numbers app and other tools available for number crunching on the iPad.

Keynote

Along with Pages and Numbers, Keynote is part of the Apple iWork application suite. Presentations created in Keynote are viewable on the iPad in the Mail app without extra software. There is a Keynote app that allows editing of Keynote files on the iPad. Learn more in Chapter 17.

Text

A text file (.txt) is the simplest file type. It contains basic text and can be read on the iPad.

Rich Text

Rich Text Documents (.rtf) are created and owned by Microsoft. This type of file is used mainly inside Microsoft applications and when dealing with different operating systems (e.g., Windows and Apple OS).

BOOK FILES

The iPad makes a great electronic book reader. To offer that service though, it needs books. The iBooks app uses the ePub file format for its electronic books. This is covered more in Chapter 4, but it's helpful to know that the iBooks app also treats PDFs as books. This means that any PDF can be read inside the iBooks app as well.

Newer versions of the Pages application allow you to export your documents as ePubs. So anyone can create a file that will be treated as a book on the iPad.

AUDIO FILES

The iPad has built-in support for a ton of audio formats. I guess this isn't much of a surprise since the iPad is part of a long line of media players that starts with the iPod, the most popular music player ever. The following audio formats are supported on the iPad and can be played through the iTunes app.

AAC (16 to 320 Kbps)

The Advanced Audio Coding format is a standard lossy compression audio format that reduces a file's size by getting rid of some of the data.

HE-AAC (V1)

High-Efficiency Advanced Audio Coding is an extension of the AAC audio format. It is mainly used when every bit counts and the file size needs to be as small as possible, as when streaming audio. Think digital radio.

Protected AAC (from iTunes Store)

This version of the AAC file is protected by Digital Rights Management (DRM), so the content bought through the iTunes Store can be played on only authorized devices.

MP3

This audio format uses a lossy data compression to make small audio files that still sound good. Many audiophiles claim that the loss of audio data harms the sound and that the trade off between size and quality just isn't worth it. But this is still a very popular format … mainly because it has been around for a long time.

It is possible to create MP3 files with different amounts of compression, resulting in different sized files with different levels of audio quality. And the iPad plays them all, including the MP3 VBR files, which have a variable bit rate and need a layer III decoder to play back.

Audible (formats 2, 3 and 4)

This is a proprietary DRM-protected format used for audiobooks.

Apple Lossless

This is a lossless audio compression that was developed by Apple and usually has the extension of .m4a. This format has no DRM built in, but many think it could have this added in the future. All Apple products, including the iPad, can play the Apple Lossless format with no problems.

AIFF

Audio Interchange File Format is an audio format developed in 1988 to store audio files on a personal computer. It was developed by Apple and is mostly used on Apple computers, so it's no surprise to see it supported here. The data in a standard AIFF file is uncompressed; therefore it takes up more space than a compressed audio file.

WAV

Waveform Audio File Format was developed by Microsoft and IBM for storing audio on PCs. The format is very similar to AIFF, and the audio data is stored in an uncompressed manner, which means larger files.

VIDEO FILES

The iPad has a great screen and can be used to play video in the following formats.

H.264

This standard in video compression is used in a variety of applications, including YouTube videos and content purchased through the iTunes Store. The H.264 compression grew from a need to provide good video quality at a small file size. It now encompasses a wide range of video types and, to get technical for a moment, the actual limitations on playback on the iPad are as follows: H.264 video provides up to 720p, 30 frames per second and a Main Profile level 3.1. Files need to be in the .m4v, .mp4 and .mov formats.

Figure 1-4
Use QuickTime to create different file types of video clips. QuickTime even has presets for different types of devices.

MPEG-4

This is a set of standards used for compressing video and audio that the Moving Pictures Experts Group (MPEG) agreed on in 1998. The iPad can play MPEG-4 video up to 2.5 Mbps, 640 by 480 pixels, 30 frames per second … with movies that use the file extensions .m4v, .mp4 and .mov.

M-JPEG

Motion JPEG is a video format that compresses each of the individual frames of a movie. It was originally developed for multimedia applications, but it's falling out of use as more advanced methods of compression are replacing it. On the iPad, the M-JPEG movies can be up to 35 Mbps, 1280 by 720 pixels, 30 frames per second and in the .avi file format.

CONTACT FILES

The address book on the iPad uses vCards (.vcf) to store information about your contacts. This is good, because .vcf files are accepted by most address book programs, and this means you can export your contacts via e-mail and share them with others. It also means you can get e-mails with attached .vcf files and have new contact information imported into your address book quite easily.

MOVING CONTENT

It's great to have content on your iPad and on your computer, but it's even better to be able to move that content from one to the other. There are two ways to do it. You can use the USB cable or move files via wireless transfer.

Sync vs. Transfer

These two actions may sound the same, but there is a real difference between syncing data and transferring data between the computer and iPad.

Syncing refers to the process of transferring data from a computer to the iPad using iTunes. When you sync data, you install content from your iTunes library to your iPad. This content includes music, movies, TV shows, podcasts, audiobooks, iBooks and even photos. Note that the photos are actually transferred from iPhoto on the Mac or My Photos on a PC ... not from iTunes.

When you *transfer* data from the computer to your iPad (or from the iPad to a computer), you're working with data that can be used on the iPad but isn't part of your iTunes library. This can include Word documents, PDFs, Excel spreadsheets, comic files, image files, and a host of other file types. These files can be transferred through iTunes, using the supplied USB cable; they can also be transferred wirelessly over the network.

USB Cable

The iPad comes with a USB 2.0 cable that connects your iPad (or iPhone, iPod etc)—directly or through a dock—to your comput-

Figure 1-5
Take a look at the transfer screen
in iTunes.

er's USB port for syncing and charging. This is the fastest way to sync information from the computer to your iPad and from the iPad back to the computer. For some content, it is the only way.

File transfers with the USB cable are done through iTunes on the computer, and this can actually be quite difficult to find. The basics are below, and information on how to transfer specific types of files with specific programs is provided later in the book.

1. Open iTunes on the computer.

2. Attach the USB cable to the computer and the iPad.

3. Select the iPad from the device list on the left side of the iTunes window.

4. Select "Apps" from the tabs across the top of the screen.

5. Scroll until you see the "File Sharing" window.

File Sharing is the area that allows you to transfer application-specific files on and off the iPad. The transfers happen without totally syncing the device. When you transfer a file to a specific app, it is indeed performing a sync, but not a system-wide one.

Wireless Transfer

There is no official method for syncing an iPad and a computer wirelessly. What you can do wirelessly is transfer files to and from the iPad using a variety of third-party apps. Some of these work better than others, but all basically do the same thing. They allow files to be transferred to and from the iPad using a wireless connection. My favorite app in this category is Dropbox. It allows me to access the same files on my computer, the Internet and on my iPad. There is a lot more about Dropbox in Chapter 15. Check it out.

iTunes

The Skim

There's a lot you can do with the iPad as a stand-alone device. But the iPad can't be used without first connecting it to a computer that's running iTunes. And while you can get away with not using iTunes on a computer much after that, it is more efficient and easier to use iTunes to manage and interact with your iPad in almost every way. So I suggest that you get the two warmly acquainted.

Yes, this book is about the iPad. Specifically, it is about how to create, manage and use content on the iPad. It most certainly is not a book about iTunes. But the two are so closely related that some talk about iTunes is more than necessary.

Now, to be clear, there are two versions of iTunes: one lives on your computer and the other is an app that you see on your iPad. The iTunes software that runs on your computer (Mac or PC) is a free program from Apple. This is basically a program that stores and organizes your media and allows your files to be used on the computer and on multiple devices, including iPhones, iPods and iPads.

There is a component of the iTunes program that's called the *iTunes Store*. (The iTunes Store is covered in the next chapter.) For now, just know that this store makes it very easy to get content, including music, movies, TV shows, audiobooks, apps and podcasts. The draw is that free content is available (like podcasts and classes on iTunes University), but there is much to buy.

Let's not kid ourselves; Apple is in business to make money. And the iTunes Store is a for-profit enterprise. So the version of iTunes that's on the iPad is the iTunes Store for music, movies, TV shows, podcasts, audiobooks and iTunes U. There is a separate app-based store for books (iBooks) and yet another for apps (App Store). These different stores allow users to buy content for the iPad—directly through the device.

Apple makes it attractive and easy for users to use iTunes, because it limits sharing of purchased content. Since an iPad can only be synced with a single iTunes account,

Figure 2-1
The iTunes interface. As you can see, on the left is a column where you can choose the type of content to view. Options include the iTunes Store, any devices attached to the computer (including the iPad), any shared iTunes libraries, the Genius menu and playlists. On the right is music shown in Cover mode by artists.

purchased content is restricted to a single user. Content is not shared among multiple accounts on multiple devices, and this helps keep the music, television and movie companies happy.

ITUNES BASICS

Remember: iTunes is an application that stores, manages, accesses and plays back your media. It is the all-in-one solution to playing your music, movies, TV shows, audiobooks and podcasts. If you're reading this, chances are you've already used iTunes, so I'll keep this really short and sweet.

SET UP AND SYNC

The first time you plug in your new iPad to your computer and launch iTunes, you'll need to name the device and decide how the iPad will deal with content when it is attached to iTunes—now and in the future.

Chances are good that you already have a healthy amount of content in iTunes, so we need to take that into account as well. My best advice is to name the iPad and uncheck the other three options on the screen.

Make sure only the box for "Open iTunes when this iPad is connected" is checked. We will add content manually and not give iTunes too much power. A fundamental problem with going the automatic route is that you probably have way more media in your iTunes library than you have space for on your iPad.

Why Sync?

You may be thinking that you won't use iTunes much since you can buy content directly on the iPad. But there are some good reasons to sync your iPad with iTunes on your Mac or PC … even though you don't have to. Keep these in mind:

- Every time you sync, the computer backs up all the data from your iPad. So if something happens to your iPad or something goes wrong (envision a case of data corruption or interrupted software update), your data can be recovered from your computer.

- It's easier to arrange the icons on your iPad screens using the iTunes interface than to do it on the iPad itself.

- Syncing is the fastest way to get data files on and off the iPad, especially when working with a large number of image files.

- Syncing is the only way to get purchased content from your computer version of iTunes onto your iPad.

- This is by far the easiest way to get your music and movies and TV shows from your computer onto the iPad.

- If you have a season pass to a TV show, syncing is the only way to get new episodes from your computer onto the iPad.

Interaction Settings

For best results, be sure to set up how iTunes and the iPad will play with each other. When they play nice together, it makes your life a lot easier. Here's how to get them going down the right path:

1. Make sure the iPad is turned on and then plug it into the computer with the included USB cable. Launch iTunes on the computer. The iPad will appear in the devices list on the left. There, click on "iPad" to bring up its info.

2. The first screen that comes up on the computer is the basic info spread. From here you can use the tabs across the top of the window to control the media that you put

on the iPad. But first things first. It's time to set your preferences on the front page.

3. You'll see that the front page is divided into three sections. The first shows info for the attached iPad, including its Name, Capacity, Software Version and Serial Number. The second area is all about making sure you're running the latest version of the iPad software. This area also gives you the ability to restore your iPad to its original settings, which is a good option if the device starts having problems that cannot be fixed easily in other ways. The third window is the Options menu. Here you'll find the main tools for managing your iPad, and these are important.

4. Two of the managing tools directly affect how much space you have available on your iPad. They are "Convert higher bit rate songs to 128 kbps AAC" (which creates lower-quality audio files that take up less space than those with higher bit rates) and the "Prefer Standard Definition" videos option (which tells the iPad to use standard definition videos instead of HD videos if both are present) This, too,

Figure 2-2

This shows the iPad summary window when it is attached to a computer and iTunes and running.

decreases the amount of space a certain file will require on your device.

4. From this menu, you can also set up iTunes to encrypt your iPad backup. This is very useful if you are connecting to a shared computer … at work, the library, etc. You can also configure the Universal Access for the iPad, if needed, here. Universal Access allows you to set a voice-over or zoom, change to a white-on-black display, speak auto-text for those with impaired eyesight, and change to mono audio for hearing devices.

ADD MEDIA

There are a few different ways to add media to your iTunes library. The first and easiest is to buy content directly from Apple through the iTunes Store. When you do, the media and all the information associated with it is loaded onto your computer—ready to go.

You can also easily transfer (or *rip*) music from a CD into iTunes by inserting it into the CD drive of your computer. iTunes will give you a pop-up box that offers the option to import the music. (Find more on this in Chapter 9: Music.)

You can use the "Add to Library" command by following the steps below:

1. Go to File > Add to Library.

2. In the Mac version of iTunes, there is one "Add to Library" command that allows you to add a single media file or a whole folder of files. In the Windows version, you choose to add either a file or a folder.

3. Select the music or video file (or folder) you want to import into iTunes.

4. On the Mac, click the "Choose" button. On the PC, this button is labeled "OK" for a single file and "Open" for a whole folder.

Yet another way to add media to iTunes is to drag and drop files right into your iTunes program from the Apple finder window or the Windows Explorer window. You can drop the file onto the iTunes interface or the desktop icon.

Note: Just because a media file (such as the one you just loaded into iTunes) will play in iTunes doesn't necessarily mean it will play on your iPad. You'll usually find out if a file is not compatible with the iPad when you sync. If iTunes tells you that it couldn't transfer a certain file because it isn't the right file type, then you know you need some help.

And good news … help is available! iTunes can convert most movie and audio files because it has access to QuickTime and can use the codec to create a compatible version of the file. Just click the "Advanced" tab and see what versions of the file iTunes can create. Menu choices include "Create iPad" and "Apple TV." Just click the best option for your needs and forget about it. Apple will take care of the rest.

PLAYLISTS

Playlists are really powerful and, if used properly, can help you organize the media that you carry with you on the iPad. The first step to benefitting from playlists is to actually set up a few. There are two types of playlists: Plain Playlists (referred to as playlists from now on) and Smart Playlists.

Make a Playlist.

It's really easy to make an iTunes playlist. Just click the (+) button on the bottom left of the iTunes window or click File>New Playlist.

In both cases, an untitled playlist folder will appear in the column on the left side of the iTunes window. It'll already be highlighted; so just type a name for your list, hit

"Enter" (or "Return"), and you'll be ready to add songs and build your playlist.

Picking the right name for your playlist is kind of important, because it acts as your visual clue when you search for a playlist later. For example, my workout playlist has an hour of fast-tempo songs, and my travel playlist is a much broader collection of music I might want for a trip … when I might not have access to my computer for awhile. When quickly searching for the right playlist, it wouldn't help to have these files named, for example, by the date they were created.

Adding content to a playlist is easy. Just drag a selected music file from the right side of the window to the playlist. Drop it on the playlist title you want to populate. That's it. Now you can click on the new playlist to open it. You'll see the list of music there, so you can re-arrange the order of the content, delete items or just listen.

Keep in mind that if you delete an item from a playlist, it does not delete the track from your iTunes library; it simply removes it from that playlist. This is because the "files" in a playlist are actually links to the real content, which is saved to your iTunes library.

There is one other way to quickly make a playlist, and that is to drag any file, album or selection of files from the right side of the iTunes window to the left side. Make sure that your selection isn't hovering over any of the already-created playlists, and when you see a small green (+) sign, let go. This will instantly create a playlist with all the content you selected.

For example, say I want a playlist with all the Beatles songs I have in my iTunes library. But, crap, I realize there are a few of these songs

Figure 2-3
When you drag an album to the left-side menu—in this case, it is the Billy Idol album—a green (+) appears. This allows you to quickly create a playlist that contains all the songs from that album.

I'm a bit sick of hearing. I could make a smart playlist, but that would be overkill for this. So I just go to my music library and select all the Beatles songs. Then I drag that selection to the left side and let go. Now I have a Beatles playlist that I can edit. I can remove the files I don't want to add to my device, and voilá! Yup, it's that easy.

Create a Smart Playlist.
The real power of playlists is with *Smart* Play-lists. These nifty creatures can change the way you use iTunes and listen to your music.

Smart playlists are created automatically using criteria that you define. This means that you don't have to spend a lot of time dragging and dropping and searching for files to popu-late your playlist. iTunes will do it for you!

Here's how to set up a smart playlist:

1. Open iTunes.

2. Click File> New Smart Playlist. This opens the Smart Playlist rule. (See figure.)

3. In this window, you define the criteria that Apple will use to create your playlist. Use

15

multiple rules together to define an ultra-awesome playlist.

4. Add rules to determine and/or limit the variable(s) iTunes will use to select content.

5. Once all the rules have been entered, just click "OK" and the smart playlist will show up in the list on the left side of the window.

6. Now, name that set of tunes and enjoy!

When you create a smart rule for iTunes, you define what type of data the rule finds and how it treats that data. And when you're done adding a rule, you can add a second or third or fourth (or more!). You can also add nested rules. Find information on building space-saving rules in Chapter 9.

Figure 2-4

This smart playlist rule set will pick out comedy albums I bought in 2010.

Figure 2-5

To find all the versions in your iTunes library of the Grateful Dead's *Sugar Magnolia* and *Sunshine Daydream*, this is the list to build.

When you add a second rule to a smart playlist, you suddenly get an option (at the top of the Rules window) to "Match all of the rules" or "Match any of the rules." So let's say you have a rule that states, "The Artist contains the Beatles" and a rule that states "The Genre contains pop." If you tell iTunes to match all the rules, then it will select only Beatles songs that are also labeled as pop. If you tell it to match any of the rules, then it will select all the Beatles songs as well as all songs labeled as pop.

The rules are definitely not limited to music. They work great for video and all the other content in iTunes. For instance, Figure 2-4 shows a multi-rule iTunes smart playlist that will select all the Comedy Albums that I bought from iTunes this year. Figure 2-5 shows a playlist that pulls out all the versions of *Sugar Magnolia* and *Sunshine Daydream* by the Grateful Dead that are in my iTunes library.

And while it's possible to mix file types in a playlist, as in putting video and audio in the same playlist, don't do it. If you do, say, combine videos with audio in a single playlist, you'll be able to see audio files in the iPod player on your iPad, but the videos will not show up in either the iPod player or the video player. So keep life simpler for yourself by not mixing audio and video in the same playlist.

There is a lot more information about smart playlists in this book, especially on how to keep the media on your iPad new and fresh. Here, I just wanted to tell you how to make them.

MANAGE CONTENT

When it comes to loading content onto the iPad, I like to be in full control. So I manually work through the options on each of the tabs (described on the next few pages) when my iPad is attached to the computer.

INFO

This section is the place for syncing your Address Book contacts, iCal calendars, Mail accounts, Bookmarks and Notes. It's also where you can replace this content on the iPad (by checking the box). This area can be very confusing to iPad users, because it seems like these items must be checked to get the info from the computer to the iPad. The truth is, it's easier and more convenient to have all this done automatically and wirelessly than during a sync. In fact, there are actually warnings with most of these selections that if you use them, you may end up with duplicate information. Since most of my information syncs wirelessly, I have none of these checked.

APPS

This is the window that allows you to add all those cool apps and data files for specific applications on the iPad. It's also easy to organize your apps and decide where they'll be located screen-by-screen on your iPad from this window. You can sort the apps by name, category, date or size. Once an application is selected to be synced onto the iPad, you can move it around and place it wherever you want. It's much easier to do all that on the computer en masse than on the actual iPad.

MUSIC

Want music on your iPad? This is the place to add it. I have the "Sync Music" button checked and, instead of trying to sync the entire music library, I select the playlists, artists and genres I want. There are lots of options here and they are covered in detail in Chapter 9. The important thing to know here is this is the place to choose what playlists to sync to your iPad.

Figure 2-6
This Sync Music window for the iPad is showing where you can select playlists versus the entire library.

MOVIES

Use this tab to add movies to the iPad. A cool thing about this area is that you can see the size of each movie file right next to its icon. This is important because the movie files are BIG and can take up a lot of space on your iPad. *Avatar,* for example, is 2.35 GB while *Sherlock Holmes* is 1.79 GB. With files this size, you can imagine how easy it is to fill an entire iPad with movies very fast.

TV SHOWS

Apple sells a lot of TV shows, and I have a season or two of my favorites on my iPad. Here is where shows can be added to your iPad. You can automatically sync a selection of shows based on rules, much like a simple smart playlist. For instance, I have my list set to automatically transfer all unwatched episodes of the shows in my library. This means that new episodes of shows that I download with my season pass will be added to my iPad automatically.

You can also add any episode or season of a TV series by using the "Show" menu. And if you keep scrolling down on this menu, you'll see a place to include episodes from playlists.

In other words, you can make a smart playlist for your TV shows! Find more on this topic in Chapter 6: Television.

PODCASTS

Listen to or watch podcasts? If so, add those to your iPad from here. It's a shame there's not a way to create a smart playlist for podcasts, but you *can* input a single sync rule. I usually have mine set to automatically include all unplayed episodes of selected podcasts, so my favorites stay updated.

iTUNES U

This is the place for syncing all your iTunes University material. It has the same layout and rules as the podcasts section, which makes sense, because this content is just another type of podcast. iTunes U is easy to use. Refer to the section above.

BOOKS

I use the iPad to read books, so I have the "Sync Books" checkbox selected. But since I don't want all my books to be loaded on the iPad at once, I also have the "Selected Books" radio button checked. This allows me to manually choose what books are synced to my iPad at a given time. I have my books sorted by author since that is usually the way I buy books. You can also sort by title.

 In this area, you can select to sync audiobooks as well. Again, I check the "Selected Audio Books" box, because I don't want all the audiobooks in my iTunes library to be on my iPad.

One interesting thing about electronic books is that, since there is no bookstore on the computer, there won't be any iBook files in your iTunes account until you buy them on the iPad and transfer them onto your computer. Note that among your book files in iTunes are any ePub books or PDF files you have imported there.

PHOTOS

The first version of the iPad doesn't have a camera. So while you can't take photos with this iPad, you can use it to look at and share your images. The device is actually really great for showing off your photos, and this area makes it very simple to add photos to your iTunes library.

On the PC side of things, you can select images from any one folder (and subsequent sub-folders) and move them to your iPad. There are many more choices on the Mac, especially if you use iPhoto or Aperture. You can add whole albums and events, or you can use the built-in Faces technology (Apple's attempt at facial recognition) to just add certain people. More on this in Chapter 10 : Photography.

TRANSFER CONTENT

It's easy to buy content for your iPad on the iPad, and it's also easy (and a good idea) to move that content to your iTunes account on a computer. Some content (like iBooks) can only be purchased on the iPad, so this is important for saving your file and retaining space on your iPad. See page 12 for the benefits of using iTunes to back up your iPad content.

When you connect your iPad to a computer, iTunes should tell you if there are purchased items on your device. It will ask if you would like to transfer those items now. If you allow it, all content purchased on the iPad will be transferred to your iTunes account. Or you can click on File>Transfer Purchases from iPad, or right click on the iPad in the Device list and then click on "Transfer Purchases."

After you purchase and transfer content to a computer from the iPad, you will find that there is a new list in the Store section of the

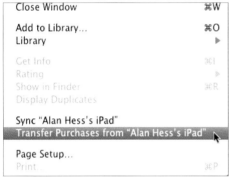

Figure 2-7

Transfer content from an iPad to a computer without having to go through a full sync by right clicking on the device or selecting File>Transfer. Both accomplish the same task.

menu bar; it's called *Purchased on iPad*. This list shows all the content, other than apps, that you've purchased on your iPad.

Note: The content that you buy on the iPad is automatically transferred to the computer when you sync your iPad.

BACK IT UP

Apple might not consider your iPad to be a personal computer; but on many counts, it is much like one. Among the similarities is potential to lose valuable information. To

avoid losing the content that's stored on your iPad, back it up once in awhile. Fortunately, backing up an iPad is very easy. The system is designed so that your iPad is automatically backed up when it syncs with iTunes. You can also back it up by right clicking on the iPad in the Devices list and choosing "Back Up."

The backup you get contains settings and some data, but the process doesn't include iTunes actually acquiring new copies of the media you have on your iPad. Instead, the media (e.g., music, movies, apps and photo content) are already on the computer and will be reloaded when the iPad is restored.

In case you want to know where iTunes stashes your backups, you can find them here:

∘ **On a Mac:**
  ~/USERNAME/Library/Application Support/MobileSync/Backup/

∘ **On Windows XP:**
  \Documents and Settings\ (username)\ApplicationData\ AppleComputer\MobileSync\Backup

∘ **On Windows Vista and Windows 7:**
  \Users\(username)\AppData\Roaming\ AppleComputer\MobileSync\Backup

RESTORE

Sometimes things go wrong. It happens. And when it does, the best course of action is to restore your iPad so that it returns to the factory settings. Then, restore your own setup from a backup. Do this by right clicking on the iPad in the Device menu and choosing "Restore from backup."

When you use the restore function for your iPad, all your data is deleted from the device, including your music, movies, contacts, pho-

Figure 2-8

When you restore an iPad, it will ask if you want to back up the info first.

tos and calendars. The settings return to the factory defaults. Once this happens, you can reload your data from a backup.

To restore your iPad:

1. Open iTunes and plug in the iPad.

2. Select the iPad from the Devices list.

3. Select the "Summary" tab and click the "Restore" button.

You will be prompted to back up your settings before restoring the device to the factory defaults. Whether or not you do this depends on when you last backed up your iPad and how valuable you think the information is that's on it.

From there, you will be prompted to restore the iPad: "Are you sure you want to restore the iPad to its factory settings? All of your media and other data will be erased." It sounds ominous, but if you need to do it and have a backup, then go for it.

When the restoration is complete, you will be asked if you want to use the backup to reload your info onto the iPad. Go ahead and use one of the backups or, if you prefer a clean slate, just say no.

There you have it, a backup and restore for the iPad. My advice is to make sure your iPad is backed up every so often; because, if you do have a crash, it can be a real pain to get everything back to the way you want it without a recent backup.

COMMIT

I have some bad news. I know this won't come as much of a surprise to many, but the iPad is a monogamous thing; it can't interact with multiple iTunes accounts. Once it is tied to an account, it can't sync to another. This is the way it is for an iPod or iPhone, too. But since a lot of people are using the iPad as a replacement for a laptop, this restriction might not be clear.

I can only hope that, at some point, there will be support for multiple accounts on a single iPad. But right now, it isn't there.

This is also true for certain types of e-mail, contact and calendar information. The iPad is meant to be used by one person, and it cannot be set to get e-mail, calendar and contact info for two separate MobileMe or Exchange accounts, for example. So, this means, the iPad can be synced to get my e-mail, contact and calendar info from my MobileMe account, but it can't get the same information from my wife's account. This can cause some problems when two people are trying to share the device, especially if both have a MobileMe account from Apple or use different Microsoft Exchange servers.

So, if you're sharing a single iPad, you have to decide whose information will live on the iPad. Of course, you can always just get a second iPad… Wait! That might be Apple's master plan after all.

MAXIMIZE SPACE

There is quite a difference in price between a 16GB and a 64GB iPad. It's a $200 difference to be precise. And even if you buy the biggest capacity iPad available, at some point you will max it out and need more space. It's just human nature to fill up the space we have available.

So the first thing to know is that even though the iPad says it is a 16GB or 32GB or 64GB model, that's not actually the amount of space you have available to you. As with any storage media, the formatted capacity of your iPad is less than the indicated memory size. For example, the 32GB Wi-Fi /3G model iPad has an actual capacity of 29.04GB—a difference of roughly 3GB, or two feature-length movies and a CD or two. When you plug in the 16GB Wi-Fi version, you actually get 14.02GB of space. This is just something to keep in mind when loading an iPad with content.

There are two things you can do right off the bat to decrease the size of the files on your iPad …and thereby squeeze a little extra space on your device. On the "Summary" page in iTunes, when you connect your iPad to your computer, you'll find "Prefer standard definition videos" and "Convert higher bit rate songs to 128 kbps AAC" in the options panel. Both of these actions reduce the size of your media files, if possible, by reducing quality. Hey, every little bit helps …

I loaded up my iPad, which is a 32GB Wi-Fi / 3G (actual space 29.04 GB), with the following media:

- Audio 6.40 GB
- Video 15.41 GB
- Photos 228.1 MB
- Apps 5.11 GB
- Books 78 MB
- Other 1.14 GB
- Free 698.6 MB

When I activated both of the space-saving boxes on the "Summary" page and clicked "Apply," the iPad automatically started to sync. This time, instead of updating, it was searching for ways to reduce the file sizes. This sync

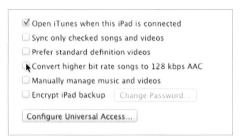

Figure 2-9

In the "Summary" tab, look for the settings to reduce the amount of space your media takes up on the iPad.

can take awhile. And when I say *awhile*, I actually mean a very. long. time. Of course, the exact amount of time it will take for you depends on how much of the data on your iPad needs to be converted and/or updated.

After Apple reduced the media as much as it could, the iPad showed the following usage.

- Audio 3.74 GB
- Video 13.35 GB
- Photos 228.1 MB
- Apps 5.11 GB
- Books 78 MB
- Other 1.12 GB
- Free 5.43 GB

As you can see, the amount of space used by the music files and the video files were reduced quite a bit, and the free space significantly increased—from approximately 700 MB to 5.43 GB. That's a lot—more than enough for a few extra movies. So be sure to use these two settings to get the greatest amount of content onto your iPad.

Okay, you had to know it was coming. There is a catch. The price you pay for space is in the quality of your media files. So if you are a true audiophile or video-quality freak, then the reduction in quality might bother you. But if you usually listen to music through the iPad's speakers or a pair of Apple earbuds, you probably won't notice the demotion of quality.

Similarly, by having the iPad choose standard definition video when possible, you remove the HD video content. Now that we're all getting used to HD, it might bother you to see video in standard format. In that case, uncheck the box and just carry around fewer movies on your iPad. This is all about choices and trade-offs. I can't tell you what to do; I'm just here to describe your options.

STREAM CONTENT

One way to maximize the storage space on your iPad is to stream media instead of loading it onto the device. Think of the difference it would make if all your video and audio content was streamed to the iPad instead of being loaded on it. It would basically give your iPad unlimited storage!

Pandora Internet radio and Netflix are both great examples of streaming media. Pandora allows you to listen to music over the Internet, so none of the music is actually taking up space on your iPad, and Netflix does the same with movies and television shows.

Streaming both music and movies is covered in other chapters, but here is the quick lowdown. If you stream music and video over Wi-Fi, it works really well. But if you go on a trip or find yourself in a place where you are not on a Wi-Fi network, then suddenly you have no content—a real bummer. And the 3G won't get you very far; the caps on 3G bandwidth make streaming with that a crappy option.

In these situations, I've come to appreciate the value of keeping content that's important to me on the iPad. I choose to use precious iPad space to have the things I know I'll want when a network is unavailable. When I'm on an airplane, for example, I want some entertainment. This is usually a book … or five, since the books take up little space … as well as a couple of movies and a few music albums. And, yes, I'll have my favorite photos with maybe a recent podcast or two. All of this fits easily into 16GB—never mind 32GB or 64GB.

OPTIMIZE PDFs

One of the more advanced space-saving techniques for an iPad user comes into play if you use the device for reading and viewing a lot of PDF files. You just need Adobe Acrobat Pro to easily reduce the file sizes. Here's how:

1. Open the file you want to reduce in size.

2. Click Advanced > PDF Optimizer.

3. In the image window, set the color and grayscale images to downsample using bicubic downsampling to 130 ppi for images above 195 ppi.

4. Save the file with a new name.

5. Check the space savings by comparing the before-and-after file sizes.

To use as an example, I tried this on a PDF that was chock full of photos. And the savings were surprisingly huge! The file started out at 103.3 MB and, after reducing the file size, it shrunk to a tiny 7.1 MB. Now this is an extreme example, but it goes to show you that it is possible to squeeze an extra MB or two here and there if you need it.

The amount of space savings will depend on the amount of images present in the original file and, more importantly, their resolution. By reducing the images to 130 ppi, you make them the right resolution for the iPad's screen. Be aware though that this resolution may not be adequate for images that need to be printed or re-sized for a specific application.

The iTunes Store

The Skim

Apple ID • iTunes Store • iTunes App • Media Treatment

The success of the iPod, iPhone and iPad is due in part to the ease of buying new content and accessing it. Apple really hit a home run with the iTunes Store. This is a one-stop online shop that allows you to buy music, TV shows, movies and apps and to download podcasts and access iTunes University. There is no way that a book about the iPad, and especially about *content* on the iPad, could miss a chapter on the iTunes Store. It is the easiest—and in the case of apps, the *only*—way to get a variety of content onto your iPad.

And just because the iTunes Store is a store and is in the business to make money—and it makes a lot of money—you don't actually have to buy anything from the iTunes Store to get content there. Plenty of free content is available for the taking; but chances are you'll end up purchasing content, so it's a good idea to know the best way to do that.

The iTunes Store exists in two different places. The first is on your computer as the iTunes program, shown in Figure 3-1 on the next page, and the second is an iTunes app that comes preloaded on your iPad, shown on the left. Apple really wants to make it easy for you to buy content for your iPad … even when you're not connected to the computer. And it is easy.

For instance, I just took a vacation to Florida and wanted to grab a movie for the trip. I didn't have to connect my iPad to a computer; I just got the movie straight from the iTunes Store on my iPad.

Figure 3-1
The iTunes Store on the computer is a one-stop online shop for iPad content.

YOUR ITUNES ACCOUNT / APPLE ID

The first thing to know before you buy any content from the iTunes Store is that you will need an iTunes account (otherwise known as an Apple ID). It doesn't matter if you never plan to buy anything there—and you only download free content, like podcasts, and use free apps—you still need to set up an iTunes account. And you can do it without a credit card! More on that in a minute. First, let's walk through signing up for an iTunes account with a payment option.

Figure 3-2
Sign in to iTunes and create a new account.

Set up an Apple ID on the computer.
You can set up your Apple ID on your computer, or you can do it on the iPad. We'll start with the process for setting it up on your computer.

1. Start iTunes on the computer.

2. Click on "iTunes Store" in the list on the left side of the screen.

3. Click the "sign in" button at the top right side of the window. (If, instead of the sign in button, you see a name there, then it means that you or someone is already signed into iTunes on your computer.)

4. At this point, you can either sign in to an existing account or set up a new account.

5. If you don't have an account, click "Create New Account." This will take you to a welcome screen. Click the "Continue" button.

6. Now it's time for that legal mumbo jumbo that no one ever reads. It's the *iTunes Store Terms & Conditions* and *Apple's Privacy Policy*, and you are required to check the "I have read and agree to the iTunes Terms and Conditions and Apple's Privacy Policy" before you can continue.

If you print the *iTunes Store Terms & Conditions* and *Apple's Privacy Policy*, it will run about 20 pages. In summary, the main points are:

- Don't sell the music you buy from iTunes.

- If a third-party app crashes, don't blame Apple.

- There are a lot of ways to send Apple money, including checks, wire transfers and money orders along with credit cards and gift certificates.

Figure 3-3
The Terms of Service. Try to stay awake while reading this. I dare ya!

- Don't let anyone use your account, because you are responsible for all charges that accrue.

- You can burn a CD playlist seven times. Want more? Delete the playlist; make another with a different name; and burn, baby, burn.

- You can't burn ringtones or video products to a CD or DVD.

Of course there's more, especially when it comes to renting movies, enjoying TV season passes and dealing with electronic books. I suggest that you actually read this. It's boring, but some of the information may be important for you.

7. The next step is to enter the information required to create the Apple ID. Your birthday is required, so that Apple can tell if you are older than 13. This is the minimum age for a person to get an Apple ID.

8. The third and final screen is where your payment info goes. It's nice for Apple to have this information, so you can purchase

content without having to constantly enter in a credit card number. That's your call though. See below for more information on completing the sign up process without a credit card.

9. Once you've set up the account, you can sign in to your account when using the iTunes Store and check out all the goods.

If you want to sign up for an Apple ID and *not* use a credit card, it can be done; it's just a little more complicated. Here's the deal:

1. Open iTunes.

2. Click on "iTunes Store" on the left side of the window.

3. Click on "App Store," located across the top of the screen.

4. Pick a free app to download.

5. Click "Create New Account" when a window appears that directs you to "Sign in to download from the iTunes Store."

6. Click "Continue."

7. Read and agree to the *iTunes Terms of Service*.

8. Enter an e-mail address. (This will be your Apple ID.)

9. Enter a password.

10. Create a security question and answer.

11. Enter your birthday.

12. Click "Continue."

13. Select "None" as payment type.

14. Fill out the name and address fields.

15. There will be a "Verify Account" screen; click "Done" and check your e-mail.

16. Once you get a verification e-mail from Apple, open and click the enclosed link to activate your new iTunes account.

17. Your account is now activated.

You can access your account information from inside iTunes at any time. To do so, just open iTunes and then place your mouse over the account name on the right side of the screen. Click on the down arrow to open the Account menu. You can now choose from the following options:

- **Account** shows your account information (At times, as a security precaution, iTunes might ask you to reenter your password.)

- **Redeem** is the place to go with an iTunes gift card.

- **Wish List** is where a collection is saved of unpurchased, but desirable, items you've marked in the iTunes Stores.

- **Sign Out**, especially if you share a computer with others, so your account doesn't get used without your permission.

If you need to change any of your account information, from payment details to your personal information, this is the spot to do it.

Set up an Apple ID on the iPad.

It is possible to set up your Apple ID from your iPad.

1. Turn on your iPad.

2. Tap on "Settings."

3. Tap on "Store."

4. If you have an iTunes account already, then sign in; if you don't, tap "Create New Account."

5. If you tap "Sign In," then you'll be asked for a user name and password. Enter the information and tap "OK." Skip the rest of

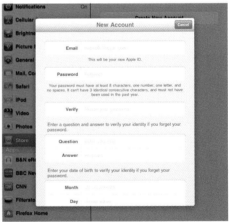

Figure 3-4

The iTunes sign up screens on the iPad are similar to those on the computer.

these steps if you already have an account; you are good to go.

6. If you tap "Create New Account," then you will enter information as noted in the next few steps.

7. Choose a country or region that matches your billing address. Tap "Next."

8. Read all 35 pages of the Terms and Conditions and then tap "Agree." You can also have the Terms and Conditions e-mailed to you to read later. For fun.

9. Once you have agreed to the Terms and Conditions, you'll need to enter:

   ◦ Your e-mail address (This becomes your Apple ID.)

   ◦ Password

   ◦ Verification of password

   ◦ A security question

   ◦ Security question answer

   ◦ Date of birth

   ◦ Opt to receive iTunes updates … or not.

   ◦ Opt to receive News and Special Offers from Apple … or not.

10. Tap "Next."

11. Now you need to enter your billing information. You can use an iTunes gift card or gift certificate to open the account; just scroll to the appropriate area to enter the information.

12. Tap "Next" to complete the account set up process.

13. Tap "Done."

Now that you're legit, you can go and use the iTunes Store, the App Store and the iBooks Store. If you want to set up an account but don't have a credit card *or* a gift card, you can—on the iPad and/ or your computer. It's a little more complicated; but once it's done, you're good to go. Here's how:

1. Open the App Store on your iPad.

2. Find a free application. I suggest the iBooks app, since you'll want that at some point anyway.

3. Tap "Install App," and a menu will pop up asking you to sign in using an existing account.

4. If you don't have one, tap "Create New Account."

5. Enter your country or region.

6. Tap "Next."

7. Read and agree to the *iTunes Terms of Service.*

8. Enter an e-mail address. (This will be your Apple ID.)

9. Enter a password and verify it.

10. Create a security question and answer.

11. Enter your birthday.

12. Opt to receive iTunes updates … or not.

13. Opt to receive News and Special Offers from Apple … or not.

14. Tap "Next."

15. Select "None" as payment type.

16. Fill out the name and address fields.

17. On the "Verify Account" screen, tap "Done" and check your e-mail account for a message from Apple.

18. When you get a verification e-mail from Apple, open it and click the enclosed link to activate your new iTunes account.

19. The App Store will open. Enter your new account information to sign in, and start downloading some apps!

Once you have an Apple ID, you can utilize the iTunes Store in all its glory.

THE ITUNES STORE: COMPUTER

The iTunes Store opened for business in early 2003 as a place to buy and download music for use on a computer and iPod. When it launched, the store had 200,000 music tracks and was available only to Mac users. PC users got the iTunes Store later that year. On February 24, 2010, Apple announced that more than ten billion tracks had been downloaded from the store since it began.

The store has now grown into so much more than music. Today, there are seven distinct parts to the iTunes Store. Each one has a huge amount of content that can be consumed on a computer or iPad (or an iPhone, iPod, etc).

Music

The Music store is the one that started the iTunes gig, and it's still growing every day. The store has a ton of content, but it tries to make it easy for you to find what you're looking for … and even suggests new music to match your taste.

When the store opened, all the music was priced at $0.99 and the files were protected by a Digital Rights Management (DRM) algorithm. This limited what you could do with the songs. But recently, Apple announced that they were removing the DRM from most of the music in the iTunes Store. (There is still DRM on the audiobooks though.)

Along with this change is a new pricing structure. No longer are all tracks $0.99; there is now a three-tiered pricing plan: $0.69, $0.99 and $1.29. And songs now download at the highest level of quality (256 kbps AAC audio), which is twice the audio quality of the older DRM-enabled songs from the iTunes Store. And … the tracks can be played everywhere. The DRM-free status means you can burn your music to a disc or play them on any computer anywhere, anytime. Nice …

One more thing you need to know about iTunes music is the iTunes LP, which is Apple's answer to the long-playing album. The iTunes LP tries to re-create the whole album experience with more artwork and bonus features. These albums cost a little more. And while I don't think they've been as successful as Apple would have liked, the iTunes LPs are cool.

Here's the thing though: The iPad doesn't support the LP format. So while you can download the individual tracks of an iTunes LP to your iPad and all the music will be available there, the interface will not have the cool LP features that you paid extra to get. It'll look

Figure 3-5
You can access the various parts of the iTunes Store using the menu across the top of the screen.

and act the same as all your regular albums. This is true even if you buy the LP album on the iPad. Once you sync back over to the computer, iTunes will go back online and get any of the missing files so you can enjoy the extras on your computer.

Figure 3-6
The Rolling Stones great album *Exile on Main Street LP* on the computer has a very slick interface.

Figure 3-7
The same album on the iPad has none of the cool extra interface elements, but the bonus tracks are still there for your listening enjoyment.

TIP

You do not need to be connected to the Internet to begin watching a rented movie. This means it works great everywhere. Keep in mind that once you start to watch a rented movie, you have to finish within 24 hours.

Movies

The iTunes Movie store has changed the way I buy and rent movies. I used to actually buy movies … on VHS tapes! Remember those? Then I transitioned to the DVD format, and now I buy digital files.

Not all the movies released on DVD show up on the iTunes Store, but there are more and more movies there every day. The movies are protected by DRM, and they need to be played on devices that are either authorized to play your purchased movies (up to five computers) or on iPads that are under the same Apple ID. So if you buy a movie using an Apple ID and transfer the movie to an iPad that has a different Apple ID, it won't play.

When it comes to the iTunes extras that are available with many movies today, it's important to understand that they are not compatible with the iPad. They'll show up on your computer but not on the iPad.

Renting movies from the iTunes Store is also a viable option, and rented movies can be transferred from a computer to the iPad. But rented movies, unlike purchased movies, can

Figure 3-8

I rented *Robin Hood* on the computer and wanted to watch it on the iPad. I knew that I had to go to the DMV soon. That is, the Department of Motor Vehicles here in California, a place where sitting and waiting is common. So I thought it would be the perfect thing to pass the time. In the iTunes window, you can move the rental over to the iPad. It does not copy the file; it moves it.

only live on a single device at a time. This means that you do not copy a movie to the iPad but rather transfer it. And this is done in iTunes. So if you have a rented movie in your iTunes library, you can transfer it to the iPad using the following process:

1. Open iTunes on the computer.

2. Plug in your iPad using the USB cable.

3. Select the iPad from the device listing on the left.

4. Select "Movies" on the iPad menu.

5. Select the move arrow that corresponds to the direction you want to transfer the movie.

6. Click the "Apply" button.

7. The movie will transfer as directed.

You can now watch the movie on your iPad. You need to have an active Internet connection for this to work, and the iTunes Store will check to make sure you are allowed to make the transfer before actually transferring the movie to the iPad.

TV Shows

I'll admit that I watch some of my favorite TV shows on my computer and iPad. You can buy individual episodes in both standard definition and in HD, and you can buy season passes (entire TV seasons at a time) ... also with your choice of Standard Definition or HD. You can buy the season pass before the season is even complete, and episodes will become available to subscribers within 24 hours of its broadcast. Apple sends season pass holders an e-mail notification when new episodes become available to download. To access a new episode, tap the link in the e-mail and iTunes will launch. The file is automatically downloaded.

Figure 3-9
Here is the error message I got when trying to download the new episode of *Terriers*, a show for which I have a season pass.

Figure 3-10
Make sure that you have selected "iPad" apps when shopping the iTunes App Store.

There are some problems with season passes on the iPad though, and you'll find more on that on page 36.

The App Store
The App Store is a goldmine for Apple and, according to some developers, it's a very profitable platform for app creators. This seems amazing sometimes, because a lot of content in the App Store is free.

There is a very important menu choice for users in the App Store when accessing the site on their Mac or PC, and that is "iPhone vs iPad." This option is positioned right in the middle of the screen at the top, and it switches between apps developed for the iPhone and those designed for the iPad. Be sure that you click on "iPad" to see the apps developed for the iPad. There are new apps in the App Store every day.

There is something very different about apps when they're compared to all the other media types. Apps get updated. Developers add new features, fix problems and generally update their apps periodically for various reasons. At least the good app developers do. When an app is updated, you can download the new version in the iTunes Store, usually for free. Then, the next time you sync your iPad, the newer version of the apps will overwrite the older versions on your computer.

You can go and check for updates in iTunes anytime by visiting the app library and clicking "Check for Updates," which is located at the bottom of the screen. This will automatically check for updates and open the App Store if it finds any newer versions of the apps you own. It's a good idea to keep your apps up to date, because many times the updates fix problems or add new features.

33

Podcasts

Podcasts have matured by leaps and bounds since they were first offered on the iTunes Store back in 2005. Users can now search for and download podcasts on a huge variety of subjects—from tech news (some of my favorite subjects) to wine-making and automotive repair. The store looks just like the other iTunes stores with one key exception: All the content is free.

Figure 3-11

The Podcast store on the iPad and the computer is formatted differently but offers the same content.

Audiobooks

There are times when a good audiobook can make a long drive go by much faster … or at least seem that way. The iTunes Store offers a wide selection of audiobooks, ranging from political thrillers to autobiographies. The store is divided much like a regular bookstore … by fiction and non-fiction. But one really cool category is "Books Made Into Films." I think this one is especially fun to browse. Check it out when you get a chance.

iTunes U

The iTunes U area of the iTunes Store was opened in 2007 and is a forum for educational materials. It allows educational institutions to distribute information through the iTunes Store for just their own institution or the general public. A ton of great free content is available in iTunesU.

THE ITUNES APP: IPAD

Buying content from Apple on the iPad is slightly more complicated than doing it on a computer … or slightly simpler, depending on your point of view. Apple has split iTunes commerce into two different stores: the iTunes Store and the App Store.

These stores mirror the content available on the iTunes Store that's accessible through the iTunes program on your computer. The stores might look slightly different and navigation is via finger instead of mouse, but the content available to you is the same … with one exception. Apple offers a book store that's accessible only on the iPad (as well as the iPod Touch and iPhone). This store allows you to purchase iBooks right on the iPad.

The iTunes Store is the place to buy and download music, movies, TV shows, podcasts, audiobooks and iTunes U content. The

App Store is dedicated to apps. Similarly, the iBooks Store is all about electronic books. Let's start with the iTunes Store on the iPad. And before we go any further, let's be clear that on the iPad, the app is just called "iTunes."

iTunes

As stated above, the iTunes app is the place to search for and buy music, movies, TV shows, podcasts, audiobooks and iTunes U material. All of this content is easy to find; the menu, organized by category, is laid out across the bottom of the screen. The different categories (or stores) look similar to the computer-based versions, but there are some small differences, and they can be really annoying.

TIP

iTunes is a term that describes two different things. On the iPad, iTunes is the place to get music, movies, TV shows, audiobooks, podcast and iTunesU content. When referencing the program on a computer, *iTunes* is the application that plays and organizes your content and provides the portal for accessing the iTunes Store to sync content from your computer to the iPad.

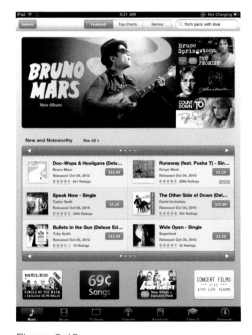

Figure 3-12
The iTunes Store on the iPad shows content categories across the bottom of the screen.

The stores available on the iTunes app include:

○ **Music**

You can search, purchase and download music right on the iPad. This works with both the Wi-Fi and 3G versions of the iPad. Find some music you want to buy by either searching for it using the search feature at the top of the screen or by navigating around like you would in the iTunes Store on the computer.

And when you find some music you like, you can download the album or individual tracks. The songs will be placed in the "Downloads" page and you get to enter your Apple ID password before enjoying the sounds. This is so Apple can charge you for your purchases.

One thing to remember is that the screen on the iPad, especially when in landscape

35

mode, doesn't show the full page of the store. So scroll down for more music choices.

Some things that are different on the iPad version of the Music store are mainly stuff you *can't* do. The extra content and cool interface of the LP version of music files are not supported on the iPad, even if you buy the LP Album on your iPad. Another strange thing happens when I click on the "Complete My Album" button at the bottom of the page: It never actually works. Instead, a dreaded "Cannot connect to iTunes Store" message pops up. But in perspective, these are slight inconveniences. The store works great most of the time.

○ **Movies**

The Movie store on the iPad allows you to purchase … or rent and download … movies right to the iPad. One thing to keep in mind is that you need to be on a Wi-Fi network to do this, because the size of movie files is far bigger than the allowable download size of the 3G.

The movie store on your iPad looks just like the one on the computer, and it allows you to buy movies in both Standard Definition and HD. My suggestion here is that if you're planning to watch the movie on your iPad, stick with the lower-cost SD movies. If you're planning to enjoy the movie on a computer, the Apple TV or an HD television, then you might want to pay the extra coin for HD. Honestly, I usually buy movies in Standard Definition because I tend to watch them on smaller devices that don't benefit from the HD quality. It's your call.

It's important to know that, right now, there are things you can't do with the movies you purchase or rent on the iPad. For one, you can't transfer them to a computer. If you

rent it on the iPad, you have to watch it on the iPad. Another thing is that the iTunes Extras that are available when you purchase some movies do not work on the iPad as they do on a computer. Only the movie content gets copied to the iPad. To watch the extra stuff, you need to be on the computer, viewing the movie thorough iTunes.

○ **TV Shows**

The way things are progressing, all of my television viewing will soon be done on-command and without advertisements. Through the iTunes TV store, you can now buy individual shows and season passes in either HD or Standard Definition on the iPad. This is great, but Apple has a bit of work yet to do on the functionality of the iPad's TV content.

For starters, with iOS3.2, renting TV shows on the iPad is not supported. Even if you rent the TV show on the computer, there is no way to transfer it to your iPad. Another glitch that currently exists is something not fully operable on TV Season Passes. Now I really wanted this to work, but I've tried to access my content on different devices in different locations … with season passes bought on the computer and season passes purchased on the iPad itself. And here's the deal: Subscribers get an e-mail when a new episode is available, but clicking on the link in the e-mail (that's supposed to lead you blissfully to the new episode) opens iTunes on the iPad … only to reveal an error message that says the connection to the iTunes Store cannot be made and that no file is available for download.

If you buy a Season Pass on the iPad (and not your computer), something slightly different happens. You still get the error message, but a new download will be available in the "Downloads" area, and you can get the show onto your iPad from here … sometimes. Other times, it never works; and the only way to get your new episode is to download it on the computer and sync it to the iPad with the USB cable. Groan …

Hopefully Apple will fix this soon.

○ **Podcasts**

I have a favorite podcast or two. Actually, I have a whole collection of podcasts that I listen to when I have the time. I subscribe to the podcasts on the computer; but if there's something specific I'm looking for, I go searching through the Podcast store. The only real downside is that there's no way to subscribe to podcasts on the iPad.

Both audio and video podcasts are available, so the size of the downloads vary widely. A podcast's size will determine if it can be downloaded on 3G or if it can only be downloaded when attached by Wi-Fi.

○ **Audiobooks**

I love a good audiobook, and having them available on the iPad just increases the value of the device in my eyes. The audiobook files in the iTunes Store are DRM-protected, so they can't just be copied and used anywhere. This means that the number of computers that can play an audiobook purchased from iTunes is limited to five; and all of them must be authorized under the same Apple ID. The good news is that your audiobooks can be played on as many iDevices as you want.

When you find an audiobook you're interested in, play a preview of it. Many times, it really helps to have headphones or external speakers to get the best experience from your audiobook.

Figure 3-13
The Downloads page on the iPad iTunes app shows items as they are being downloaded.

○ **iTunes U**

Here is a great reason for students to have an iPad. You can access all of the iTunes U materials right here. A really nice element of the iTunes U store on the iPad are the three buttons in the middle that allow you to search by "Universities & Colleges," "Beyond Campus" and "K-12." Tap on any of these three buttons and scroll through a list of school names. Tap on a school to see a listing of the content available from that school. What a great use of iTunes and a great use of the iPad!

App Store

I have no idea why Apple made the App Store a separate app on the iPad, but I like it. The setup makes it really easy to find and buy new apps. You can even check to see if the apps on your iPad are up-to-date and, if they aren't, the app will ask you to download the updates. Some updates will not be available unless you are on a Wi-Fi network (and not connected over 3G). This happens when an app is bigger than the 20MB per-app limit for 3G downloads.

Remember that if you've previously purchased an app anywhere else using your Apple ID, you can re-download it for free. Just go into the App Store and tap "Buy." The iPad will act as if you are buying the app for

Figure 3-14
The App Store interface on the iPad. Notice that I have an update to an app waiting to be downloaded. That's what the little red and white "1" represents on the bottom right.

the first time until it starts to download. Then it will tell you that you have bought the app before and ask if you want to download it again for free. This is really nice. It means that you can delete an app from your iPad; and, if you reconsider, you can just visit the App Store and get it again … for no additional cost.

iBooks Store

The iPad's iBooks Store is the most challenging of the stores to find, because it is not standard on the iPad. It is an extra app that has to be downloaded. Even then, it is still a semi-hidden part of the app.

In the library view of the iBooks app, there is a "Store" button on the top left. Tap this button to gain access to the iBooks Store, a rapidly growing electronic bookstore and the only place to buy books from Apple.

I'm not sure that anything will ever replace the feeling I get when I wander through a bookstore, looking at new books. But the iBooks Store comes close.

The store allows you to wander around virtually and even download samples of books for free. Flip through them just like flipping through a paper one.

A really nice thing about the iBook Store is that the book files are small, so they can be

Figure 3-15
The iBooks Store looks just like all the other Apple stores. But you won't find it on your computer. It can only be accessed through the iBooks app on the iPad (and iPhone and iPod Touch).

downloaded over 3G as well as Wi-Fi. This means you can grab a new book just about anywhere. Another very cool thing that is starting to show up in the iBooks Store are enhanced books that contain extra content, like timelines, photographs and author Q&A for an extra fee.

DIFFERENT MEDIA. DIFFERENT RULES.

This is important: Apple treats different types of iTunes content differently depending on format. Here's the deal:

Say you buy content in the form of music, movies or TV shows on the computer or your iPad … and they get deleted or lost, or

Figure 3-16
Good thing that Apple warned me;
I wouldn't want to spend another
$14.99 to buy to buy a movie I
previously purchased.

Figure 3-17
Since I had already purchased the
Exposure Digital Field Guide in iBooks, I
was able to re-download it for free.

you just decide to download the file a second time. When you go to download previously purchased media of these types, either on the computer or the iPad, you will get charged a second time for the content.

I need to make this really clear, so here is a real-world example. I went to the iTunes Store on the computer and bought *Hot Tub Time Machine* for $14.99. (I have a soft spot for anything with John Cusack in it.) Then, I decided to download the movie on my iPad, so I went to the iTunes Store on the iPad, brought up the same movie and tapped "Buy Movie." I got a message saying that I've already purchased the movie and the question, "Do you want to proceed with the purchase?" If I tap "Buy" then I WILL PURCHASE THE MOVIE AGAIN. That is, iTunes will debit my credit card for another $14.99. This is true with music, TV shows and movies.

It's a different story when it comes to apps and eBooks. If you buy an app in the computer's version of the iTunes Store and then try to buy the app again on the iPad, Apple will allow you to download it the second time for free. For some reason, Apple has decided to keep track of your app purchases and allow

you to re-download them at no additional charge ... as long as the device is logged in with the Apple ID that was used to purchase the app initially.

Now let's talk about iBooks for a minute. Apple has lumped them into the same category as apps. You can re-download any previously purchased book on the iPad as long as you are signed in with the Apple ID that was used to first purchase the book. This makes it really easy to have the same book on multiple devices if they all have the same Apple ID associated with them. For example, I have an iPad and my wife has an iPad, and both are tied to the same Apple ID. This means she can download to her iPad any iBook I buy on my iPad ... for free. The same goes for apps but not music, movies or TV shows.

To recap, iBooks and apps can be re-downloaded at any time for free, but music, TV shows and movies cannot. If you re-download content that's not an iBook or app, then you will get charged for it again.

PART 2

Content Consumption

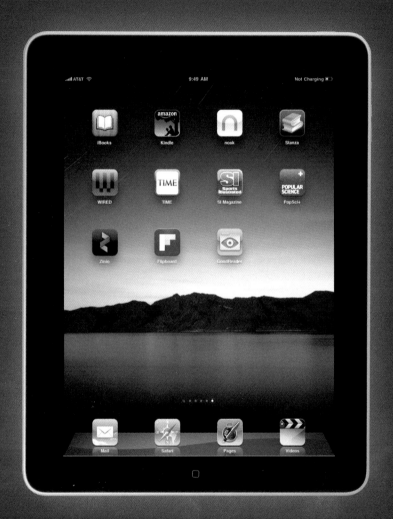

Electronic Reader

The Skim

For me, one of the most exciting features of the iPad is its electronic book reader. Like many people, I enjoy the convenience of reading books electronically, and I searched far and wide to find a gadget to allow me to do this. My problem with some of the options on the market is that they limit users to a single book store. I want to be able to shop where I want to shop, not just at the Amazon Kindle store or the Barnes & Noble Nook store.

Well, Apple not only added a new book store to the electronic book marketplace vis-à-vis iBooks, but the company allows other electronic book makers to write apps for the iPad. This is cool. It means there are many more eBook options for the iPad than other electronic readers. Not only is there an iBooks Store but also a Kindle app and a Nook app for the iPad, which offers iPad users a variety of books at an even wider variety of prices.

The iPad also enables users to read their own books and get free books. These capabilities interest me in part because I write books for a living. The more places people can access and read my books the better! And who doesn't like *free?*

GET IBOOKS

iBook is the name Apple uses for electronic books, generically called an *eBook*. iBooks is also the name of the online bookstore where iBooks and other eBooks are available for purchase. The iBooks app is where you access the iBooks Store and it's where you can read and store your iBooks.

The thing is, you won't find iBooks on your iPad when you take it out of the box. You have to install the iBooks app just like most other apps—either through the iTunes Store on your computer or the App Store on your iPad.

Acquire the iBooks app on the iPad.

When you tap on the App Store icon, you'll see an offer to download a free copy of iBooks. Tap "Download" to get the iBooks app.

If you don't get the invitation, just click in the search bar on the top right of the screen and enter *iBooks*, and then click "Search." The iBooks app from Apple will be the first choice. Tap the "Free" button (and, if prompted, enter your iTunes password) to download the app.

Download the iBooks app from iTunes on a Computer.

Start iTunes on your computer and click "iTunes Store" on the left side of the window. Select "App Store" at the top of the screen and search for iBooks. Once you've downloaded the iBooks app, you'll need to sync your iPad to install it there.

With the iBooks app on your iPad, you can start using your iPad as an electronic book reader.

USE IBOOKS

The first time you run the iBooks app, you'll be asked if you want to Sync Bookmarks. Doing so allows you to keep the same bookmarks and notes on multiple devices ... as long as they are all associated with the same

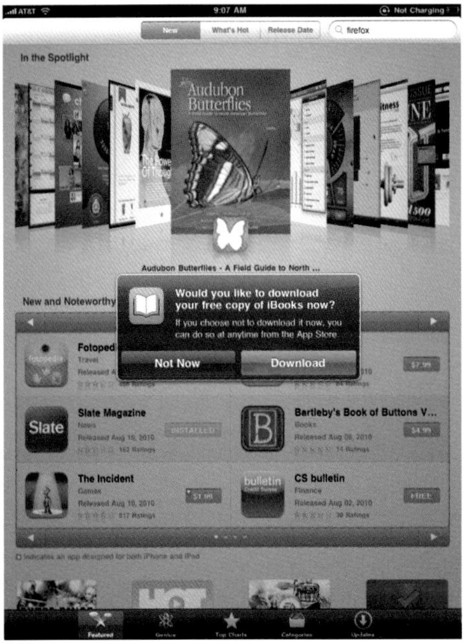

Figure 4-1
The App Store on the iPad is asking if you want to download iBooks.

Figure 4-2
The Default bookshelf view shows the free *Winnie the Pooh* book.

iTunes account. There is more on this a little later in this chapter. For right now, just tap "Sync" or "Don't Sync." You can always change this setting later in the Settings app on your iPad.

iBooks comes with a free book so you can see how it works without buying anything. Just tap the cover of the book you see on your bookshelf. I know it looks pretty lonely there all by itself, but I'll bet it won't be that way for long.

When an iBook is opened, the screen shows a menu bar across the top and a slider (with a page identifier) across the bottom. Both of these tools will fade from view after a few minutes, but they can be brought back by tapping on the top of the page.

Use the controls at the top of the page to navigate this app:

- Tapping the "Library" button will get you back to your collection of books.

- The "Table of Contents/ Bookmark" list brings up a menu that allows you to choose between the Table of Contents, which has links to the start of each chapter, or to a list of bookmarks that you've set in the current book to mark the place where you stopped reading. To set a bookmark, just tap this button. There are other ways to set bookmarks, too; we'll cover them a little later.

- The "Buy" button is visible when reading a sample chapter. It allows you to immediately buy the book with a simple tap.

- Tap "Brightness" to change the lighting of the page. This is really useful when reading in low light, since the device doesn't need to be very bright in this situation. This brightness level only affects iBooks though—not the whole iPad. There is a

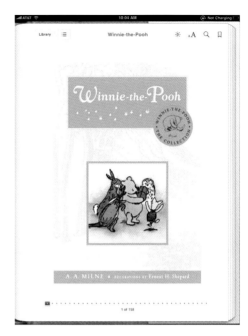

Figure 4-3
The *Winnie the Pooh* book has all the menus visible.

different brightness setting in the System Menu that affects the brightness of the iPad in general.

- Use the "Type Size," "Font" and "Page Color" settings to change the size and font of the text and to change the color of the paper from white to a sepia tone.

- Tap the "Search" bar to look for specific terms.

The control on the bottom of the page is a quick and easy way to flip through a book until you get to a specific page. There is a small brown slider that can be moved left or right to page quickly through the book. As you drag the slider left and right, you'll see the page count on the bottom of the page and the chapter numbers, keywords and page numbers above the little brown box.

To turn a page in iBooks, just swipe your finger across the single page in the direction you want the page to turn. You can also turn a page by tapping on either the left or right side of the

Winnie-the-Pooh

"Nothing, Pooh Bear, nothing. We can't all, an/ don't. That's all there is to it."
"Can't all *what?*" said Pooh, rubbing his nose.
"Gaiety. Song-and-dance. Here we go roun/ bush."
"Oh!" said Pooh. He thought for a long

Figure 4-4
On the page being turned from right to left, notice the realistic-looking page curl on the bottom.

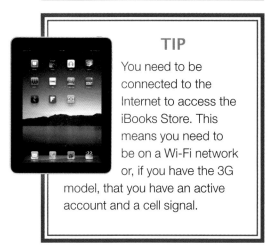

TIP

You need to be connected to the Internet to access the iBooks Store. This means you need to be on a Wi-Fi network or, if you have the 3G model, that you have an active account and a cell signal.

page you want to turn. One little thing to be conscious of: If you tend to swipe across the bottom part of the screen to turn a page, there is a chance you will inadvertently activate the slider. So instead of turning one page, you will suddenly find yourself jumping back or forward by whole sections. I know it seems like that wouldn't happen much; that's what I thought anyway, until I did it by mistake. Twice.

IBOOKS STORE

There is only one iBooks Store, and it is part of the iBooks app. This is the only place to go for Apple iBooks. There is no place to buy iBooks on your computer or through the iTunes Store. To access the iBooks Store, tap the "Store" button on the top left of the iBooks library view.

If you've used the App Store or the iTunes Store, then the iBooks Store will look very familiar to you. You won't see any video or music offerings; instead, a growing selection of electronic books is available here.

Use the menu across the top of the screen to navigate this store:

○ Tap the "Library" button to return to your book collection on the iPad.

○ "Categories" allows you to jump directly to a category that you find interesting … be it "Classics" or "Nonfiction." Picking a category here will change the information presented in the main part of the window.

○ Choose "Featured/ Release Date" to determine whether your content is displayed by what Apple wants to feature or by the most current selections.

○ "Search" enables you to filter the whole iBooks Store for just the information you're seeking. Type in an author's name or subject and see what pops up.

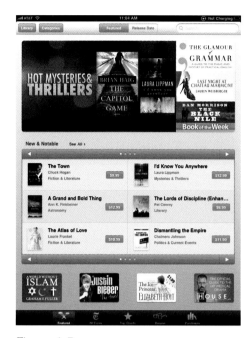

Figure 4-5
The iBooks Store

The middle section of the screen shows a display of books available for purchase. One odd thing about the navigation here is that swiping your finger across the page doesn't work. You need to use the little arrow icons to browse the pages of book listings.

The menu across the bottom of the screen offers the following information:

- "Featured" is the main display in the iBooks Store. It gives you the latest and greatest offerings in the store.

- Tap "New York Times" to see this publication's Best Seller lists. This iBooks list gets updated when the *New York Times* updates its list: once a week.

- These "Top Charts" show you what is popular and selling well in the iBooks Store—both the paid and free books.

- Tap "Browse" to bring up a search feature that allows you to scroll through the Top Authors, both in the paid and free books sections as well as the other categories. This is very much like browsing the shelves of your local bookstore.

- The "Purchases" button shows you which books you've already purchased. You can re-download these files if you want.

When you find a book that looks interesting, just click on the book's icon to bring up more info about it. Buy the book by tapping on its price, which turns into a "Buy Book" button, or get a sample chapter by tapping "Get Sample." I usually get a sample before I buy a book … to make sure I'm getting something I'll really want. I really love the try-it-before-you-buy-it concept, and iBooks has done it right.

Figure 4-6
My bookshelf is filled with sample downloads.

When you click "Get Sample," the bookstore automatically changes back to your library view, and your sample is placed on the shelf with a *Sample* banner across it. Click on the book to read the sample chapter.

If you decide you want to purchase the book, click the "Buy" button. You will be asked to enter your iTunes password so Apple can charge the right account. If you decide you don't want to buy the book, you can delete it from the iPad easily by tapping the "Edit" button on the top right of the screen. Then tap on the "X" that appears on the top left corner of the book. That will remove the book from your library immediately.

That's how easy it is. You can download as many sample chapters as you want and keep them until you get around to reading them. Apple understands that you are much more likely to buy a book once you've read a chapter or two. I like Michael Connelly books, so I downloaded a sample chapter from all of his available books. I can start to read one and then just click on the "Buy" button. Voilá, the book is added to my library.

Speaking of the iBooks library, it has a few neat features. The first is that it has two different views. For those who like the visual approach of a bookcase, with all the books set with covers facing out, that's the default look. And for those who prefer a vertical list with small icons, that look is also available. In the top right area of the library are buttons for both the shelf view and the list view. When in the list mode, you can sort books as they

Figure 4-8

I held my finger on the *Echo Park* book until it got larger, and then I moved it around the bookshelf.

Figure 4-7

The list view of the bookshelf. Notice the three sorting options across the bottom.

appear on the bookshelf: by title, author or category. These options are available at the bottom of the screen.

There is a way to sort your books when in bookshelf mode, too, and it's pretty cool. Just hold your finger on the book you want to move and wait for it to get bigger. Then, drag it around the bookshelf and drop it into position. It's like sorting books on a real bookshelf. This is really useful when you have a lot of books and want to keep them in a specific order that's more personal than the options provided by Apple.

As a side note, any iDevice can re-download previously purchased iBooks content at any time … for no additional charge, as long as the device is using the Apple ID that was used to purchase the book. This is great—for families who have more than one iPad, for example—and it means you don't have to pay for the same app or book for each iPad. And if you bought a book and delete it from your iPad, you can re-download it later at no additional fee.

KINDLE APP

The most popular electronic book reader on the market is the Kindle from Amazon. But that might change very quickly now that there is an iPad app that turns the iPad into a Kindle—with color.

With the iPad's Kindle app, you can read Kindle books on the iPad, buy Kindle books, browse the Kindle bookstore, add your previously purchased Kindle books to the iPad Kindle app and get all the advantages of a Kindle … on an iPad.

One main difference between the iBooks app and the Kindle app is that the iBooks app is a stand-alone store, while the Kindle app

TIP

Only iBooks and apps can be re-downloaded for no charge. Movies, music and TV shows cannot be downloaded multiple times for free.

Figure 4-9
The main page of the Kindle app offers a free Dictionary.

launches the Kindle Web site, a subset of the regular Amazon.com site. Once you've found your book through the Kindle app, you can buy it at Amazon.com and the book will automatically be loaded into your Kindle app on your iPad.

49

Remember that you don't need to actually own a Kindle to run the iPad Kindle app. The Kindle app will allow you all the benefits of this device on your iPad, including an ability to shop for eBooks at the Amazon Kindle store.

If you do own a Kindle and have the same books on both your Kindle and your iPad's Kindle app, then the two eBooks will automatically sync to your place in the book. This means that if you read a chapter or two on the Kindle, and then switch to the iPad, the book on the iPad will automatically be set to open at the last place reached on the Kindle. The same is true if you start reading on an iPad and continue reading on a Kindle. Just keep in mind that the Kindle doesn't sync all your bookmarks and notes like the iPad does with its iBooks app, but it's pretty seamless nonetheless.

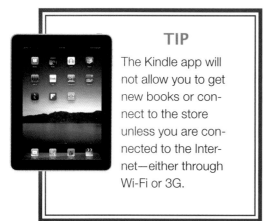

Figure 4-10
Setting up your Kindle app on the iPad is straightforward. Just enter your Amazon account information and you're good to go.

> **TIP**
>
> The Kindle app will not allow you to get new books or connect to the store unless you are connected to the Internet—either through Wi-Fi or 3G.

Figure 4-11
The Kindle bookstore is a special Web page that runs in Safari.

NOOK APP

The Barnes & Noble eBook reader is called the Nook, and it too has an app on the iPad. The Nook app allows you to shop in the Barnes & Noble online store on your iPad, download sample chapters, sync books over multiple devices and, of course, read your electronic books.

Tap the first button to visit the Barnes & Noble Nook online store. This is very much like the Amazon online store and allows you to search for and buy eBooks; all you need is a credit card. Once you've purchased an eBook, you get a list of devices to which you can download the book. When you tap

Figure 4-13
The Barnes & Noble Nook online store allows you to purchase and download eBooks directly to your iPad.

Figure 4-12
The Nook app opens to your purchased books. The opening screen also offers suggestions from Barnes & Noble … along with opportunities for you to download book samples.

Figure 4-14
Here are the choices available to you after purchasing a book.

"iPad," you get a submenu that allows you to "Download in iTunes." Tap the "Download in iTunes" link, and the Web page will change to the Nook app site. Close Safari and open the Nook app on your iPad. The book you just bought will automatically be available on your iPad.

There is one thing that the Nook app offers that iBooks and the Kindle do not. The Nook app allows you to share books with other Nook/ Nook app users. That is, you can lend a book out for 14 days. This doesn't mean that you can lend out your books over and over again; you can lend out a book once, and for a period of two weeks.

Once you lend out a book, you can't access it—just like a real book. The recipient has seven days to either accept or decline the book loan and another 14 days to finish reading it. Once (s)he is finished reading your book, you can re-download it and return it to your library. It's a shame you can't loan out the book again, but the limit at this time is one loan per book.

Figure 4-15
When you tap on a book in the Nook app, you can lend the book to a friend for two weeks. The "LendMe" button is right below the "Read" button.

STANZA APP

Less well-known than the Kindle or Nook apps is Stanza. It's a really nice eBook reader, but its distinguishing feature is its ability to access a high volume of different bookstores, including a wide range of free books. This is by far the easiest way to access a huge amount of free content. Just tap the "Get Books" icon at the bottom of the page to get started.

Once you have installed the Stanza app and synced the iPad to your computer, you can transfer eBooks from your computer to the iPad (and from the iPad to your computer). Because you can transfer files in and out of the Stanza app, you can actually get the free books in the Stanza app and read them in

TIP

The Nook app will not allow you to get new books or connect to the store unless you are connected to the Internet, either through Wi-Fi or 3G.

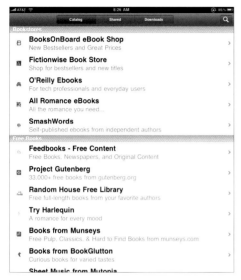

Figure 4-16

The list of bookstores associated with the Stanza app includes a great selection of free books.

iBooks. Just transfer them from your iPad to your computer and into iTunes, and load them back onto the iPad into the iBooks app.

Plus, using the iBooks app to read your books from Stanza allows you to keep all your books in one place. Here's how to do it:

1. Download the Stanza app on the iPad.

2. Open the Stanza app and tap "Get Books."

3. Download the books you want to read.

4. When you are back at your computer, plug in the iPad and launch iTunes.

5. Click on File > Transfer Purchases from iPad.

6. Click on "iPad" in the Devices list on the left.

7. Click on the "Apps" tab.

8. Scroll to the bottom of the page to find the "File Sharing" section.

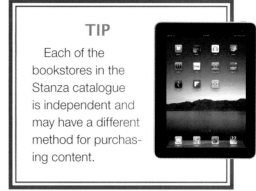

TIP

Each of the bookstores in the Stanza catalogue is independent and may have a different method for purchasing content.

9. Click on the Stanza app on the left under "File Sharing," and you'll see all the books you've downloaded to your iPad using Stanza.

10. Select the books you want to transfer and click the "Save To" button.

11. Select a spot that you will be able to find later. I use a folder called "Stanza Books."

12. Once the files have been saved, click File > Add to Library… and navigate to the saved books.

13. Now click on the "Books" tab to see the books you bought on Stanza. Make sure they are selected, and sync your iPad.

14. The books you acquired with Stanza are now in your iBooks library and can be read like any other book in there.

An additional note about Stanza: Not only can Stanza read ePub-formatted books, it can also read PDF files, HTML documents and even Comic Book Reader (.cbr) books as well as a variety of document types, including Microsoft Word. This is something that iBooks can't do, because it is limited to ePub and PDF files. More on comic book files in Chapter 7 and Word documents in Chapter 15.

FREE IBOOKS

Access free iBooks right from the iBooks Store on the iPad. The first place to check is the "Top Charts" area for the Top Free Books.

Just tap on "Top Charts" at the bottom of the page. The Top Paid Books and the Top Free Book lists will appear. Free books range from *Pride and Prejudice* by Jane Austen to the *United States Bill of Rights*. Most are older publications, and many are out of copyright and in the public domain. This means you've probably seen or read some of these books. In fact, many are on high school and junior high school reading lists.

You can also do a search for the word *free* in the iBooks Store. This will bring up not only books with the word *free* in the title but also the collection of free books in the iBooks Store. Take the time to check this out. There is a lot to read in the free lists, and some of it is well-worth the time it takes to search and download.

PUBLIC DOMAIN BOOKS AND EPUBS

Don't overlook other places to get your eBooks, especially if you're shopping on a budget or really just like free stuff. Since the iBooks app uses the very popular ePub electronic book format. Many of these types of books are available online and can be synced to your iPad using iTunes. I already talked about Stanza, which has the ability to search for free books, but if you want to do it on your computer, you can … with just a web browser.

First, let's look at where to find ePub books. Then, just so you know where this is going, we'll cover getting the books onto your iPad and how to get a good-looking cover on the books you select. 'Cause, seriously, a book-

Figure 14-17
Look for the settings in the Summary tab to reduce the amount of space you're your media takes on the iPad.

shelf with a well-considered look is just more fun than a plain one.

There are many places on the Web that offer free and easy-to-access electronic books. Below are some of the most common sources for free books:

Project Gutenberg (www.gutenberg.org) is home to more than 33.000 books, all of which can be downloaded and read on your iPad for free. The thing with Project Gutenberg is that it stores the book files in many different formats. Be sure to download your books from this site in the ePub format.

ePub Books (www.epubbooks.com) is a great resource for free electronic books that are published in the ePub format. Since the Apple iPad and iBooks use the ePub format, the books from this site work great on the iPad. Many of the books here are also available from Project Gutenberg; but on this site, you don't have to worry about making sure you have the right format. Files from ePub Books, as expected, are all in the ePub format.

Web Books (www.web-books.com)
was started by Frank Lee, a textbook author who wanted to help other authors publish their work and, at the same time, build an electronic book library that now has more than 1400 free ePub format books. Most of the books here are non-fiction.

Once you've downloaded an electronic book to your computer, you'll need to add the book to iTunes. To do this, open iTunes and click on "File." Then, select "Add to Library" and navigate to where the electronic books are stored on your computer. Click "Continue."

The books will automatically be added to your books section in iTunes. The problem is that they won't look really nice. You'll see a grey box with an image of a book—not very pretty.

Improve this by clicking on the book file. Select "File" and click "Get Info" to bring up the file information. From here, you can add the book cover artwork. All you need to do is find an image file of the cover that you want and copy it into the artwork section of the "File Info" window.

All that's left to do is sync the iPad with iTunes, and your free ePub books will be available in your iBooks library.

PUBLISH IBOOKS

When Apple released iTunes years ago, independent musicians rejoiced. There was finally a way to get their music out to the masses without a big record label. And now there's a

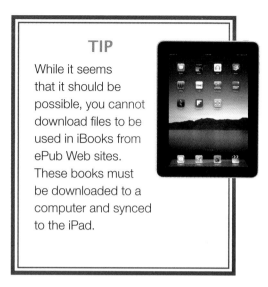

TIP

While it seems that it should be possible, you cannot download files to be used in iBooks from ePub Web sites. These books must be downloaded to a computer and synced to the iPad.

good chance that iBooks can do the same for authors. At this time, the iBooks Store isn't taking independent submissions, but this is likely to change.

Lulu.com
One of the easiest ways to write your own book is to use the Apple Pages application (a part of the Apple iWork app). This is especially true now that you can export Pages files as ePub documents. Find more on this in Chapter 1.

And right now, one of the smoothest options for publishing your own books is to use the Lulu self-publishing service. Lulu will allow your book to be available in the Apple iBook Store, because Apple is a certified aggregator for the iBooks Store.

There are two options for authors:

Make your own ePub
With this option, an author submits a fully finished document in the ePub format. Lulu then assigns the book a free ISBN, which is needed if the book is to be sold in the Apple iBooks Store.

Leave it to Lulu

With this option, Lulu handles the conversion of your file from Pages to ePub so you don't have to.

If you publish a book through Lulu in the iBooks Store, Apple will retain 30% of the revenue from the book's sales. The author and Lulu split the remainder 80/20, so the lion's share goes to the author. For more information on publishing your own books on Lulu, check out lulu.com.

Other Options

Since the iBooks app uses the ePub format, which can be created by anyone, aspiring authors can publish a book that can be read on an iPad.

But I'm not going to lie; the process of creating a nicely formatted ePub file that displays properly is complicated. But it's getting easier all the time, as more and more automated processes are becoming available for creating ePub documents from files in other formats. In fact, one of the big players in the content creation game is Adobe. This company's layout program is InDesign and it can be used to create an ePub. But the program has a steep learning curve and high price.

The easier option is to create a PDF.

PDF BOOKS

The Adobe Portable Document Format, or PDF, is used as a way to share documents across platforms and devices. It allows users to create clean and stable documents that contain a combination of text, photos, graphics and special formatting. What's more, a PDF document doesn't need a special program to read it. Just about all Web browsers have built-in PDF support; iBooks supports PDFs, too.

Figure 14-18
When PDFs are present in your iBooks library, a button at the top of the screen appears. This button allows you to switch between the iBooks …

Figure 14-19
… and the PDFs.

What this means is that you can put PDF documents on your iPad and treat them just like you would an iBook or ePub file. They are readable in the iBooks app and there is even a special shelf in the iBooks app library for PDFs.

You can add PDF files to your iTunes library, and they will automatically show up in the Books section. Once a PDF is synced to the iPad, you'll see a new button in the iBooks library. This is an iBooks PDF access point that's positioned on the top left of the Bookshelf page (right next to the "Store" button). One click on the PDF and a new shelf is shown; this time it has all of the PDFs you've loaded to your iPad.

Reading a PDF in iBooks is very similar to reading a book in iBooks, but there are some differences. Among the most noticeable is that when you turn a page of a PDF, it slides over and doesn't have the well-loved page flip of an iBooks book. Another main difference is that you can't change the font or text size of a PDF. Instead, you use the two-finger pinch and zoom.

SYNC BOOKMARKS

One of the best things about electronic books is that you can have multiple copies of the same book on different devices. Now, in the last section, I said that there was no way to share books with others; but there is a very easy way to share your books with yourself across multiple devices. This is especially true when your intent is to share between your iPad and iPhone. You can sync the bookmarks across devices seamlessly if they're on the same iTunes account.

This is a great little feature for those of us with both devices. I always make sure that I've loaded a book or two on my iPhone. It comes in handy for times when I'm standing in line or waiting around somewhere.

Just open your iPhone, start iBooks and continue reading where you left off on the iPad. When you're done reading, there's nothing special you need to do. Your bookmark is in place, so when you get back to your iPad, the new starting point is ready—as if you never switched devices in the middle of reading.

Note: Since this only works by connecting to the iTunes server, you must be online for the updates to take place.

MAGAZINE AND EBOOK APPS

Traditional magazines continue to struggle. For strictly print-and-paper publications, it's been tough to sustain advertising and readership amidst the electronic and ultra-mobile

SHARING IBOOKS

One of the best things about a great book is recommending it to friends, family, colleagues, etc … and being able to loan it to them. Many people read a book once and then pass it on.

Well, the iPad allows you to do this—but with severe restrictions. Actually, the restrictions are so severe that you can really only share iBooks with other iPad users who share your iTunes account. You can't even read your own iBooks on your computer, even the one you use to sync your iPad. Only if you have multiple iPads using the same Apple ID can you share your iBooks. That is, books purchased on one can be downloaded and read on the others for free.

This only applies to the books purchased through the iBooks Store. It does not hold true for free ePub books that you find online or the PDFs that you've loaded into iTunes. These can be shared without restrictions.

If you really want the ability to lend your eBooks, then your best bet right now is to use the Nook app by Barnes & Noble. It's the only one with the lending feature built in. Hopefully, other eBook vendors will take note of the popularity of this feature and add it to future versions of their electronic readers.

culture evolution. That's why publishers are getting creative and finding new formats for their readers to easily access the content they want to circulate.

When the iPad was announced, a future unfolded in which magazines would be available on demand via mobile media. Not only that, the possibility was born for these magazines to contain a blend of text articles, video clips and interactive elements. This future is obviously not yet here, but it's getting closer all the time.

Some magazines have started down this path with iPad apps, which offer more multimedia features than eBooks. Some of my favorites are described below.

Wired® **Magazine**

Wired was one of the first to jump onto the iPad eMag bandwagon, and it has done a great job balancing traditional articles with advertisements and new media that take advantage of the iPad's video and audio capability. The *Wired* app also acts as a virtual newsstand, allowing you to purchase individual issues of the magazine as they become available … as well as back issues.

The good news is that the first issue, the iPad issue, is free. Each of the subsequent issues cost $3.99. To purchase an issue, just tap on the "Buy" button and enter your iTunes password. You'll have a chance to confirm your purchase, and then you can download the issue by tapping the "Download" button.

As I write this it's still not possible to buy a *Wired* magazine subscription on the iPad. So you have to wait until the app is updated with a new issue before you can purchase and download it. *Wired* is usually made available for purchase on the iPad at the

Figure 14-20
The cover to an issue of *Wired* magazine has the date and price of the issue on one side and the "Buy" button on the other.

same time it shows up in stores, about a week after subscribers receive it in the mail.

If you delete this app without backing it up, your purchased issues will disappear and you'll have to download it again from the *Wired* app. This can be a real pain, as some of the *Wired* issues are hundreds of megabytes in size.

There is no way yet to share *Wired* magazine over multiple devices. Downloading the app on another iPad—even one that uses the same Apple ID—doesn't give you access to previously downloaded magazines.

The *Wired* magazine iPad navigation is important to review, because there is a really good chance that by the time you read this,

Figure 14-21
Preview of *Time* magazine for August 16, 2010, has the option to buy.

Adobe will have publicly released the software used to develop the electronic version of this magazine. This will make it possible for anyone to use the same layout and navigation elements to create a good-looking electronic magazine without re-creating the wheel.

Wired magazine allows you to jump straight to an article just by tapping on the story headlines on the cover. A vertical navigation bar lists articles, and a slider across the bottom of the page provides yet another tool to help you explore the magazine. There are also embedded video and music clips in this publication, and some of the ads even have embedded video in them.

You need to be connected to the Internet to download the magazine, since it is many times bigger than the 20MB cap that Apple

has placed on the 3G download. The *Wired* app requires that you keep the app open while the magazine downloads, and it can take a long time.

Time Magazine and *Sports Illustrated*

Time Magazine is another app that was available as soon as the iPad was launched. Since then, the app has gone through some very big changes. Now, the app functions as a newsstand. It allows browsers to preview issues to decide whether or not they want to spend the $4.99 per issue price. The preview is basically a list of stories in each issue. It doesn't really give you a taste of the articles. The *Sports Illustrated* app operates much like the *Time* app, but each issue costs $5.99.

As with *Wired* magazine on the iPad, there is no subscription service that automatically pushes a new *Sports Illustrated* or *Time* magazine onto your device when it becomes available. You must manually find out if a new issue is available and buy it.

The **Popular Science** app costs $4.99 in the App Store. For that, you get the current issue and access to buy earlier issues at discounted prices. The *Popular Science* app sends notifications to let you know when new issues are available. These notifications can be turned off in the Settings app of your iPad.

The *Popular Science* app is actually not very intuitive to use. It makes use of more than one finger swipe actions; and it can be confusing to read, as the text seems to flow over the photos. This app is included here because it shows that a digital version of a magazine isn't always a copy of the paper version … and while the e-version might be snazzier than the print one, it can be more difficult to read. Just goes to prove that electronic doesn't always mean easy.

Figure 14-22
These are the most popular magazines on Zinio.

Figure 14-23
Flipbook makes anything look good.

Zinio Magazine Newsstand & Reader

If your favorite magazines don't have their own app, your best bet is to look at **Zinio Magazine Newsstand & Reader.** This app is available for free on your iPad and acts like a storefront for a growing number of magazines. Here, you'll find everything from *Fader* to *National Geographic.*

Many publishers will allow you to switch from a paper subscription to a digital subscription using Zinio, so if you want to save a couple of trees and get your latest magazine in digital format, this is the way to do it. For more info, go to **www.zinio.com.**

There are one or two things to keep in mind when dealing with Zinio. The first is that you won't find any "adult content" here for your iPad. That is because Apple guidelines prohibit content they deem as *mature*. The second is the 20MB cap for downloads on the 3G network. This means you need a Wi-Fi connection to download most magazines.

Flipboard

When is a magazine not a magazine? The answer is **Flipboard**, an app that turns social media streams and Web streams into a magazine-like experience. This app really is beautifully done and can make the most mundane updates look great. Think of Flipboard as your personal magazine filled with your own news. You can set Flipboard to get the updates from your Twitter and Facebook feeds, or you can flip through the tweets by a single person.

Flipboard is your social magazine. I believe there is definitely a place for this on your iPad. Find more information on this type of app in Chapter 8.

SET UP FLIPBOARD

When you open Flipboard for the first time, there are six pre-formatted sections. The first two allow you to add your Facebook feed and your Twitter feed. The other four sections focus on Flipboard content: Inside Flipboard, FlipTech, Flipphotos and FlipStyle. To add your Facebook and/or Twitter feeds, just tap on the respective button and enter your account info. It's that easy … and worth every step.

Magazines are in their infancy on the iPad, and there's still a long way for them to go. I don't think they'll really take off until there is a subscription service. When subscriptions download automatically … or the magazine at least sends a notification e-mail about new issues (the way Apple does with TV show season passes), iPad magazines will be a hit. It would also be great if there was a way to easily transfer magazine issues to the computer to keep old issues and spare space on the iPad.

So while I love being able to have magazines on the iPad, I have great hopes for what this can be. For now, most of the magazine apps allow you to download a free issue or at least a free preview, which lets you try before you buy. And I definitely like that.

Movies

The Skim

Buying Movies • Renting Movies • Ripping DVDs • Home Movies
Streaming Movies and Video • Projecting Movies

The iPad is a great device for watching movies. The screen is sharp and bright, and movies are easy-to-see. The only downside is that the screen is not the same aspect ratio (widescreen, or 16:9) as that of a movie theater. So you either need to live with the black bars on the top and bottom of the screen or adjust the view.

To adjust, you can double tap the screen to zoom in and fill the screen. Doing this will obscure part of the movie, which means you won't see the film the way the director intended. But you don't have to see the black bars.

One of the best movie-related features of the iPad is its ability to be used as a movie player. You can use the iPad to watch movies on your television screen. I cover this at the end of the chapter, but here is a sneak peak. You need an extra piece of equipment to make the connection from the iPad to the TV. Both the Apple Component AV Cable and Apple Composite AV Cable will do the trick and allow you to connect your iPad to a television.

The iTunes Store is Apple's preferred source for your movie purchases. The company really wants you to shop for your movies at iTunes and forget about buying actual DVDs or Blu-Ray movies. Why spend your money on buying the actual DVD or Blu-Ray when you can spend it in the Apple Store?

WARNING:

If you have a 3G-enabled iPad and you want to buy or rent movies, you must connect to a Wi-Fi network or use iTunes on your computer to download it. This is due to the cap on 3G data transfer.

Figure 5-2
The iTunes Movie store on the iPad offers many choices.

Figure 5-1
You will get a warning if you try to buy or rent a movie on the iPad when on a 3G network.

And iTunes continues to evolve. When the iTunes Movie store first came out, you could only buy movies there. None of the cool extras that come along when you buy the actual DVD were included. But that has all changed now that iTunes has added iTunes Extras, which come with some movies. Just be aware that the extras are not available for every movie, and they don't come with rentals.

BUYING MOVIES ON THE IPAD

Apple makes it very easy to get content on your iPad. In the case of movies, all you have

to do is visit the iTunes Store and tap "Movies," which is located at the bottom of the screen. This brings up the Movies store, which is set up just like the iTunes Music store and the iTunes Television store.

Explore the options. When you see a movie that interests you, tap on it to bring up the information page. From here, you can see a preview of the movie and switch between Standard Definition and HD, if available.

A weird thing about the different iTunes stores is that not all versions of a movie are available at all stores. For example, I recently looked for the movie *Repo Men* (unrated), 2010, in iTunes on my iPad and the iTunes Store on my computer; and I got different options. On the computer version, I could buy the movie for $14.99 or rent it for $3.99—

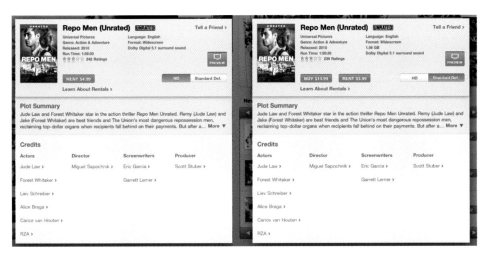

Figure 5-3
The difference between the HD and Standard Definition versions of the same movie from the iPad iTunes Movie store.

neither option was in HD. On the iPad, I could buy the movie for $14.99 or rent it for $3.99 in Standard Definition, and I was given the option to rent the movie in HD for $4.99.

If you buy a movie from your iPad, the movie file will be placed in the Download folder on the iTunes app. It will start downloading immediately if you are connected to a Wi-Fi network. Depending on your Internet connection and the speed of the Wi-Fi network you're on, movies can take awhile to download. Think: a half hour or more.

Once a movie is downloaded, you can start watching it by tapping on the Video app, which is where the movie will be listed. Unlike the computer iTunes Store, you can't begin watching a purchased movie on an iPad until it has finished downloading.

When the download is complete, you can transfer the movie to your computer. You'll notice a new category in your iTunes account called "Purchased on the iPad." This helps

you keep track of what you've purchased and where you purchased it.

BUYING MOVIES FROM THE ITUNES STORE

Buying movies at the iTunes Store through your computer is really easy. Just click on the iTunes Store button (located on the left side of the window) and select the "Movies" tab. Pick a movie and buy it.

Once the movie has started to download, you can begin to watch it on the computer. That's right, you don't have to wait for it to finish downloading.

The next time you connect your iPad to a computer, make sure you add the movie to the Movies page, so it loads onto your iPad during the next sync. Just select the iPad from the device list and then click on "Movies" at the top of the screen. Check the newly purchased movie. When you sync, the movie will be loaded onto the iPad.

RENTING MOVIES

Does anyone go to a store to rent movies anymore? I know I don't. I used to take big hits with late fees because I never managed to get the movies back in time. And sometimes I had late fees on movies I never even got around to watching! Well, renting digital copies of movies is so much easier. Just pick out the movie you want to rent from the iTunes Store, start the download, watch the movie and you're done. No errand necessary.

There is one thing to know about renting movies on your iPad though. You can play them on a television via the component video or VGA cable, but you can't transfer them to any other device. So if you rent a movie on the iPad, you need to watch it on the iPad (or projection device from the iPad).

You have 30 days to start watching a rented movie, and you can watch it as many times as you like within the first 24 hours, which begins the first time you hit "Play." When the 24 hours are up, the movie will delete itself. Poof! No need to return anything.

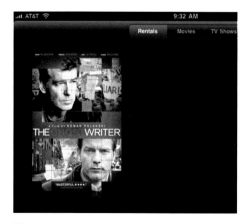

Figure 5-4

Rented movies have their own page in the Video app on the iPad.

RIPPING DVDs

It's really easy to get your music into iTunes and onto your iPad. Music ripping is built into the iTunes program, but DVDs are another story altogether. While it can be done, iTunes does not have built-in support for ripping DVDs. You have to rely on an external, third-party program (e.g., Hand-Brake) to do this.

Now I want to make sure you understand what I'm talking about here. What I'm *not* saying is that you should go download the latest Hollywood blockbuster from some shady part of the Internet for free or that you should go to a friend's house and copy all his/ her movies. I am saying that there is a way to take the movies you've legally purchased and play them on your iPad—legally.

This gets a little sticky when it comes to copying copy-protected content. But the new ruling that declared it legal to jail break your iPhone also made it legal to copy your DVDs in "Fair Use" scenarios such as this. (The ruling is based on updates to the Digital Rights Millennium Act that happen every three years.)

If you own a legal copy of a CD, DVD or movie, then you have the right to make a version of that content to play on your iPad. That's according to U.S. Copyright law, so you should be good to go.

The confusion comes with another section of the law that states if there is some type of copy protection on the media, you are not allowed to break it. So this means that part of the law says you are permitted to copy the material to a different device, but other parts of the law state that you cannot do it if you break the special encryption.

I'm not giving you legal advice here, as I'm not a lawyer. I just want to show you how to watch your movies on your iPad.

I believe that you should be allowed to make copies of your legally purchased material as long as you don't turn around and sell the copies or even lend them out. Just think of the copies as being part of the original. And just as it is impossible to read the same physical copy of a book in two places at the same time, it's not good judgment to have the same DVD playing in two places at the same time.

I'll try to make it even easier to understand. Here's a situation: I have a copy of *Almost Famous: The Bootleg Cut* (one of my favorite movies) on DVD, and I am going on a trip. I want the movie on my iPad and don't see why I would need to buy the same movie a second time just because my iPad doesn't have a DVD drive. So I make a copy of the movie and put it on the iPad to watch while travelling. As long as my DVD is sitting in the rack at my house and isn't being used, how can this be wrong? I think it's not.

So how do you get your movies onto your iPad?

The first step is to "rip" the DVD from the disc and create a movie file on your computer. This file can then be loaded into iTunes and synced to your iPad. One of the best programs to do this is called HandBrake, which describes itself as "an open source, GPL-licensed, multiplatform, multithreaded video transcoder, available for Mac OS X, Linux and Windows." Let's look at what that means and how this program, which seems to do something frowned upon by the movie studios, manages to stay around.

Figure 5-4
The HandBrake interface shows the Apple Universal setting.

HandBrake is *open source* and thus free, meaning that no one actually owns it and no one profits from it. It's updated and maintained by a worldwide group of developers that gives the movie industry no real target for a lawsuit. Now while HandBrake can rip DVDs, it cannot rip copy-protected DVDs all by itself. For that, it looks for a separate program for some help, and—here is the cool part—it will point you to where that program is on the Net. So you can download a movie file and have the two programs work together to get the content you own onto your iPad.

Help for Mac Users

When working on a Mac, the key to making a copy of media on a copy-protected disc is a program called VLC. VLC is a really powerful video player, and when paired with Hand-Brake, it's awesome!

VLC contains a code library that HandBrake can access, and HandBrake knows to look for this code to remove the copy protection. VLC installs the components that work around a DVD's copy-protection technology onto your Mac. And when HandBrake sees that these components are present on your Mac, it can get past the disc's copy protection.

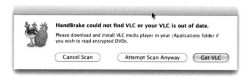

HandBrake could not find VLC or your VLC is out of date.
Please download and install VLC media player in your /Applications folder if you wish to read encrypted DVDs.

Cancel Scan   Attempt Scan Anyway   Get VLC

Figure 5-6
HandBrake will ask for VLC if it's not installed on your computer.

Get VLC at **www.videolan.com**. Or, if you run HandBrake with a copy-protected disc, it will ask if you want to download and install VLC automatically. It's that easy!

Copy DVDs with a PC

When you want to copy a protected DVD on a PC that's running Microsoft Windows, you'll need a little extra help. The process is nearly as easy for PC users as it is for those on a Mac, but it's a little more expensive.

While Mac users get DVD-ripping tools for free, PC users will pay about $52 or EUR 41. This is because the best program for the PC to get around copy protection is the AnyDVD application from **www.slysoft.com**.

This program runs automatically in the background; so when you start your computer, a copy-protected DVD looks like a regular disc that can be copied. When AnyDVD is running, HandBrake can rip any DVD that you put into your computer.

USING HANDBRAKE

At this point, let's assume that your Mac is equipped with VLC in the applications folder and your PC is running AnyDVD. So it's time to run HandBrake and rip your DVD.

There are no iPad-specific settings for this operation yet, so here are the ones I've found work well. To rip a movie using HandBrake:

1. Start HandBrake.

2. Insert the movie you want to rip into the computer's DVD player. If the DVD starts to play, press "Stop."

3. Set the source by clicking the "Browse" button and selecting the DVD.

4. Now tell HandBrake what type of movie to create from your DVD. There are no iPad presets, but both the Mac and Windows versions have an Apple Universal preset that works great. (Check the iPad's on-screen presets occasionally to find out if better presets become available.)

5. Pick the content you want to rip.

6. Add chapter names to movies if you want them.

7. Choose a destination for your movie files.

8. Click "Start" and be prepared to wait … for a long time.

Ripping a movie can take hours. Of course, the speed and power of your computer will determine how long it actually takes. The faster and more powerful the computer, the faster HandBrake will rip your disc. Regardless, if you're thinking ahead, set up a movie to be ripped overnight. That way, you don't sacrifice time on your computer and iPad.

When ripping a movie, it's best to convert it to one of two formats. Which format you choose depends on how important image quality is to you. For good quality, use the AppleTV 720x352 standard setting; for max quality, dial in 960x540 custom resolution setting. A large movie file will end up being approximately 2GB, which will look very nice on an HDTV.

For best compression, which will give you a smaller file size and a quicker conversion,

Figure 5-7
This HandBrake window shows the different audio streams for the *Almost Famous* DVD.

the iPhone/ iPod Touch setting at 496x208 will work fine. More advanced users can, of course, dial in these settings for better compression, better resolution and other considerations; but regular users can use these predefined settings with no problems.

Once your movie has been ripped to the computer, all you have to do is drag it into iTunes to load it into the movie library. Then you can add the movie artwork using the same process you do for books and album covers. See page Chapter 9 for step-by-step instructions for loading artwork into iTunes.

Some things to know about HandBrake to help you get the best results.

- Pick the right audio track. Many movies have multiple audio tracks, and few things are as disappointing as spending hours waiting for a movie to be ripped and then finding out you have the director's comments instead of the movie's soundtrack.

- Get the entire movie. If you're converting a DVD that contains separate episodes or

multiple versions of a movie, you can copy them all by adding chapters to the queue instead of just running the program. This way, when you run the HandBrake queue, all the chapters or episodes will be ripped.

HOME MOVIES

It is so easy to create videos these days. From those little Flip video cameras and cell phone video cameras to regular cameras with video capability … anyone can be a moviemaker. If you have "home" movies that you've made, it's easy to watch those on the iPad as well. Wouldn't it be great to have the movie from your last vacation with you … or maybe your wedding video, so you can show family and friends?

The obstacle to loading home videos on an iPad is that some movies are not in the proper format to be recognized by the iPad or iTunes. As a result, when you try to sync the movie to your iPad, you get an error message that tells you the movie is in the wrong format.

No worries! HandBrake can help by converting a movie from one format to another. Just follow the directions from the previous section. But instead of picking a DVD as the source, navigate instead to your movie file.

It's also possible to use QuickTime to convert a movie to the correct format.

1. Open the QuickTime player.

2. Open the movie you want to convert.

3. Click on the "Share" menu.

4. Choose "iTunes."

5. Pick the preset you want and go for it.

When the movie is converted, it will automatically be added to iTunes and can then be synced to your iPad.

STREAMING MOVIES

Streaming movies from your PC/ Mac/ Internet is a great way to maintain free space on your iPad and still have a ton of content. When steaming from your computer, movies aren't technically on your iPad; rather, they're being sent over the Wi-Fi network to your iPad using an app on your Mac or PC that links them.

Another option is to stream movies from the Internet with a service like Hulu Plus™ or Netflix®. These services allow you to watch movies without actually having them on your iPad or your computer. The thing with this option is that Netflix costs money and so does Hulu Plus.

Let's start with Netflix.

Netflix

Netflix originally started as a way to get DVDs in the mail and avoid the troublesome late fees that would add up so quickly with rentals from video stores and kiosks. And it's a smooth operation.

Basically, Netflix sends subscribers a DVD that they request … in those now-famous red envelopes. Subscribers watch the movie and then pop the disc back in the postage-paid envelope and off it goes, back to the Netflix mothership. There are never any late charges, and subscribers pay a monthly rate depending on how many DVDs they want to have out at any given time.

Well, Netflix has added a service that allows you to watch certain movies instantly via the Internet on a variety of devices, including the iPad. The service for iPad viewers is controlled through the Netflix app. What is really amazing about the Netflix app and its content streaming is the speed at which a selected

Figure 5-8

The Netflix app shows which movies you can watch instantly and which movies you've already watched. The difference is the buttons: "Play" to stream and "Add" to put the movie in your DVD mail queue.

movie will start to play. In my personal and very unscientific tests, it took less than a minute for a movie to begin after I selected it.

Here's how this works: After you install and launch the Netflix iPad app, enter your Netflix account information. If you don't have an account, you can sign up for a new account and enjoy a free one-month trial. Then you can start building a queue of movies to have sent to you as DVDs in the mail. And (insert drum roll …), you can start streaming movies and television immediately.

One really nice feature is that you can start watching a movie on one device and fin-

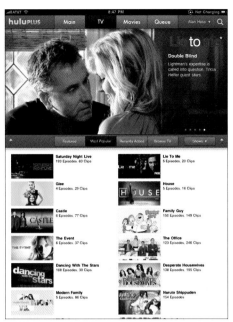

Figure 5-9

The Netflix app allows you to easily search its huge library of movies.

Figure 5-10

The Hulu Plus interface is easy to navigate and find shows you want to watch.

ish watching it on another. Also, since your Netflix account is separate from your iTunes account, you can log in to Netflix and watch movies and TV shows from any other iPad or computer with Internet access. You can even watch Netflix using the 3G capability of the 3G-enabled iPad. But the quality will depend on your signal strength, and streaming video can use up your data plan quite easily.

And Netflix streaming isn't free. It costs roughly $9 per month to get one DVD in the mail and unlimited streaming. Not a huge amount of money, but it can add up over time.

Another thing that can be frustrating is when the Internet connection or Wi-Fi gets over-loaded for whatever reason. When this hap-pens, the movie will freeze. This happened to me when I was watching a Netflix movie on my iPad while also downloading content to iTunes on a computer on the same Internet connection. There was nothing I could do to unfreeze the movie. I just had to wait until the movie started playing again.

Hulu Plus

Another player in the streaming industry is Hulu Plus. Since Hulu Plus has a lot more television content than films, I cover it in-depth in Chapter 6: Television. The main thing to know about this app for now is that Hulu Plus streams content right to your iPad. It also costs about $9 per month. But instead of just getting content, you get content and advertising. There is also a big discrepancy with what is available on the Hulu Plus Web site and the Hulu Plus iPad app. The Web site has a lot more content than the iPad. Hope-fully that will change as Hulu Plus continues to convert its files into a format that the iPad can use.

STREAMING VIDEO

The first thing to know about streaming your self-made videos from your computer to your iPad is how to set up a server app on your Mac or PC that allows you to send movies out over Wi-Fi. And basically all streaming apps work as follows:

1. Install a "server" application on your computer.

2. Let the server know which movies/ folders you want to access and stream.

3. Make sure that your iPad and computer are on the same local Internet network.

4. Run your iPad server app and pick a movie to watch.

Air Video

A great streaming video app is called Air Video. This app allows you to stream movies from your computer to your iPad over Wi-Fi. It's available as a free app, and there's a $2.99 version. The free version is great as a tester, to find out if the app works well for you. But of course, the free app has a usage limit. You can

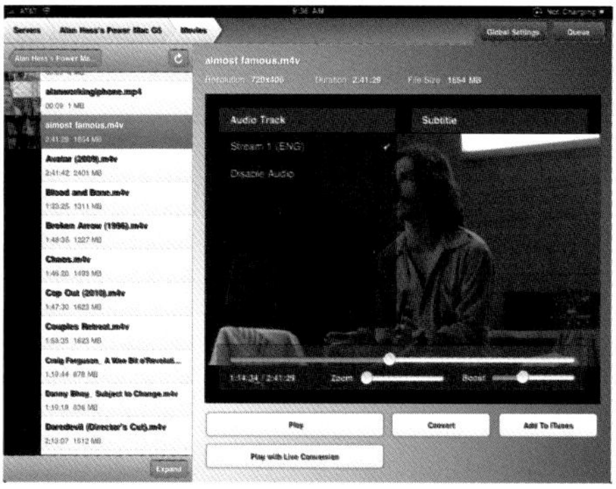

Figure 5-11

The Air Video interface is showing the *Almost Famous* movie I ripped using HandBrake.

only see 3-5 videos per folder for playback. I bought the $2.99 version because I have a lot more videos than that, and I really like the Air Video app for streaming my video content to my iPad.

After you install the app on your iPad, you need to download and install the server software on the computer that has your video files. Just go to **http://www.inmethod.com/ air-video/download.html** and download either the Air Video Server for Mac OS X or the Air Video Server for Windows XP, Vista or 7. Follow the installation instructions on the screen for your computer.

Then, you will need to run the newly installed software on the computer that turns on the Air Video server and point to the folder(s) that contain your video files. One important note: You cannot use the Air Video program to stream any video content that you've purchased in the iTunes Store, because it is copy protected with a DRM algorithm. That means if you buy or rent a movie from the computer's iTunes Store, you will not be able to stream it to your iPad. Sorry.

Once you have the Air Video server up and running on your computer, just tap on the Air Video app. This will enable you to browse the files on your computer, right from the iPad, and play any of the videos listed. Movies that have been ripped with HandBrake will stream to your iPad just fine.

StreamToMe

Another strong contender in the "Best Tools for Video Streaming" category is StreamToMe. This app, like Air Video, allows you to stream video files from your computer to your iPad. The similarities between Air Video and StreamToMe are many. Like Air Video, StreamToMe costs $2.99 in the App

Figure 5-12
Here is the StreamToMe interface.

movies and music. iTunes works great and everything else runs just fine on this machine, but it doesn't support StreamToMe. You need Air Video for streaming movies to this oldie.

To get the server application on your Mac or PC, you need to go to **http:// projectswithlove.com/streamtome/ servetome.html** and download ServeToMe (free) for either the Mac or Windows computer. Just follow the directions on the screen for installation.

PROJECT MOVIES

Since you have a collection of movies on your iPad, it doesn't mean that you have to watch them on the small screen. It is possible to watch your iPad video files on almost any television or projector. You just need an extra piece of equipment to bridge the gap between the iPad and the television set. Any of the following will do:

- Apple Component AV Cable: Enjoy 576p and 480p with this cable.

- Apple Composite AV Cable: You'll get 576i and 480i when using this setup.

- Any third-party connection kit made for the iPad: Output will vary.

- Apple iPod Dock Connector to VGA Adapter for use with a projector or TV with a PC/VGA input: You can get 1024 x 768 pixels when using the dock connector to VGA adapter.

All these tools are available at the Apple Store, either online or at a retail location.

Once you have your cable, connect your iPad to the TV and do the following:

1. Tap "Settings."

2. Tap "Video."

Store and it requires you to run a server program (called ServeToMe) on the machine that has your video files.

A big difference is that StreamToMe runs in both landscape and portrait modes, while Air Video runs only in landscape mode. So using Air Video and a dock connector at the same time is impossible. Again, since your iTunes-purchased content has DRM, it will not play using StreamToMe, but movies ripped from your own collection with a tool like HandBrake will work ... like a charm.

One other key difference between Air Video and StreamToMe is that the server application ServeToMe does not run on the older G5 Mac architecture. It only operates on the Intel machines. This is not a problem if you bought your computer in the last few years, but I have an older G5 Mac that I use just to store

Figure 6-4
Here is the TV Show transfer window on the computer-based iTunes.

Figure 6-3
When buying the TV show *Haven* from the iTunes Store on the computer, I first had to find the show. Seeing that it is the HD version, I switched to the SD version and then previewed the episode before buying it.

- The oldest unwatched episodes of all shows (or selected shows)

  Or you can just pick the individual episodes you want to load onto your iPad.

8. Then click "Apply."

If you've purchased TV episodes on the iPad itself, you can transfer those files to the computer. This will free up space on your iPad and is a smart move, especially if you have already watched the show. The quickest and easiest way to move episodes from your iPad to your computer is described below:

1. Turn on your iPad.

2. Attach the iPad to the computer with the included USB cable.

3. Open iTunes on the computer.

4. If iTunes does not prompt you to transfer purchases automatically, click on File > Transfer purchases from iPad.

5. The content that was purchased on the iPad will be transferred to iTunes.

These solutions allow you to buy individual episodes of television shows on the iPad or computer … and watch them anywhere.

Buy television seasons.

If you really like a certain television show, you can make sure you never miss an episode by buying the whole season with a single click or tap. This is the Apple Season Pass solution. And while it might sound like a waste of money—cause the show is available on television for free (or for the price of your monthly cable bill)—there are reasons to do this.

The Number One reason to buy a season pass is that you could actually eliminate your cable bill by buying all of your TV from iTunes or watching it on the Internet. I haven't actually managed to do that yet, but I do envision a day when my television will be completely on demand.

The Apple Season Pass allows you to buy a whole season of a television show at one time, and you do get a price break for your bulk purchase. For example, the Season Pass for NCIS, Season 7, is $59.99 for the HD version, and this includes all 24 episodes. Individually, the season would cost you $71.76 (24 x $2.99 = $71.76). So the Season Pass saves you $11.77. The SD season pass is $39.99, which offers a savings of $7.77 over what it would cost you to buy each episode individually (24 episodes x $1.99 per episode = $47.76).

Once you've decided to purchase a full season of a television show, the available episodes will be downloaded immediately. All future episodes will be available for download usually within 24 hours of the show being broadcast. Every time a new episode is available, Apple will send you an e-mail to let you know. This message will include a link for you to download it.

It's here that the service seems to run into problems. I had purchased a season pass for a show at the iTunes Store on my computer.

Figure 6-5
This is the Season Pass menu for the show *Terriers* … right on the iPad.

Figure 6-6
See the Season Pass menu for the show *Terriers* as it appears in the iTunes Store.

When I received an e-mail on my iPad that said a new episode was available, I clicked on the link and the iPad iTunes Store opened. I was asked to enter my password so that iTunes could go and check for new content. All good so far. But then I got an error message that stated that my iPad could not connect to the iTunes Store. Great!

Right now, the Season Pass does not seem to work on the iPad. You can buy a Season Pass, but new episodes need to be downloaded to the computer and synced over individually to the iPad. Not ideal but do-able.

Rent television shows.

A relatively new feature offered by Apple*— available only if you upgrade the iOS of your iPad to 4.2 or later—is an option to rent instead of buy television content. So instead of paying $2.99 to own a TV show episode, you can rent the episode. Renters have 30 days from the rent date to start watching the episode and 48 hrs to finish watching it.

* *At the time of this writing, it is unconfirmed whether or not this new feature will be offered by Apple when the new operating system is released. The service upgrade seems likely but may not be available with iOS 4.2.*

TIP

If you click on the Home button, the video will stop playing and the spot you left off will be saved. If you tap on the episode again, it will start playing from the last place you left off. If you swipe across an episode in the episode list menu, you will be able to delete it from the iPad. Be careful with this. If you buy an episode on the iPad and don't transfer it to the computer … and you delete it from the iPad … it is gone. Gone for good, never to return — unless you buy it again.

Figure 6-7
The Videos app icon is easy to find.

WATCH IPAD TELEVISION!

Once you have loaded television shows onto your iPad, you can access and play them just like you would any other kind of video content. Here's how:

1. Start by opening the Videos app.

2. Tap on the TV Shows tab at the top of the screen.

3. Tap on the show you want to watch.

4. Pick the episode from the list on the left.

5. Tap on the screen to bring up the controls.

FREE IPAD TELEVISION

There are ways—though not as many as you'd think—to watch television for free on the iPad. When I started to write this, I really did think there would be tons of different ways to get free, legal, television shows on the iPad. Turns out I was wrong. But there are some options.

If you search for "television" in the App Store, you'll find a lot of apps. The problem is that most of them are not ready for prime time or have anything to do with television. Many of the search results are either games based on television shows or television guides … or remote controls for your television. Of those, by the way, most are terrible. I can only hope that the developers of television-related apps start to look at the ABC Player and follow its lead.

Figure 6-8
Watching your favorite show is three taps away. Just pick the show, choose the episode and tap "Play." The controls during playback are the same for all video content.

ABC Player

The ABC Player was one of the first apps available on the iPad, and I still use it all the time. In my opinion, all networks should follow ABC's lead and offer this type of app.

The ABC Player allows folks to watch a variety of ABC shows for free on the iPad. The selection ranges from specials and daytime shows to primetime programs. But nowhere is a com-

WI–FI VS 3G

The ABC Player runs over a 3G connection, which means you can get TV anywhere. The quality isn't perfect, but it's really good for television that's streaming over a 3G network. If you can, use Wi-Fi; the cost will be lower (no 3G data plan to buy), and the quality will be better.

Figure 6-9
The main screen of the ABC Player features the most popular shows available.

plete season available. Usually just two or three of the latest episodes are available there.

The ABC Player is free, but it comes at a different kind of price. By that I mean that the shows are commercial-supported and the content is very limited. Still, if you're looking for a free way to watch TV on the iPad, this is the best app available by a network. While

83

other networks have talked about iPad apps, none have delivered.

The interface of the ABC Player is really easy to use and makes watching shows a breeze. The main screen opens with an overview of featured content, looking a lot like the iTunes Store. From there, you can pick either the featured show in the header or look at the Most Popular, Most Recent or Staff Picks—all on the Featured page. If you look across the bottom of the page, you'll see that you can change the view:

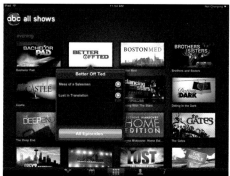

- **Schedule** shows what is on ABC for the upcoming day or week.

- **All Shows** is a list of shows available for viewing in the app.

- **Me** shows your viewing history.

- **Info** gives you the opportunity to send your feedback to ABC.

I like the All Shows view, because it allows me to look at the current offerings. When you tap a show title, it opens a pop-up window that lists available episodes. This window also allows you to start watching an episode with a single tap.

When you are watching a TV show in the ABC Player, a single tap brings up the player controls, which consist of a play / pause button and a scrub slider that shows where the commercial breaks are. It is also possible to zoom in with a double tap, so that the video content fills the screen and the black bars on the top and bottom disappear. You can watch in either landscape or portrait modes, but you get more screen real estate when you pick landscape.

Figure 6-10

Using the All Shows menu, I picked out the show *Better Off Ted* and started to watch an episode.

THE FLASH ISSUE

When Steve Jobs said that the iPad wouldn't need to run Adobe Flash player and it would still be the best Internet device, he obviously didn't take into account those of us who watch TV on the Internet. Or maybe he did and just prefers that we buy or rent our TV content from the iTunes Store. Regardless, just about every network has its own Web site where you can watch recent full episodes of television shows. But they all need Adobe Flash Player to work.

It is possible that, as the iPad becomes more popular, the TV companies will make it so that the content now available on Flash-enabled devices will also be available for the iPad—as ABC has done. But right now, the choices are extremely limited due to the lack of iPad support for Adobe Flash Player.

In an open letter dated April 2010, Steve Jobs made the claim that there was a lot of video content from providers and iPad users wouldn't be missing much. He stated "… video from Vimeo, Netflix, Facebook, ABC,

CBS, CNN, MSNBC, Fox News, ESPN, NPR, *Time, The New York Times, The Wall Street Journal, Sports Illustrated, People, National Geographic,* and many, many others [are available in a format viewable on the iPad]. iPhone, iPod and iPad users aren't missing much video." And while there might be content from all those video sources on the iPad, most of the television shows hosted by the broadcast companies still use Flash, making them impossible to view on the iPad.

STREAM TELEVISION TO THE IPAD

Wouldn't it be great to watch television on your iPad without actually taking up precious space on your device? You can, but the options are limited.

An option I've already covered in a previous chapter is Netflix. I am not going to cover Netflix here again … even though it does have TV content. Go check out Chapter 5 for the details on that.

The other real option is Hulu Plus. I was introduced to the regular Hulu awhile back,

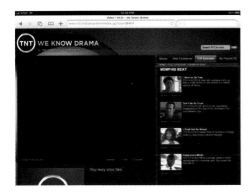

Figure 6-11

The TNT Web site on the iPad shows a black square where TV content would be if the device was Flash-enabled.

Figure 6-12

This message shows that the Hulu service is disabled for the iPad.

and it was/ is a great service. To access it, just point your Mac or PC Internet browser to hulu.com and watch a wide variety of TV content for free.

The Hulu service is free to viewers and supported by advertisements. The problem is that there is no Hulu on the iPad. If you open the built-in Safari Web browser on your iPad and type in *hulu.com*, the Web site will load but a message will pop up directing you to the Hulu Plus service.

Hulu Plus

It seems that there are two sides to Hulu Plus—a good side and, regrettably, a bad side. Let's start with the bad.

The longer I watched television on Hulu Plus, the more problems appeared. This has nothing to do with lack of content, but more with the Hulu Plus app crashing on a regular basis. It seems that the app crashes about 25% of the time, especially when it switches between commercials and the actual TV show. The most frustrating and common of these crashes is usually at the last or second-to -last commercial break, right at the end of the

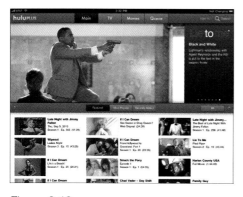

Figure 6-13
The Hulu Plus main screen is pleasantly simple.

Figure 6-14
This shows the process of searching for a show by studio, picking the show and, finally, playing the episode. The video player looks a lot like the ABC Player and should be really easy to use.

show. So after watching 40 minutes or so of a drama, the show just quits. To see the end, I had to find the episode and start over.

Yes, there are commercials here *and* you have to pay for the service—a business model that I fail to understand. The Hulu Plus service costs $9.99 a month and there are commercials embedded in the show … not just at the beginning and at the end but in the middle of the show, too. For example, a 42-minute show has six commercial breaks. Each break is only about 30 seconds, but that's still six interruptions on content you are paying to get.

Now for the good news: There is a ton of content on Hulu Plus. The player works well most of the time, and navigation and controls are well-placed and make sense. I really love being able to grab my iPad, tap on Hulu Plus and, within moments, be watching a TV show. There is content from a wide variety of providers, so it doesn't matter if the show originally aired on Fox or NBC or ABC or a variety of other sources / networks; it's on Hulu Plus … and more content is made available all the time.

The Hulu Plus content is a streaming solution. This means that the content is available only when you're connected to the Internet. The service works with both the Wi-Fi and 3G connections, but it definitely works better on Wi-Fi. When watching on the 3G connection, the stream freezes more frequently, which gets frustrating. And the quality of the video is automatically lower on the 3G network than on Wi-Fi.

Slingbox

Slingbox is a device that allows you to watch what's playing on your television anywhere. Just attach the Slingbox device to your television in your home and the programming

will be available on your iPad by using the SlingPlayer app. The primary downside of this option is the initial cost of buying the Slingbox hardware.

There are two different Slingboxes available right now: the Solo and the Pro-HD. The Pro-HD has everything the Solo has as well as multiple inputs, built-in TV tuner and HD. These items are priced at $179.99 and $299.99, respectively. Both options hook up to your existing television setup and you need to have television content coming into the box. If you travel a lot and want to be able to watch your home television on the road, then this might be a good solution for you.

The SlingPlayer app for the iPad is the window into your Slingbox media. Here is a little piece of bad news: The SlingPlayer Mobile app is $29.99. This truly is a solution for only those who really want to be able to watch their own television while out and about.

There are no subscription fees with Slingbox, and you can watch your content on any compatible Internet browser or the SlingPlayer app. Just keep in mind that if you're connected to the Internet by 3G, then you'll need a data plan for this. Your costs for that depend on the size of the plan you buy.

EyeTV

EyeTV is a hardware and software solution for watching television on your computer—and now on your iPad. The EyeTV products are made by Elgato, and I have been using one to watch TV on my computer for years. I really like it. (No, I didn't get anything to say that.)

Different products are available for the different types of television systems; the one I've been using is for basic cable and TV antennas.

The EyeTV hardware takes the signal from your TV cable and plays it though your computer via a USB port. I found this to be a great solution in my office, where I wanted to watch TV once in awhile but didn't really need another screen.

The coaxial cable that would usually go into the back of a TV goes instead into the small hardware device, and then the device plugs into any open USB port on the computer. The EyeTV software now acts as a tuner and allows that signal to be shown on the computer screen.

There are three EyeTV hardware products:

• EyeTV HD for digital cable and satellite boxes

• EyeTV Hybrid for basic cable and TV antennas

• EyeTV One for TV antennas

All of these products use the same software, EyeTV 3. It is the EyeTV 3 software that allows users to export TV recordings automatically to iTunes for playback on an iPad. And it allows live TV viewing on the iPad with the optional EyeTV app, which costs $4.99.

NOTE: To watch live TV, you'll need a Mac with an Intel Core 2 Duo processor or better.

STREAM TELEVISION FROM THE IPAD

With the arrival of the new iOS4, you can stream television shows right from your iPad to the new Apple TV. This is a feature available only with iOS 4.2 and later, and it requires a newer Apple TV. The idea is that you can take the TV shows that you've purchased or rented and play them on the regular

television through the Apple TV box … right from your iPad.

THE FUTURE OF TV ON THE IPAD

There is a lot of press about Verizon allowing TV streaming to the iPad from the FiOS TV service. This app will allow the Verizon FiOS TV subscribers to stream live TV from the service to the iPad using a home Wi-Fi connection.

Comic Books

The Skim

Before the iPad was even announced, there were rumors that the comic book industry was going to use the new platform as a way to deliver a better electronic comic book experience. Well, the big comic book companies and some of the independents have made this possibility a reality.

I am a huge comic book fan and have been for many, many years. I have many long white boxes filled with old comics, and every year I spend a week at the San Diego Comic Con International. I have also written articles on comic coloring and am lucky to be close friends with some great comic color artists. I really enjoy reading comics and look forward to new arrivals on Wednesdays. I do most of my comic reading on the iPad now. The size is right, and the touch screen controls seem to be made for turning comic pages, making reading comics on the iPad a real joy.

There are lots of apps out there for the comic fan. But as you'll see, when it comes to buying comic books on the iPad, there really are only two options: the comic store apps built by Comixology and those built on the Comics+ platform by iVerse Media.

COMIXOLOGY

If you're a comic book fan and want to read comics on your iPad—and let's say for some really strange reason, you can only have one app (thank goodness that's not true)—then Comixology Comics is the app for you. It is the only app that has Marvel, DC, Boom! Studios and numerous independent comics … all in the same place. What's strange is that Comics+ will make a very similar claim, but you'll find more on Comics+ a little later.

It's simple to get started with comics.

1. Search for and download the Comixology app (titled "Comics").

2. Tap on the "Comics" icon to launch the app. (It has the word *Comics* with a big X in the background.)

Figure 7-1

The storefront of the Comics app by Comixology is similar in layout to the Apple iBooks Store.

3. Sign up for an account; it's free and very useful. (More on that in awhile.)

4. Go shopping for free and paid content.

5. Download your comics.

6. Read your comics.

When you start using Comics, click on the "Settings" button (located at the bottom of the screen) and either sign in to your Comixology account or sign up to create a new account. This will allow you to access the comics, both the paid and free variety, from the Web site, your iPad and your iPhone. And here's the best part … at least in my opinion: If you use the DC comic app along with Comixology, the comics that you purchase from one of these apps will show up on the other!

Strangely enough, this doesn't seem to work with the Marvel Comics app. If I buy a Marvel comic in the Marvel app, then I have to read it in the Marvel app. It doesn't show up in the Comics app. And if I buy a Marvel comic in the Comics app, it doesn't show up in the Marvel app.

The Comics store is really easy to navigate and, while it isn't an Apple product, it does

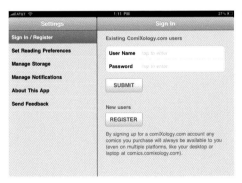

Figure 7-2

Entering your information in Comixology is quick and easy.

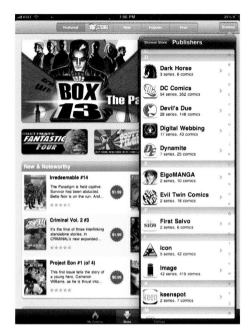

Figure 7-3

You can search the Comics app by publisher. Tapping on any comic brings up its information. Tap the "Buy Now" button to buy the comic from inside the app. Once you buy it, you can download and enjoy.

have the same feel as the iTunes or iBooks Store. So if you use these stores then you'll be able to use the Comics store.

When you click on "My Comics," you will see the comics you've purchased. If you purchase and download an issue while in the DC store, for example, and then go into the Comics app, you'll see the issue in your comics. But you'll need to download it again to be able to read it in the Comics app. No worries; you won't need to pay again.

Each of the comics apps seems to use a different storage location on the iPad, and there is no way to access this right now. So the apps download the comic book issues to the iPad and you can access them from inside the apps, but you can't access the actual files. This makes it impossible to move the files around outside of the app and to back up the files on your computer … which stinks.

Hopefully a future version of the iPad will allow the apps to move the individual com-

Figure 7-4

Seeing what you have already purchased is easy. Just click on "My Comics" at the bottom of the page.

Figure 7-5

This is the full-page view of the third issue of *Team Zero*.

Figure 7-6

Here is the same page, zoomed in to make it easier read the comic's credits.

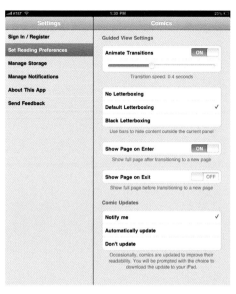

Figure 7-7

This is the Settings page on Comixology. I keep the "Show Page on Enter" checked.

ics off the iPad and onto your computer—the way you can manage iBooks.

Reading comics on the Comics app is really easy. Just swipe your finger across the page to go back and forth, just as you would expect. A really cool feature is the Guided View™ Technology that Comixology developed. This was originally designed for reading comics on the iPhone, but it really works well for the iPad, too.

Each page usually shows up in the full-page view. You can pinch to zoom, as with any image on the iPad. This works great if you want to get a closer look and check out some of the detail, but there is another way.

Sometimes it's easier to double tap on a panel in a page to zoom in. This triggers the Guided View, which zooms in so that the single panel fills the screen. Then, when you swipe to change

Figure 7-8
See the difference between a full-page view and the close-up of a panel.
The close-up makes it easier to read the dialogue.

pages, you'll move to the next panel in the correct order. If there are one or two big panels on a page, the view will follow the text; so you'll read each page in the order that the author intends.

I have this app set so that once I get to the end of a page, it shows me the next full page. Do this in the Set Reading Preferences menu on the Settings page, which is accessible from the bottom of the screen when in the Comic app. At this setting, the first thing I see when I turn a page is the full comic page laid out in front of me, just the way it would be if I was looking at an actual comic book. Then I swipe to start reading, and it automatically zooms into the first panel. With every swipe, I follow the panels until it turns the page and I see the next full page of the comic book. This is how I read naturally, so this is comfortable.

If you don't want to use the Guided View technology, you can just double tap on the screen to turn it off and go one page at a time. A single tap on the screen brings up the "Close" and "Settings" buttons as well as a full-page scrub slider across the bottom that makes navigation to a certain page really quick.

DC, MARVEL, BOOM!

When you look at the DC Comics app, the Marvel Comics app or the Boom! Comics app on the iPad, they should look really familiar, especially if you've used the Comics app. They are built on the same Comixology platform as the Comics app, and they all allow you to sign into your Comixology account.

The differences among these apps are in their content and custom buttons. The apps look

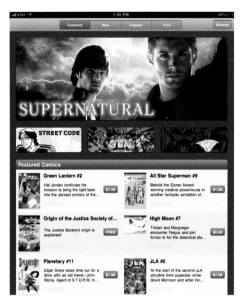

Figure 7-9
The DC Comics app's main page
shows the DC branding.

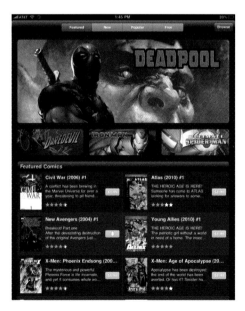

Figure 7-10
The Marvel Comics app main page
shows the Marvel branding.

Figure 7-11
Check out the Boom! Studio app. Notice
how the main pages look of DC Comics,
Marvel Comics and Boom! Studio look
the same as the Comics app.

and feel the same, but each has only content
from its own comic line. This makes sense
because the comic companies are in it for
themselves. Just like you won't see Apple selling the Zune or Microsoft selling the iPad,
you won't see Marvel selling DC comics. Ever.

All these apps have both free and paid comic
books, and the selection is growing all the
time. For example, I was just able to download *Blackest Night* Issue 0 in the DC store for
free. All 22 pages of comic goodness on the
iPad for free! That's a great deal.

As mentioned, the DC Comics app, the Marvel Comics app and the Boom! Studio app are
built on the Comixology platform and they all
support the Guided View technology, which
makes reading comics on the iPad a really
enjoyable experience.

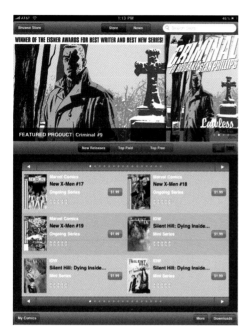

Figure 7-12

The storefront of Comics+ looks really familiar, because it too is based on the iTunes Store. One nice feature is the ability to finger swipe to navigate the store.

Figure 7-13

Comics+ is great for full-page viewing; but to look closer, you have to manually zoom in and out. If you double tap on a page, it zooms in; and every time you double tap, you zoom in closer.

COMICS+

If there is any real competitor to Comixology, then it is the Comics+ app by iView Media. Obviously, I'm going to cover Comics+ here; but after reading comics on both the Comics and Comics+ apps, I find myself only using the Comics app. In my experience, it's just a better product. That's not to say that the Comics+ experience is terrible; it just pales in comparison. Comics+ does not offer the Guided View technology, and I think it makes all the difference in the world.

What Comics+ does have is a lot of comics and there are a lot of other comic stores built on the Comics+ framework. Among the stores you'll find here are the IDW app, the Archie Comics app, the GI JOE Comics app and the Transformers Comics app. Good stuff.

FREE COMICS

Who doesn't like *free*? And I mean free … as in *it doesn't cost anything*. Well, believe it or not, there are lots of free comic books out there, and many of them are available right inside the most popular comic reader apps. They are easy-to-find, because the creators of these apps realize that you're more likely to buy stuff if you get free stuff as well. Right now, all the comic apps mentioned above offer some free content … be it an entire free issue of a comic or a free preview.

A great resource for free comics is the website **www.lorencollins.net/freecomic/**. This is attorney Loren Collins' compilation of 200-plus comics that you can read online at no cost. It's a great starting point to see what is available.

Many of the comics listed here are in PDF format and can be used in any PDF-reader program, like iBooks. Just download a comic, add it to iTunes and then sync it over to the iPad … as a book. Because these are PDF files, you have many viewing options. There are also other choices when it comes to free comics.

Long before the Comics and Comic+ apps came onto the iPad, actually long before the iPad even existed, there were free comics available on the Internet. It was much more difficult to find them then, but if you knew what you were doing, you could locate free comics by searching Google using custom search strings.

The idea was to find the CBR or CBZ files and download them to a computer. Now, comic fans can download the CBR or CBZ files from the Internet, and then load them onto the iPad for portable reading. So before we go any further, let's discuss the CBR and CBZ file types.

CBR AND CBZ FILES

CBR and CBZ are file formats that are commonly used for comic books and other graphically rich documents. These formats are open standards for comic book files based on the compression of the file structure. Basically, digital versions of comic books consist of the scanned pages of the comic all bundled together. The tough part is finding these files on the Internet, because they are usually on private servers and not too easy to find.

> ### TIP
>
> Many times a comic file will download as a .rar-compressed file. Just rename the file with a .cbr extension to view the comic on your Mac or PC in order to ensure it's working properly and is the comic you thought it was.
>
> There are many free comic book readers available online; just search Google for them.
>
> For reading the comic on your computer before transferring it to the iPad, I recommend using Comic Reader Pro, a cross-platform reader that works for Mac, Windows and Linux. Find this at http://www.fantastic.me.uk/comic.html. It's free!

A word of caution here about digital comics: Since the CBR and CBZ comic files are usually stored on private servers, you won't always know what you're getting and whether or not it's legal. Let me put it this way: A lot of the content out there isn't legal. Just because someone scanned a comic and then put it on the Internet in a place where it could be downloaded, it's not necessarily legal. There are many people who work on comic books who consider this stealing, because it is. Don't do it.

The key to finding legitimate and free comics on the Internet is to be able to search using those custom search strings I mentioned earlier. Using a search engine, no matter how good, will bring back a wide variety of results for any search. Using search strings narrows the search results. So instead of getting a wide array of results, you get a narrow, focused, useful list of results. Google is a very powerful search engine and can be made to jump through hoops to find lists of comic books ... and any other books for that matter. To use Google to find the comic files, you need to enter the custom search into Google.

Open Google and type the following in the search box:

-inurl:htm -inurl:html intitle: "index of" +("/comics"|"/comic book") +(cbz|cbr|pdf|zip)

Now let's break down this custom string so you can understand it and use it to modify or refine your search. This will help you get the results you want.

The "**-inurl:htm**" and "**-inurl:html,**" along with the intitle: "index of" is used to remove regular Web pages and hit only index pages.

The pipe (|) lets Google know to search for something OR something else. In this case it's (**"/comics"|"/comic book"**) which represents "comics or comic books."

Then we add the most common types of files to look for. When it comes to comics, that's "**cbz|cbr|pdf|zip**".

You'll find that the list of sites you get from this process is very different from your usual search results. But with a little practice and some poking around, you'll find free and legal comics in the CBR and CBZ file types. Just download the files to your computer, pick a comic reader and transfer the files to your iPad.

CLOUDREADERS

CloudReaders is a simple reader app for viewing PDF, CBZ, CBR, ZIP and RAR files. The best part about the app is that it's free. You can send documents to CloudReaders by USB and through the same process you use to send documents to Comic Zeal. Find step-by-step instructions for this in the next section.

Figure 7-14
The list of files loaded onto the bookshelf of CloudReaders is displayed here.

Figure 7-15
Here are the warning and directions used to send files to the iPad over Wi-Fi, as shown inside the CloudReaders app.

Figure 7-16
The user interface of Comic Zeal is showing the comics currently available in the reader.

A great thing about CloudReaders is the online cloud bookshelf, where volunteers are starting to upload free public domain books and comic books. You can also upload your documents over Wi-Fi. And while this is much slower than using a USB cable, it does allow you to transfer files from different computers to the iPad without having to worry about iTunes settings or cable tethering.

To upload files over Wi-Fi, just click on the Wi-Fi icon (located at the bottom of the screen) and follow the directions. You will need to use your computer's Web browser to connect to the iPad and then upload the file to the iPad. This is super easy and works like a charm.

COMIC ZEAL

Comic Zeal is the best reader for comics in the in App Store right now. It will import CBZ, CBR, RAR, ZIP and PDF files and display them nicely on the iPad. The only downside is that the app costs $7.99. But if you can swing it and have a lot of comics on your computer,

Figure 7-17
The background of the Settings menu in the Comic Zeal reader looks just like a printed page, because it is a scan of one.

this is the way to read them on the iPad.

With Comic Zeal, you see your collection stored in traditional comic boxes, which allows you to store issues of the same title together. This makes it easy to find the issue you want to read.

To add comics to the Comic Zeal reader to your iPad, just:

1. Connect your iPad to the computer and launch iTunes.

2. In the left column under devices, click on the iPad.

3. Click on the "Apps" tab at the top of the window.

4. Scroll to the file sharing section of the page.

5. Select "Comic Zeal" from the list.

6. Drag and drop the comic files from your Finder or Explorer window directly into the Comic Zeal documents section.

7. The comics will be imported into the Comic Zeal app immediately.

The reading capability of Comic Zeal is really well done, too. While the comic reader experience here isn't as polished as Comics, Comic Zeal does a great job, especially since the content can be in different formats.

Use the finger-swipe method to turn pages in Comic Zeal and the pinch zoom to bring

out the details of each page. Since each comic is produced by scanning in the pages of the print version, the quality can differ from book to book and even from page to page. This is a result of the care (or lack thereof) taken by the person who scanned in the comic book originally. Some are almost unreadable, but … *you get what you pay for.*

STAND-ALONE COMICS APPS

There are other options when it comes to reading comics. You don't need to download a comic reader; there are many comics that are their own apps.

One of the big problems with these apps is finding them. There is no "Comics" category at the App Store on the iPad. While cumbersome, the best way to find stand-alone

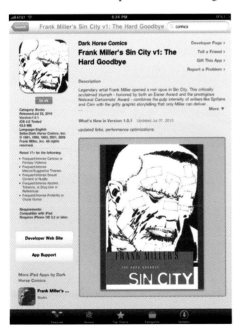

Figure 7-18
Frank Miller's *Sin City* takes a 200-page comic novel and turns it into a very slick comic book app.

Figure 7-19
Easy controls in the Sin City app allow you to scroll though one page at a time, but the lack of a good zoom is really a hindrance to the reading experience here.

News

The Skim

Traditional News Apps • News Aggregator Apps • Instapaper

All the news I see, I get on my iPad now. It's not that I have anything against newspapers or TV news; it's just that I believe the news reading/ watching experience on the iPad is superior in every way… and has been from Day One.

The iPad lends itself to news like no other device. It can be used to read a newspaper or magazine as well as watch news programs on television and the Internet. And since the iPad allows you to have push notifications, important stories can be pushed right to your device. You don't have to go look for them.

There is no news program built into the iPad though. There's not even an Apple-branded solution, so all the news apps available … and covered in this chapter … are from third-party vendors. The good news is that many of these apps are free.

There are two different types of news apps on the iPad. They are those from traditional news sources (e.g., newspapers) and news aggregators that go out and collect news from a variety of sources. The one thing that I never do anymore is go out on the Web, using a browser, to get my news. Why? Because the news apps work so much better!

The news apps don't actually load content onto your iPad; instead, they access news and information from the Internet. This means that an Internet connection is needed to use these apps to get your news.

105

TRADITIONAL NEWS APPS

By *traditional*, I mean these are apps from established, well-known news sources and organizations. I've been using these apps for awhile and I've found that they all have some plusses and minuses. Overall though, the iPad and news go together really well. The apps I consider to be traditional news applications are listed below in alphabetical order.

ABC News

The ABC News app is very cool, especially in the "globe" view. This view gives users a 3D sphere with news stories on its surface, and the sphere can be rotated in any direction. This lets a user spin the globe and grab stories they want to read. But if you'd rather have a more traditional view, ABC still has you covered. At the top of the screen is a button that allows you switch between the normal view and the globe view.

The ABC News app has a lot of features that you'll see again and again when reviewing news apps on the iPad. For starters, you can share a currently selected story with others by sending an e-mail with a link to the story or by sharing a link to the story on Twitter or Facebook. You can also mark a story as a "Favorite" so that you can easily retrieve it and view it again later. The buttons for these features are located at the bottom of the page. They are only active when you've selected a story.

The ABC News app has a lot of great video content as well. This makes sense, as the app's content is drawn from a variety of ABC news sources, such as Good Morning America, World News, 20/20 and ABC Nightline. And the *really* good news is that the ABC News app is free.

Figure 8-2

The regular interface to the ABC News app isn't heavy on style, but it offers a lot of content.

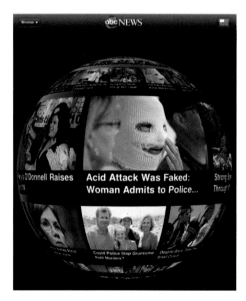

Figure 8-1

The spinning ball interface of the ABC News app lets users spin and grab.

Figure 8-3
The ABC News app has video sources from other ABC news shows.

AP News

The Associated Press (AP) has long been one of the leading names in news. You can pick up any newspaper and see the AP byline. Well, the AP app for the iPad is like having a personal AP feed whenever you want it.

The stories are updated quickly and the articles are usually very short pieces, being just a paragraph or two (perfect for my short attention span). The AP News app isn't perfect and it does have quite a few negative comments on the iTunes Store; but on the whole, I've found it to be really good at showing the latest news stories.

> **TIP**
>
> Don't always believe what you read when it comes to App Store ratings. Everyone has different expectations and needs, so an app that works well for you might not be right for someone else. The good thing is that a lot of apps are free, so you can try them without any real investment … aside from your time.

When you first run the AP News app, it asks for permission to identify your current location. I usually allow it to do so, because this lets the app give me the current temperature, weather and time for my location—not New York City.

Figure 8-4
The AP app is asking to use my current location when it first starts up.

Figure 8-5
The AP app is showing the photo, video and article layout.

When you open the AP News app, you'll see a menu across the top of the screen that consists of the following options:

- **My AP** brings up the main page of the app. A better description for where this takes you is *Home*.

- **Local** is the place to tell the AP News app to go out and get your local news. Within seconds of allowing this app to use my current location, I received ten news stories from my local newspaper. You can add other locations by entering the zip codes.

- **Categories** offers you the top news stories by category, ranging from "Top News" and "Sports" to "Wacky." Just tap on the category you want, and the latest news stories in the category will be displayed.

- **Saved Stories** is, you guessed it, where the stories you've saved to read later are stored. When you're reading any of the articles in the AP News app, you can save the article to read later with a single tap. This is where you go to read them.

- The **Settings** tab allows you to adjust the placement of photos, videos and articles. It also gives you the ability to add your Twitter account, so you can easily tweet links to news stories and even contact the app manufacturer. This, too, is where you can change the weather reporting, so it uses centigrade instead of Fahrenheit.

The main page of the AP News app is divided into three parts. There is a Photo section, a Video section and an Article section. Between the Photos/ Videos sections (at the top of the screen) and the articles (on the bottom) is a menu bar that slides sideways, allowing you to pick a category of stories to display.

Figure 8-6
The main article window is showing. This is where you can rate an article, Tweet it, share it via Facebook, save it, e-mail it and change the text size.

The news categories in this menu bar are based on your selections in the Settings menu (described previously).

To access the photo or video content, click on a photo or video thumbnail on the main page. A new screen will open, showing the current photos (or videos). You can then scroll through the files and tap on any of them to see the full file.

In the case of photos, your tap opens the photo along with a full caption. You can rate the photo, send it out in a Tweet or e-mail, share it on Facebook or save it for later.

Tapping on a video thumbnail opens the video screen and allows you to watch the video as well as rate it, share it via tweet, Facebook or e-mail, or save it for later.

Two things are nice and consistent in the AP News app. The first is that the navigation is very intuitive, and you can see new stories by swiping sideways on the screen. Want to see more videos or photographs? Swipe sideways.

Another nice feature is the side menu that appears when viewing a video, looking at a photo or reading an article. This menu allows you to rate the article with a star system—one to five stars. You can save it to view later, send the story/ video/ photo out as a tweet or in an e-mail, or you can share it via Facebook. When it comes to articles, you can also change the text size.

BBC News

BBC News was one of the first apps I installed on my iPad, and it's still the news app I read more than any other. I enjoy the style and delivery of the news I get here, and I stay really impressed with the app's functionality.

When the BBC News app launches, the main window is divided into two parts: the story picker and the selected story's coverage. There is also a news ticker at the top of the screen that reveals the latest headlines. The news ticker is refreshed every five minutes as a default, but this can be changed from the BBC News settings screen in the main iPad Settings app. To access these settings:

1. Turn on the iPad.

2. Tap on "Settings."

3. Look on the left side of the screen and scroll until you see the "Apps" heading.

4. Tap on "BBC News."

5. You can now adjust the ticker Refresh and the default font size for news articles. You can also choose to share statistics with the app developers, so they can improve future versions. As well, this screen shows you what version of the BBC News app you are running.

Figure 8-7
The main page of the BBC app offers lots of options.

Figure 8-8
Tapping on the "Live Radio" button brings up a bandwidth warning.

One unique feature of the BBC News app is the "Live Radio" button that's located on the top left of the screen. Tapping this button starts a free live feed from BBC radio. Note the warning: If you are using the 3G network, this could cost you; it uses your data plan to deliver content. Better to use this feature when you're on a Wi-Fi network.

Now back to the main window of the app. Story selections are on the right, and each category has a series of stories that can be scrolled through sideways. The categories scroll up and down.

Figure 8-9
The Settings panel shows the BBC News app settings.

At the top of the screen are menu buttons that allow you to change the default size of the font and share news content by e-mail, Facebook or Twitter.

Tapping the "Edit" button at the top of the screen allows you to pick and choose which categories of stories are listed on your BBC News home page. If you keep scrolling down, you'll see more categories of news stories as well as options to read news stories in various languages, including Chinese, Russian, Persian and even Urdu.

The BBC News app is free, and while it does contain advertisements, the ads are positioned in a way that minimizes distraction to news reading.

CNN

I struggled long and hard about whether or not to include the CNN app in this book. Why? Well, this is actually an older iPhone app—not an iPad native. In fact, it doesn't even have the higher resolution of the newer iPhone 4 apps. I don't understand why CNN hasn't released an iPad version of this app. I just hope at some point, they will.

Because this app was made for the iPhone screen, it looks pretty horrible on the iPad … especially in the 2x view. This is why I use the CNN app for one thing, and that is the push

Figure 8-10
The Notifications panel for the CNN app is a convenient way to receive news alerts.

Figure 8-11
Here is the CNN Breaking News alert in action.

notifications that CNN offers. This means that CNN notifies me via pop ups on my iPad of current breaking news. I don't have to go look for them.

Of all the different news apps I've used, right now this is the only one that offers push notifications. So while I rarely use the CNN app on my iPad, the push notifications make it worth keeping around.

To access Notifications on the iPad:

1. Turn on your iPad.

2. Tap on "Settings."

Figure 8-12

The Notifications screen shows which apps have this feature activated on my iPad.

3. Tap "Notifications" on the left. (Note: If the Notifications choice is not there, then none of the apps on your iPad have Notifications turned on.)

4. At the top of the screen, you can turn notifications on or off for all apps, or

5. Select specific apps and turn notifications for each one on or off individually.

The CNN app is free and works great. I just wish that it was made for the iPad. I'm sure I'd use the app more if it was designed for the iPad screen. As it is now, you need to run the app in the 2x mode, and this makes the text difficult to read. In fact, the whole app looks pretty shoddy on an iPad, especially compared to apps made for the higher resolution screen of this device.

USA Today

The iPad version of this popular newspaper is free and filled with great content … in *USA Today* style. If you have ever picked up this newspaper, then the iPad app will look very familiar to you. It looks and feels just like the newspaper. The layout is clean and simple with very few settings but lots of content.

Figure 8-13

The USA Today app has a very "blocky" style of design—similar to the actual dead-tree print edition.

Figure 8-14

Tapping on the *USA Today* logo brings up a menu that offers access to the rest of the "newspaper" sections. Not clear at first, but handy.

The *USA Today* app opens to the "front page" of the newspaper with a headline story and main photo in the center. Under the main story is a list of news articles that can be scrolled through with a simple flick of your finger. See an article you like and a tap of the finger brings it up full screen.

At the top of the screen in any article are three buttons:

1. The first sends you back to the newspaper.

2. The second allows you to change the size of the text in the article.

3. The third allows you to share the currently selected story by e-mail, Twitter and Facebook.

Scroll up and down to read an article, and scroll sideways through the rest of the content in that section of the newspaper. Speaking of sections, *USA Today* has four of them—just like the paper version. These are accessed by tapping on the big blue *USA Today* logo in the top left corner. The four sections are:

∘ Main (Blue): This is the main section of the newspaper with the "real" news. In addition to headline news, this section carries the weather, recent scores, the Day in Photos and a news snapshot on the left side of the screen. Like the print version of the newspaper, the iPad version of *USA Today* is ad-supported. The main page has a banner ad across the bottom. That's good news for us, because the app is free and ads aren't distracting. In the most valuable place on the screen, across the top, is a banner that shows stories from the other sections of the newspaper. If you tap on one, that section of the paper will open and the selected article will also open.

Figure 8-15
The Money page shows the stock market reports.

∘ Money (Green): The money section has finance-related articles as well as a graph that shows the latest Dow, S&P 500 and NASDAQ markets. You can also customize lists of My Stocks so that this section shows results for the companies you are interested in. Just tap on the stock you want to change, and you can edit a whole list of different stocks right inside the app.

∘ Sports (Red): The sports section carries sports news and scores. On the left side of the screen are the latest scores as well as a Day in Sports photo section and a Sports Snapshots section.

∘ Life (Purple): The Life section is the Hollywood news and entertainment section. It is also where you'll find the crossword puzzle and the Day in Celebrities photos.

Figure 8-16
The Sports page shows the Sports Snapshot section.

Figure 8-17
The crossword! Ahhh … it's a good one.

One of my greatest addictions on the iPad is the free crossword puzzle inside the *USA Today* app. It's a very nicely done piece of programming, and I would honestly pay to have it as a stand-alone app on the iPad. (Did you hear that *USA Today*?) The crossword puzzle is located in the Life section (just like in the paper version), and there is a new puzzle every day, six days of each week. Heaven …

NEWS AGGREGATOR APPS

This is a genre of news app that breaks the mold of the traditional news source application. In an aggregator, the news doesn't come from one source; it is compiled by the reader in real time from many different Internet sources. This allows you to pick your favorite news sources and have them all show up in the same place at the same time.

The following apps take advantage of RSS feeds to pull information from the Internet into its results. Learn more about RSS feeds in the sidebar on the next page.

Pulse

Pulse is my favorite news reader on the iPad; and at $3.99, I find it well worth the money. One of the things you should know about me is that I am a gadget fan, and I really like to know what's going on in the tech world. I read a variety of tech-related blogs every day, and what used to take a large chunk of my morning now takes only an hour or so … thanks to Pulse.

I use Pulse to collect the RSS feeds from the tech blogs I read, so I can see at a glance what's new and catch up on a whole slew of articles without ever having to open a Web browser or even turning on a computer.

113

Since the Pulse reader allows you to manage the RSS feeds it displays, let's look at the process for organizing, finding, adding and removing RSS feeds.

When you open the Pulse reader, you'll see an icon on the top left that looks a lot like a gear. Tap this to bring up the Pages view, where you can organize your feeds and add/ remove the feeds already there. You can just drag and drop the feeds to the various pages.

As you can see from image 8-21, I have a whole page of Apple-related feeds and a whole page of news feeds that bring in news from everywhere—from CNN.com to the

Washington Post print edition. To add a new feed to any of your pages, just tap on the (+) on the blank feed at the bottom of any of the pages.

To search for an RSS feed:

1. Open Pulse.

2. Tap the gear icon on the top left.

3. The Pages view will open, showing any and all feeds.

4. Tap (+) on the blank feed at the bottom of any of the pages.

5. A pop-up menu appears, allowing you to add feeds by the following choices:

Figure 8-18
This is the Web view of a blog entry.

- **Featured** gives you a list of featured sources, including feeds from diverse interests, including as *Advertising Age* and *Instructables*.

- **Categories** lets you search for feeds by category—from Business to Technology. This is really useful for finding new feeds that might interest you. You don't have to know about the feed, you can just look under a category and pick from the list that appears.

- **Search** is where you can enter a name or subject, and the app goes out to find all the feeds that match your criteria.

- **Google Reader:** If you have a Google Reader account, you can transfer your feeds to the Pulse reader by entering your username and password here.

Figure 8-19
The text view of the same page is less colorful but just as informative.

Figure 8-20
My personal blog in the Pulse reader app has all the information I seek.

Figure 8-21
The page sorting view of Pulse. makes it easy to organize your feeds.

Figure 8-22

The adding a feed popup menu allows you to pick the method of finding feeds.

- **Bump** allows you to get feeds from other devices, like an iPhone or another iPad. (By the way, this has been the least effective way to get new feeds in my experience. In multiple attempts to bump between two iPads, the service failed every time.)

6. Once you're done adding feeds, just tap the "Done" button on the top of the menu.

7. To go back to the main screen, tap on the Home button on the top left. (The button looks like a little grid.)

To delete a feed:

1. Open Pulse.

2. Tap on the "Manage Sources" icon.

3. The Pages view will open, showing all the feeds in their columns.

4. Tap on the "Edit" button on the top right or just hold your finger on a feed (any feed) for a few seconds.

5. A small "x" will appear at the top left corner of each feed.

6. To delete a feed, tap on the "x" of that feed.

7. The feed will be deleted immediately.

To rearrange the order of your feeds:

1. Open Pulse.

2. Tap the "Manage Sources" icon.

3. The Pages view will open, showing all the feeds in their columns.

4. Tap the "Edit" button on the top right or just hold your finger on a feed for a few seconds.

5. A small "x" will appear at the top left corner of each feed.

6. Place your finger on the feed and drag it to a new place on the screen.

7. When the feed is in its new location, lift your finger.

You can also rename the individual feeds as well as determine on what page your feeds appear in the app. Both of these edits are handled on the Manage Feeds page. Just tap on the "Manage Feeds" button and then tap on the name of the feed. The keyboard will pop up, allowing you to change the name.

Use the same process to change the names of your pages. So instead of Home, Page01, Page02, etc, just tap on the page name and change it using the keyboard. I've renamed the pages to "Apple" and "News," so I can easily see which page I'm on.

The main screen of the Pulse reader is divided simply. Each of the feeds has a single line of previews, so you can either scroll through the feeds by swiping your finger up and down, or you can look through the stories from a particular feed by swiping left or right on that feed. If you see a story that you like, just tap on it to access the full content. You will see the word *Home* at the top of the screen on the left side. Tap the

Figure 8-23
The main screen of the Pulse app is showing five pages with the news page selected.

"Home" button and the other pages will be accessible. Now tap on one of those to bring up its list of feeds.

Once a story is on the screen, you have two options for viewing it: text view and Web view. For a lot of stories, the text view might be the better choice, because it removes all images and just gives you the plain text view of the page. If you want to make sure you get to see all the images, use the Web view. You can change the view by tapping the "Text" or "Web" buttons on the top right.

Keep in mind that the text view saves bandwidth when on 3G. If you determine that a story is worthy of seeing in all its graphic glory, just switch to Web view.

A tap on the grid button (top left) will take you back to looking at the list of articles from your feeds.

Among the reasons I really like Pulse is its integration with the Instapaper app—a separate program that's covered on p. 120. I also like that the articles are loaded onto the iPad, so they are available later … even if my iPad isn't connected to the Internet. Obviously that means that the news content can't be updated until the next time you go online, but it does give you options that don't exist in other apps. The Pulse app's offline functionality isn't perfect and images from the feeds aren't loaded with the text, but the basic information is there for you.

One last thing that makes Pulse enjoyable is the effort its developers have made to ensure that the app behaves well when rotated. I like to read a lot of things on the iPad in portrait mode. I think it's more comfortable, because it reminds me of reading a book. But sometimes a wider view is better. And many apps seem to lose my place if I rotate my iPad from portrait orientation to landscape or from landscape to portrait. Pulse does a great job of keeping the view consistent even when the orientation is switched back and forth.

Early Edition

If you want your electronic news aggregator app to look more like a traditional newspaper, then Early Edition is the app for you. I like this app for a couple of reasons, but the most compelling is that the newer stories from all the feeds are on the front pages while the older stories are further back. What this means to me is that the most current stories are always the first ones I see.

When you first open the app, there are 41 news feeds already built in. These feeds are

Figure 8-24
The opening page of the Early Edition app shows the newest stories.

divided into different categories: Business, Design, Food & Wine, Politics, Technology, World News, and Uncategorized. You can remove these built-in sources and add any other feeds you like to the app. All of this management is handled in the Feeds menu that's accessible from the "Feeds" button on the top left of the app.

To add a new feed:

1. Open the Early Edition app.

2. Tap the "Feeds" button.

3. Tap (+).

4. Tap the "Add a news source (feed)" button.

5. Enter the URL of the site you want to add.

6. Type in the feed name if you want.

7. Tap "Test URL."

8. Pick the URL that you want to add.

9. Add the sections in which you want the feed to be displayed.

10. Tap "Done" on the top right of the menu.

You can also add news sections that allow you to keep your feeds organized by type as well

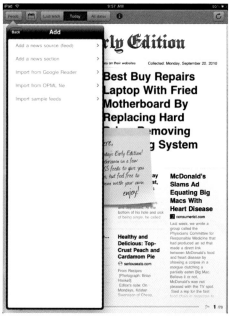

Figure 8-25
Adding a news feed is a simple step-by-step process. Just follow along and you can add a wide variety of news sources.

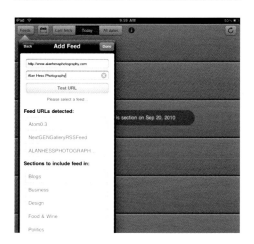

Figure 8-26
The Early Edition checks the feeds you enter and gives you all the options for adding feeds to your news hits.

as import your Google Reader feeds and even import from an OPML file.

OPML files are used to transfer lists of feeds between different news readers. If you use an OPML file, you'll need to have the URL for the file's location on the Web. Just enter the URL when you tap on the "Import OPML File" option.

To import your Google Reader feeds, just enter your username and password … and you're good to go.

If you want to delete a feed, it's really very simple:

1. Open the Early Edition app.

2. Tap the "Feeds" button.

3. Tap the "Edit" button on the top left.

4. Each of the feeds will now have a white minus sign inside a red circle next to them on the left.

5. Tap on the minus sign of the feed you want to delete, and the "Delete" button will pop up on the right side of the feed.

6. Tap the "Delete" button, and the feed will disappear.

7. Tap "Done" when you are finished deleting feeds.

When you've loaded all the feeds you want for the app, you can decide which of them to show. Tap on the "Feeds" button and tap on either the feed section or on an individual feed. I tend to keep the setting on "All Feeds." This is shown in the circle around the folder next to the text.

Let's now check out the actual interface for the Early Edition app. When it opens, you get a newspaper look with headlines and small snippets of the story along with its source. Tap on

Figure 8-27

Select the feed you want by tapping on it in the menu.

Figure 8-28

Check out the article view on the Early Edition.

the story you want to read, and it'll open up in a full-page view. From there you can send the article to Instapaper (covered in the next column), e-mail or copy the link, or open the story in Safari. You can also view the original source with a tap of the finger on the "View Original" button.

To move to the next page, just swipe from right to left (or left to right to go back), or use the slider at the bottom of the page to go to any page immediately.

Two more important buttons are the "Reload" button on the top right of the page and the "Last Fetch," "Today" and "All Dates" selections that will contract or expand your search. This app needs to be connected to the Internet to provide its delivery services, and while $4.99 isn't a lot, it isn't nearly as nice as free.

Flipboard

I cover Flipboard in Chapter 4 (which focuses on books and magazines) as well, because this reader looks just like a personalized magazine. In reality, Flipboard is a really slick news reader, and I have a lot of fun reading and browsing with it. The problem is that it isn't a great way to get up-to-the-minute actual news. Rather, it seems better suited for social media and feeds for stuff on Twitter. But that doesn't mean you can't use it for straight news; you can.

Want to add a section? Just tap on it and pick the feeds you want. You can even add a news feed from traditional news sources (described above), like *USA Today*.

To navigate in Flipboard, just swipe your finger across the page to turn it and tap on an article to read it. It really is a slick-looking app, but for serious news junkies (like me), it is just a little too haphazard in getting the real news to me in a timely manner.

Figure 8-29

Take a look at the Flipboard version of the *USA Today* news feed.

INSTAPAPER APP

I have mentioned this app prior to explaining it, because some of the other apps take advantage of Instapaper. So apologies if you've had anxiety or confusion about not knowing more about this app when you've come across these references.

Instapaper isn't an actual news reader. Instead, it is where I store articles to read later. It's like having a folder for news clippings that can be accessed on the iPad when you have time to go through your stuff. There is also an Editors' Pick section for when you have no articles waiting to be read but want to read.

Instapaper is simple to use … within the apps that support it. Just send an article to Instapaper, and it'll show up when you launch the Instapaper app. For example, I mentioned a

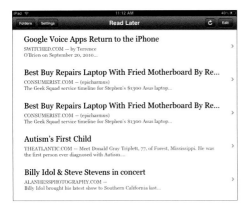

Figure 8-30
Here is a list of articles I saved in the Instapaper app to read later.

Figure 8-31
One of the articles I want to read is shown in Instapaper.

little earlier in this chapter that the Early Edition app could send an article to Instapaper. All you do in Early Edition is tap "Send to Instapaper" in the export menu. Doing this reveals your username and password along with the article description and URL. Tap "Save" and the article will be available inside the Instapaper app.

When you launch the Instapaper app, you'll find that the articles you've saved are listed. Just tap on one of the articles and it will show in full-screen mode in a plain format. Don't worry; you can open photos with a built-in browser.

Other reading tools include options for changing the font, size of type and even the spacing. You can also share the article, move it to a folder or open it in a browser. Opening the article in the browser shows the original page, formatted as it was intended. This allows you to see the article as it was originally presented on the Web.

After reading an article, you can either keep it or delete it. You can also rate the article and recommend it to others if you wish. If anyone knows your username, (s)he can access your most recent 20 starred articles. Neat way to rise to Group Thought Leader for the ambitious.

NEWS RECAP

There are many other news apps for the iPad, and you might find your favorite among the ones I've described—or not. I don't want to give the impression that the apps mentioned in the chapter are the only way to go; they just happen to be the ones I use to get my news.

Fortunately, a lot of the news apps are free or really inexpensive, so you can try out as many as you want before settling on the ones you want to keep using. It's also important to note that the apps themselves are updated regularly with new features and controls, so the app that was just okay last time you tried it might be great this time. And once you've purchased an app, the updates are usually free, so check out some news apps and stay informed.

Music

The Skim

iPod App • Buying Music • Ripping CDs
Sharing and Syncing • Smart Playlists • AudioGalaxy
Pandora • Last.fm • BitTorrent • iOS4

When Apple released the original iPod on October 23, 2001, it changed the way people listen to music. The iPad is not as focused on music as the iPod ... mainly due to the big screen and the video capabilities of the device. But that doesn't mean that audio is forgotten on the iPad. On the contrary ... the audio capabilities of the iPad are exceptional.

I love music. With the tracks I keep loaded on my iPad along with apps like Audiogalaxy and Internet radio powerhouses Pandora and last.fm, there is always great music on my iPad.

THE IPOD APP

The iPad comes preloaded with an iPod app. This gives your iPad all the functions of the iPod music player, including an ability to create playlists right on the device.

The iPod app gives you complete control over your music, podcasts and audiobooks. The main window of the app is divided into four parts. The top of the screen has the basic controls: volume, playback functions and search. The left side shows your library of music, podcasts, audiobooks, items you've purchased on the iPad and any playlists. The bulk of the screen displays the navigation window, which shows the currently selected content. And the bottom of the screen offers sorting choices, including Songs, Artists, Albums, Genres and Composers—many different ways to look at the same data.

Using the iPod app is easy. Find a song you like and tap "Play." So let's get on with getting music onto your iPad.

Figure 9-1
The iPod app is running on my iPad. I like the Album view, because it feels like I'm searching for music in my physical collection.

TIP

The iPod app will also list videos. But when you tap on a video file, the iPod app will close and the iPad's video player will launch.

BUYING MUSIC

The easiest way to get music onto the iPad is also the most expensive. Just buy the songs you want at the Apple iTunes Store on the iPad. The store app on the iPad is called *iTunes*.

Apple makes it easy to buy the music it sells— both on the computer and on the iPad. Just launch the iTunes Store and click on "Music." You can shop to your heart's content. Honestly, shopping in the iTunes Store for music is the same as shopping for movies or television shows, so I'm not going to cover it here again. For a lot more on the Apple iTunes Store, check out Chapter 3.

Amazon Music Store

What I do want to cover are alternatives to the iTunes Store for music. One of the easiest

Figure 9-2
The iTunes app on the iPad makes it really easy to buy music right on the device.

Figure 9-3
The Amazon MP3 Store has lots of music for sale, with new specials all the time, like the 100 albums for only $5 each.

to use is the Amazon.com MP3 site. This off-shoot from the Amazon.com online store has more than 12 million songs and albums. And with a little extra program (that's free), the site will add songs directly to your iTunes library so they can be synced to any of your devices, including the iPad.

Go to **http://www.amazon.com/** and select Digital Downloads> MP3 Downloads from the list on the left. You can now look through the huge MP3 library of music that's available on Amazon. To make life even easier, get the MP3 downloader that will add your new music to your iTunes library automatically. Just visit **http://www.amazon.com/gp/dmusic/help/amd.html/** and download the downloader.

Once the music is in your iTunes account on the computer, you can sync it to your iPad. The iPad has no problem playing the MP3 music files from the Amazon store.

RIPPING CDS

I have a lot of CDs. And while I buy most of my music through iTunes or Amazon now, there is still something very cool about the

packaging for CDs. I dig those cool booklets with the lyrics, the extra photos and the extra tracks you sometimes get. Moving the music you have on CDs to your iPad is actually very easy, but you need a computer that's running iTunes ... and has a CD drive. Preferably this is the computer that you use to sync your iPad.

Basically, you're going to take (or rip) the music off the CD and make it part of your iTunes catalog. There are some little things to consider in order to make the process go smoothly, especially if you have a huge CD collection.

The basic process is pretty simple. Just insert a CD into the computer's drive. Answer "Yes" when iTunes asks if you want to import the CD. The music is then imported into iTunes. When this is complete, eject the CD. Repeat with a new CD as many times as you want ... or can stand. It's a pretty boring process.

Okay, so I made that very simple, and it really is; but let's look at the full process and some of the things that can trip you up.

Figure 9-4
When you put an audio CD into your computer, iTunes wants to know if you want to import the audio tracks into your iTunes library.

The first troubleshooting move is to set your preferences in iTunes, so all your importing efforts will go as smoothly as possible.

1. Open iTunes on your computer.

2. **Mac:** Open the iTunes preferences by clicking on iTunes > Preferences.
   PC: Choose Edit > Preferences from the drop-down menus.

3. In the General tab, there are some choices to the right of where it says, "When you insert a CD":

   - Check "Show CD" so your CD will be included in the Devices list on the left side of the screen.

   - Select "Begin Playing" if you use your computer as a stereo and just want the CD to play when inserted.

4. **Ask to Import CD** is the default setting and prompts the program, when you insert a new CD, to ask if you want to import the music to your iTunes library.

   - "Import CD" triggers an automatic import of the music from an inserted CD into the computer without a separate directive from you.

   - "Import CD and Eject" is the setting to use if you're going to rip a bunch of CDs. It will automatically import the music from an inserted CD, eject it when done and wait for the next.

4. The next box is maybe the most important; it's the "Import Settings" menu. Settings include what encoder to use and how it should function. It also offers an error correction feature when reading CDs that are giving you problems. The settings attempt to balance out file size vs. quality. Available encoders are described next.

AAC ENCODER
Advanced Audio Coding is the latest and greatest audio conversion process that trades quality for space. This format does a great job of getting the best quality with the least space, and it's the encoder I use on a regular basis. But if you want the best possible audio quality in the music files you're ripping, then look closely at the next two options.

AIFF ENCODER
Both the AIFF and the Apple Lossless Encoder (below) copy the CD as a perfect duplicate. This gives you the best quality available, but these files also take up the most space.

APPLE LOSSLESS ENCODER
For all intents and purposes, this option is the same as the AIFF Encoder. It produces a perfect copy, but you pay for that in its large file size.

MP3 ENCODER
This encoder imports a music file as an MP3. Skip it. MP3 is old and tired. There are better options, like the AAC Encoder (above).

WAVE ENCODER
WAV files usually have uncompressed audio that sounds great, but the files are huge, so I recommend skipping this one as well.

5. After you pick an encoder, select the quality setting for your audio files by choosing a bit rate for your imported music. The higher the bit rate, the more information the file contains. More information means better sound and larger file size. I use a bit rate of 256 kbps, because it gives me the best quality for the required space.

6. Use error correction when reading CDs that have been scratched or damaged. This will slow down the import process, but it's

Figure 9-5
The general preferences window
shows the options available when
you insert a CD into the computer.

Figure 9-6
The import settings here show
my choices.

better to spend a little extra time to make
sure your audio is imported correctly.

Now you are ready to insert a disc and import
some music into iTunes.

1. Open iTunes.

2. Insert a CD into your computer's CD drive.

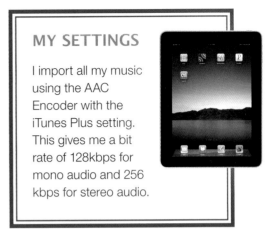

MY SETTINGS

I import all my music
using the AAC
Encoder with the
iTunes Plus setting.
This gives me a bit
rate of 128kbps for
mono audio and 256
kbps for stereo audio.

3. Depending on the settings you created,
the CD will wait to import or import
automatically.

4. If you're asked, go ahead and import the CD.

5. When the CD is done importing, it will
automatically eject or you can eject it
manually … again, depending on the
settings you entered earlier.

If everything went well, you should now have
a new album in your iTunes library with the
right track listings and the album cover art
automatically inserted. Life isn't always perfect
though, so here is the best way to get that new
music looking and acting the way you want.

Since I usually import one CD at a time, it's
easiest for me to find the new content by
sorting the music in my iTunes library by
Albums. Just click on the Music tab on the
left, and then click on the Albums tab. Each
album in your iTunes library is now shown as
an album cover. The albums that don't have
any artwork are just generic squares with big
music notes in them.

To get the artwork, right click on the album and
click "Get Album Artwork." This works… sometimes. When it doesn't, there are other options.

127

The most useful of these options is the Cov-erHunt Web site: **http://www.coverhunt.com/**. Once there, type in the album name. There's a good chance you'll find the artwork you need. If not, use any of the music sites on the Internet or try the band's official Web site. What you're looking for is an album cover image of the music that you just imported into iTunes.

Once you have the artwork on the screen, you need to:

1. Copy the image file to your computer's clipboard. To do this, right click on the artwork and select "Copy."

2. Back in iTunes, right click on the album and select "Get info."

3. After Apple warns you that you are about to edit multiple tracks, click "Yes" and then click on the Info tab.

4. You'll see a box here on the right called "artwork." Highlight the box and press ctrl-z on the PC and command-z on the Mac to paste the image into the box.

Figure 9-7
Albums without artwork show up as generic gray boxes in the iTunes library, but you can fix it. First, try the built-in "Get Album Artwork" menu option. You must be logged in with an iTunes Store account for this to work.

5. Then click "OK."

If all went well, the album now has the right artwork when it appears in your iTunes library.

The other problem with music files that can occur is that the album and tracks don't have the right name … or any name for that matter. Usually, iTunes will know the name of every album you import as well as every track on that album. It does this by looking up the info in a really big Internet database called Gracenote.

If the computer you're using isn't connected to the Internet or the album is one of the really rare ones that isn't in the Gracenote database, then you have a little work to do to get the information into iTunes. Here's what you're facing:

1. Select the first track in the album.

2. Choose File > Get info.

3. Click the Info tab.

4. Enter all the information for the track.

TIP

I have a lot of live concerts on CD from my years collecting live Grateful Dead shows. These and other live shows don't always show up on Gracenote, so entering the track info is important … if you want to have an easily searchable iTunes library.

Figure 9-8
Since the Beatles are not in iTunes, I need to import my collection and go through the tracks manually to make sure they are listed correctly.

5. For live albums, click on the Options tab and check the box next to Gapless Album. (This option removes any break between songs, giving you seamless playback.)

6. Click "Next" to get to the next track.

Now you have the right info for your music tracks and the album cover is showing in iTunes. When you sync your iPad and computer, all this info will be in both places.

SHARED LIBRARIES

Shared libraries are a relatively new addition to iTunes, and they can really make a big difference to folks with more than one computer with an iTunes library. Here's how it works.

With iTunes sharing, you can listen to music that others are sharing and you can share your iTunes library with yourself on a different computer as well as other iTunes users on your local network. To find and listen to music others are sharing:

HELPING HAND

If you have to enter track information for a CD, please do everyone else a favor and submit the info to Gracenote. Do this by selecting all the tracks and clicking Advanced>Submit CD Track Names. Done. In advance, THANK YOU!

1. Open iTunes.

2. Choose iTunes > Preferences (Mac) or Edit > Preferences (Windows).

3. Click the Sharing tab on the top of the window.

4. Click the checkbox labeled "Look for Shared Libraries."

5. You can also click "Share my library on my local network."

6. Then choose to share the entire library or only selected playlists.

7. You can enter a password to keep the library accessible to only those with the password.

8. Click "OK."

9. There will now be a Shared menu on the left side of your iTunes window.

10. Click the name of an iTunes user to see a list of all the music available for sharing.

11. You can also click on the little arrow next to a user's name to see his/ her media in a more organized manner.

12. Double-click a song to play it, or click a playlist and the "Play" button to hear an entire playlist.

Figure 9-9

I can access my main iTunes library on my desktop computer from my laptop iTunes application. Even better, I can show only the tracks that aren't already on the laptop by clicking the "Show items not in my library" at the bottom of the window.

Figure 9-10

Select the music you want to transfer from the shared library and then click "Import," which is located on the bottom right of the window. This works if both computers are on the same iTunes account.

There are certain things that can be shared and others that cannot. You can share video, MP3, Apple Lossless, AIFF, WAV and AAC files, audiobooks purchased from the iTunes Store, and shared radio station links. You can even share music that was purchased from the iTunes Store. But first you need to authorize your computer to the same iTunes account that originally purchased the music.

What you can't share is content from Audible. com, QuickTime sound files and QuickTime movie files.

One of the best features of shared libraries is that you can transfer content from one iTunes library to another. When you're looking at the shared iTunes library and you see something you like, select the song or album and click the "Import" button on the bottom right of the window. Now it's yours.

SYNCING

So far all your music that has been imported or ripped is sitting in iTunes on your computer and not on the iPad. To get the music from your computer to the iPad, you have to sync it through iTunes via the USB cable. Good thing this is easy.

1. Open iTunes.

2. Connect your iPad to a computer with the USB cable.

3. Select the iPad from the list of devices.

4. Click on the Music tab.

5. Check the "Sync Music" box.

6. Select the "Selected playlist, artists and genres" button.

7. Select the music to be synced from playlists you've already created.

130

Figure 9-11
The iPad sync window shows what music I want to sync to my iPad.

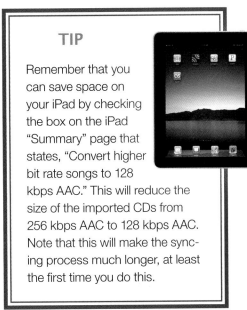

TIP

Remember that you can save space on your iPad by checking the box on the iPad "Summary" page that states, "Convert higher bit rate songs to 128 kbps AAC." This will reduce the size of the imported CDs from 256 kbps AAC to 128 kbps AAC. Note that this will make the syncing process much longer, at least the first time you do this.

8. Click Sync.

9. The music from your computer will be copied to the iPad.

I had you choose the selected playlist choice, because usually people have more music in their iTunes library than their iPad can hold. This is also the best move for those who want to leave space on their iPad for things other than music. Either way, if your iTunes music collection is small enough, you can simply leave "Entire Music Library" enabled.

PLAYLISTS

Back in Chapter 2, I promised there would be more about smart playlists here. I know it's been a long wait, but here it is. If you set up smart playlists properly, iTunes will put new music onto your iPad automatically every time you sync it. This will keep your iPad music collection fresh and, hopefully, you won't be listening to the same old songs over and over.

The key to using the playlists to automatically change your music is using the smart playlist function that removes music you've heard and to add music you haven't. If you take the time to actually rate music in your iTunes collection, you can generate a playlist filled will music you really like. By using smart playlists to describe the type of music you want on your iPad, instead of identifying the actual music itself, your iPad music collection can be updated every time you sync.

Figure 9-12
These are the smart playlist options that will put new music on your iPad every time you sync.

Let's break down the smart playlist.

- This first rule looks at the music library and picks only music files.

- The second rule chooses media that has a rating between none and five stars.

- The third rule removes all the comedy tracks.

- The fourth rule removes all the books.

- The fifth rule removes all the Fiction & Literature; I want this playlist to be music only.

- Finally, I limit the amount of songs to 100, since my iPad has limited space. If I was creating this playlist for a 16GB iPad, I'd change this to 75. If I was doing it for a 64GB iPad, I'd increase the number to 150 or 200. You can do more or less of course; it's up to you.

- The tracks are then selected by the "least recently played," which means that the list will select new tunes.

- I also make sure that the live updating feature is turned on, so when songs have been played, the smart playlist will update my collection automatically.

Then I sync this playlist onto my iPad. The key to making this work more efficiently is to rate your music. When you've rated enough of your library, change the rating setting in the smart playlist to filter your music choices. Give this a shot; it's really very powerful … and rewarding.

STREAMING MUSIC

So far we've covered buying music on the iPad and transferring your music from your computer to your iPad. All these functions place music files on your device and take up space. Fortunately, there is another way to play music on your iPad; and it doesn't take up much space at all, because the music lives somewhere else. There are a variety of ways to get music to stream onto the iPad.

Stream Music from a Computer

Wouldn't it be great if you could access your whole iTunes library from your iPad … without loading it and taking up precious space … and just stream the music to your mobile device? While this isn't built into iTunes (yet), there are third-party applications that can handle it.

One solution is **Airfoil**, a program from Rogue Amoeba that costs about $25 and includes the free Airfoil speaker app, which basically turns your iPad into a speaker for music from your iTunes library. The problem with this solution is that the controls are on the main computer and the Pad becomes a glorified speaker. This is a really simple solution to get music playing through the iPad, but it doesn't really work if you are sitting away from your computer, like in another room, with your iPad while trying to listen to music from your computer's iTunes library.

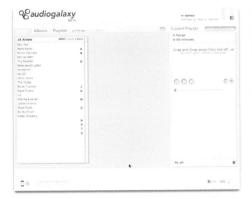

Figure 9-13
On the Audiogalaxy Web site, you can see your music when the application is running on your computer.

A much better solution is a service called **Audiogalaxy**. As I write this, Audiogalaxy has just come out of beta development and seems to work really well. This product is a combination of a server application that runs on your computer and an app that runs on your iPad. For the record, I love this app for the simplicity in setup and ease of use.

To set up Audiogalaxy, go to **http://www. audiogalaxy.com** and sign up for a free account. Then, on the computer that holds your music, download the Audiogalaxy helper app and run it. It will search through your computer and find the music files. (Seriously, I didn't do anything and the helper app found the audio files in my iTunes library on my computer.) From there, download the free Audiogalaxy app and sign in with your free Audiogalaxy account info.

I can now access all the music from my computer via my iPad. Here is the best part: It works anywhere. It doesn't matter what Wi-Fi network you're on, and it works on 3G as well.

Figure 9-14
Audiogalaxy has a great interface. Just find your music and then play it. One nice feature is that you can look through your music while a track is playing.

133

TIP

When streaming music over 3G, your data plan will be eaten quickly. So keep an eye on your usage, so you don't overdo it.

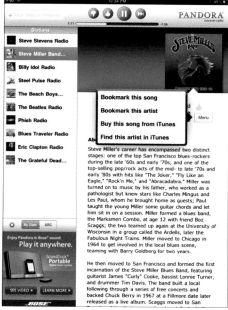

Stream Music from the Internet

Another option for listening to music on your iPad without loading it there is to stream it from Internet radio stations. This gives you a massive amount of content without any of it actually living on your iPad.

There are dozens of streaming services on the Net, so I'm going to cover only the two big players. They are Pandora and Last.fm. These really seem to be the best providers for Internet music streams right now. You can find plenty of other services, but why bother? These two have kept me very happy.

Pandora

The biggest player in the Internet music streaming arena is Pandora. There is a reason so many people like Pandora and have it on their computers, iPhones and iPads. The reason is that it works really really well. Download the free Pandora app; sign in or create an account; search for an artist, song or composer; and enjoy the sounds.

Now, since Pandora is free, there are audio ads; but you can avoid them by upgrading from right inside the app to Pandora One for $36 a year—a great price if you use the service all the time. I would love to spend hours going on and on about how great Pandora is,

Figure 9-15

The Pandora interface is really simple and, as an added bonus, you can pause playback and even skip songs using the very simple controls at the top of the screen.

but instead, just go try it for yourself. There's no risk … except you might like it so much that you won't be available to listen to your grouchy neighbor anymore.

Last.fm

Another big player in Internet radio land is Last.fm. My biggest complaint with Last.fm is that there is no iPad app yet. This means you have to use the iPhone app, and it just doesn't look anywhere near as polished on the iPad as Pandora. But looks aren't everything and it really couldn't be simpler to start getting music onto your iPad with Last.fm. Just download the Last.fm app; sign in or set up a free account; search for an artist or song; and tap on the radio station to play.

Figure 9-16
The Last.fm interface is still rather primitive, since it is designed for a smaller screen—the iPhone and not the iPad. This is displayed with the 2X scaling feature on.

MUSIC PIRACY AND BITTORRENT SITES

I'm going to step onto my soap box for a moment here and discuss BitTorrent and music (and video). I know it's easy to go out on the Internet and get music (and movies) for free at numerous BitTorrent sites. But this is called *stealing* and I'm sure you, my readers, know that's wrong and wouldn't want to do that.

I know how easy it is to get this free content, but I also know how hard musicians work on creating their art. In my other life as a photographer, I spend a lot of time photograph-

ing musicians; and I've seen the change in the music business firsthand. So even though it is tempting and really easy to grab cool stuff from swarthy places, first go and check iTunes or Amazon for the content you want. Sampling on these sites gives you a good idea of the songs available to help you avoid purchasing stuff you don't like.

iOS 4.2 AND MULTITASKING

When the iPad updated to iOS4.2, multitasking was finally implemented. One of the really great uses of multitasking on iOS devices is streaming music while doing other tasks. In other words, being able to listen to music and check e-mail at the same time is fantastic. This has been a reality for many iPhone users since iOS version 4 came out in parallel with the iPhone 4. The only downside is, since more than one thing is running at the same time, multitasking can slow certain apps and drain your battery more quickly. But I say it's definitely worth it!

Photography

The Skim

Photography is my *thing*. When I'm not writing books, I am out taking photographs—as often as possible. I actually spend far more time photographing, writing about photography, and teaching photography than I do writing about other subjects. But when the iPad was announced, I—along with photographers everywhere—started to imagine the possibilities of this device on our professional lives. To people of this ilk, the iPad can seems to exist primarily to serve as a portable portfolio and photo viewer.

It turns out that the iPad is both of these things and more. It has great resolution and a super-sharp screen, but what the first iPad doesn't have is a built-in camera (or even a USB/ SD card port). So the first hurdle for photographers—enthusiasts and professionals—is to actually get your images onto the iPad.

RESOLUTION

Before you transfer any images to the iPad, it's important to discuss resolution. The iPad has a 9.7-inch diagonal LED-backlit glossy LCD screen with a resolution of 1024x768 pixels at 132 pixels per inch (ppi). That's a lot of numbers that don't mean much for casual users, but they mean a great deal when it comes to photos.

137

Figure 10-1
Who doesn't want to carry their favorite photos with them? The iPad does a great job as a portable digital portfolio.

Traditionally, computer screens have had a resolution that was 72 ppi or 96 ppi. With the iPad at 132 ppi, the pixels are closer together than they are on a typical desktop display. This makes the images look sharper. But the more important numbers are the 1024 and 768, because these define the size of the screen, so this is the size to make images if you want them to fit the iPad perfectly. Remember this later when we talk about preparing images for the iPad.

LOAD PHOTOS WITH ITUNES

The easiest and quickest way to get images onto the iPad is through iTunes. This works really well if you keep your images sorted on your computer using a program like iPhoto, Aperture (Mac) or Adobe Photoshop Elements (PC or Mac). It also works well if you keep your images in a specific folder on your computer. To transfer images from your computer using iTunes:

1. Connect the iPad to the computer with the USB cable.

2. Open iTunes on your computer.

3. Select the "iPad" from the device list.

4. Click on the "Photos" tab.

5. Click "Sync Photos from" checkbox.

6. In the drop-down menu, select the source for your images.

7. This is where you have specific options, depending what software you use to organize your photos.

- iPhoto: You can select all photos, albums, events and faces ... but I don't recommend it, especially if you have a lot of images. This will fill the space on your iPad rather quickly. Instead, choose to select albums, events and faces and automatically include events, using a drop-down list of choices. If you pick this option, you can go through your collection and choose certain albums or events to get only the images you want on your iPad at the time.

- Aperture: With this program, you can select all photos, projects and albums or, as above, choose to transfer only selected photos, projects and albums. Once again, I recommend picking selected

Figure 10-2
The iTunes photo window makes it easy to transfer the images you want on your iPad.

images to retain some control over the amount of space you use for photos on your iPad.

○ Photoshop Elements: Again, this program allows you to choose between a full transfer of all photos and albums or only selected albums. At the risk of being repetitive but cautious, I'll remind you that if you choose all photos and albums, it can fill up your iPad very quickly, so I advise against this option unless you have very few image files on your computer.

8. Click "Sync." (If this is the first time you are syncing photos, click on "Apply" instead.)

iTunes will now optimize your images for display on the iPad. This means that larger images will be compressed in order to make the best use of the limited space available.

CAMERA CONNECTION KIT

Apple has a Camera Connection Kit available for the iPad. The Apple iPad Camera Connection Kit costs $29, which might seem like a lot, especially after buying the iPad. But if you want to get your images onto your iPad directly from your camera (or memory card), then this is the best way to go, and it's well worth the price … in my opinion.

This kit is two separate pieces: one for importing images directly from an SD card into the iPad, and the other for using your camera's USB cable to import photos into the iPad. The camera kit plugs directly into the iPad connector and, when it sees images, it allows you to save them on your iPad.

When you plug the Apple Camera Connection Kit into the iPad and either attach a cam-

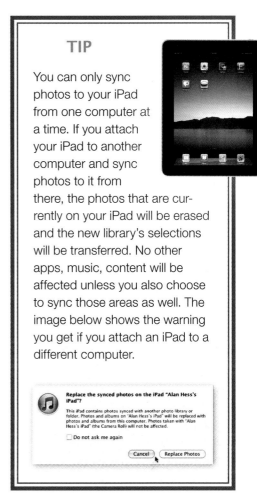

TIP

You can only sync photos to your iPad from one computer at a time. If you attach your iPad to another computer and sync photos to it from there, the photos that are currently on your iPad will be erased and the new library's selections will be transferred. No other apps, music, content will be affected unless you also choose to sync those areas as well. The image below shows the warning you get if you attach an iPad to a different computer.

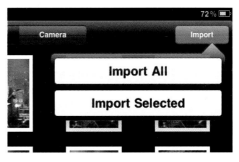

Figure 10-3
The images from the camera can be imported either selectively or as a full collection.

139

Figure 10-4
After your images are imported to the iPad, you can delete them from the camera (memory card) if you like.

era with a USB cord or insert an SD (Secure Digital) memory card, the Photos app on your iPad will launch automatically. The iPad supports most standard photo formats, including JPEG and TIFF. Find more on the file formats supported by the iPad in Chapter 1.

You can now either import all the images or select the ones that you want. The iPad will ask if you want to keep or delete the photos on the memory card or the camera. This is your choice. I usually like to keep them on the card or camera until the photos are backed up onto my main computer. That way I know they are safer than when they're just on the iPad.

A word of caution when it comes to transferring photos from your camera to the iPad: Photo files take a lot of space and you can fill the iPad quickly. This is especially true if you use the RAW file type when photographing.

I use CompactFlash memory cards in my camera that are 16GB apiece, and there is no way to

load a full 16GB card onto the iPad unless you have a 32GB or 64GB model that's empty.

And what happens if a person fills two or three cards, as many would on vacation or a photo job? While it is possible to load images from the camera to the iPad, I seldom add more than a handful at a time due to the space limitations. And once I have the images loaded onto my computer back at home, I'll sort and resize the images and load just the "keepers" onto my iPad.

E-MAIL PHOTOS

One tried and true method of moving photos to a different device is to use e-mail. I e-mail photos all the time, and people frequently send me messages with attached photos. It's really easy to use e-mail to get photos onto and off of your iPad.

When you receive an e-mail with a photo you want to save on your iPad, just press your finger on the image and wait for the "Save Image/Copy" menu to pop up. Tap "Save Image" to copy the photo to the Saved Photos album in the Photos app.

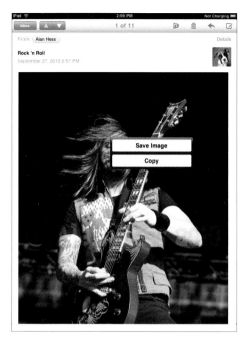

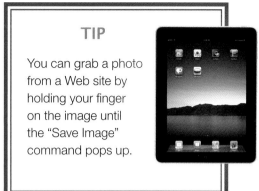

Figure 10-5
Hold your finger on an image in an e-mail and the pop-up menu will allow you to save the image to your iPad.

At times you might receive an e-mail with multiple images; don't worry. Apple understands this happens. If there are multiple images attached to a message, the pop-up dialogue box will ask if you want to save them all.

SCREEN CAPTURES

Want to share something on your iPad screen with someone else? You can do this by taking a screen capture of your iPad screen. It's really useful; at least it is for me, as most of the images in the book were created using this feature.

Just press the Home button and the Power button on your iPad at the same time. The screen will flash white; the iPad will make a camera shutter click sound; and you're done.

Figure 10-6
Here is a screen capture of my Photo page on the iPad.

Now just go back to what you were doing. The screen capture is saved in your "Saved Photos" folder, which is accessible by opening the Photos app, tapping on the "Albums" button at the top of the screen, and then opening the Saved Photos album.

9. Add a new collection in the ShutterSnitch app.

10. Now when you take photos with a camera using the Eye-Fi card, the images will appear instantly on the iPad.

11. Remember that at some point you will run out of space on your iPad, so make sure that you download the images from your iPad to a long-term storage device, like your PC or Mac.

I love what this technology represents. For example, think about walking around an event taking photos. The images appear automatically on your iPad, so your customer can see the photographs in real time. This could save a professional photographer lots of time that would otherwise be required days later for a photo preview meeting.

THE PHOTOS APP

The Photos app on the iPad is one of the built-in, free and really useful apps that you can't delete. Who'd want to anyway? All the methods for storing and sharing photos that are described in this chapter use the iPad Photo app. This is where an iPad user can view images on the device.

Figure 10-8
The Photos app is clean and easy to use.

The Photos app is really clean and simple to use, and it shows off your images very well. You don't have to use any other portfolio apps, but there's more information on those options a little later in the chapter.

The Photos app is divided into five sections, if you happen to use all the features of iPhoto 09. If you use a different program or are on a PC, then some of these will not appear.

Each of the sections lets you look at your photos in a slightly different way. When you first tap on the Photos app, it will open in the Albums view if there are albums present. If not, it opens in the Photos view.

- The "Photos" view shows all your photos that are on the iPad in a thumbnail view. If the photos were not sorted into albums before you loaded them on to the iPad, then this is the only view you get.

- The "Albums" view shows all the albums on your iPad. If you have used the Camera Connection Kit, there will be an additional two albums that the iPad created automatically. Those are the Last Import album and the All Imported album. These two albums contain images that have been imported into the iPad using the Camera Connect Kit. Another album created by the iPad is called "Saved Photos." It contains images saved to the iPad from e-mail, grabbed from Web sites, images transferred using the Photo Transfer app, and screen captures.

- The "Events" section is for iPhoto users only. In recent versions of iPhoto, you have the option to sort your photos by events. This is very much like an automatic album creator, and if you sync an event or events to the iPad, then they will show up here.

Figure 10-9
The Places interface is pretty slick.

Figure 10-10
See photos in the Photos app.

- "Faces" in iPhoto 09 has a very interesting face-recognition feature. You can tag people in your images and the program will try to find other photos you may have with the same face. If you use the Faces feature in iPhoto 09, then it will show up here … as long as there is at least one image that has a face tagged in it.

- The "Places" section might be one of the coolest interfaces available for viewing images. If you geo-tag your images—either by using a camera that is GPS-enabled or by using the map tool in iPhoto 09—then, when you load your images onto the iPad, you can search for them by location. The Places view shows, on a map, where your images were taken. Each location is marked with a red pushpin. Tap on a pushpin to see the photos from that location.

Viewing Photos

The real fun with the Photos app is in viewing individual photos. No matter which view you use to access the photos you want to show, just tap on the thumbnail to open the image. With the image open, you can do the following:

- **Filmstrip:** When you first tap on an image to open it, you'll see a filmstrip view across the bottom of the screen and some menu

options on the top. These will fade from sight after a few seconds but are easily brought back up by single tapping on the screen. You can now use your finger to scroll through the images and release on the one you want to pick that image and display it in full-screen view.

- **Scroll:** With an image file open, slide your finger from right to left to go to the next photo or from left to right to go to the previous photo. Just keep in mind that when you are at the first image, you can't swipe left to right; and when you're at the last image, you can't swipe right to left.

- **Slide show:** One of the menu choices here is to run the images as a slideshow. More on this feature in the next section.

- **Double tap:** Double tap on an image to fill the screen with that image. Note though: If you are holding the iPad in landscape mode and looking at a photo taken in portrait orientation, there will be black bars on both sides of the photo. Double tap the screen and those bars disappear, as the image zooms to fill the screen. But this does not change the proportions of the image. The problem is that you are now missing the top and bottom

145

Figure 10-11
You can zoom in really close with the Photos app.

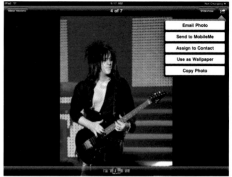

Figure 10-12
Here's a peek at the menu options available in the Photos app when a single image is being shown.

of the image. You can use a finger to move the image around, but you won't be able to see all of it at the same time. Double tap the screen again and the view will return to a size that fits inside the screen.

○ **Zoom in:** To zoom a photograph, put two fingers on the screen close to each other at the same time, and then move your fingers apart.

○ **Zoom out:** To zoom out on a photo and see the whole image, place two fingers on the screen far apart and "pinch" them together. If you zoom out further than the photo boundaries, it will "release" the image and go back to the thumbnail view.

Moving Photos

When a photo is open in the Photos app, on the top right of the screen, is a menu button. When you tap this, choices appear for how you can move the currently visible image. These options include:

○ **E-mail Photo.** Tap on this button to copy the image into an e-mail message. That's it. Really nice and simple. More on e-mailing photos a little later.

○ **Send to MobileMe.** This button publishes the image to your MobileMe account and adds it to a gallery. If no other images are there, MobileMe will ask you to create a gallery and name it.

○ **Assign to Contact.** This allows you to use the current photo as the image for any of your contacts in your Address Book.

○ **Use as Wallpaper.** You can change the wallpaper background of the iPad's home screen or the lock screen (or both) by just tapping on the Wallpaper button.

○ **Copy Photo.** This button allows you to copy the photo into the iPad's memory to be pasted later.

Managing Multiple Images

There are times when you'll want to select multiple images ... maybe to e-mail them out together or to delete them. Apple has you covered here, but the controls are a little difficult to find.

In the thumbnail view of your images, tap the icon at the top right of the screen. (It's the little box with an arrow coming out of it.) This

146

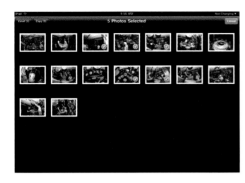

Figure 10-13
The "Select Image" window shows the E-mail and Copy options. Since this album was loaded by syncing from iTunes, there is no "Delete" option.

brings up the "Select Photos" screen, which looks just like a regular thumbnail screen except for the words *Select Photos* across the top. Tapping on the thumbnails now selects them. (Each selected image will have a blue and white check mark in the bottom right corner.) Tap an image a second time to deselect it.

When you have selected at least one image, the "E-mail" and "Copy" menu choices are suddenly active. So you can now e-mail or copy the images that have been selected. There is a catch though: If you select more than five images, the e-mail option disappears. You can e-mail up to five images at a time.

If you want to delete photos from your iPad, you can … except for those synced directly from iTunes. The only way to delete or remove those photos is to uncheck them in iTunes. The next time your iPad is synced, they will be removed.

To delete images that you've imported into the iPad using e-mail or the Camera

Connection Kit or the Photo Transfer app, follow the steps below:

1. Open the Photos app on your iPad.

2. Tap on "Albums" in the menu across the top of the screen. (If Albums is not present, then you have no saved images on your iPad that can be deleted.)

3. Tap on the "Saved Photos" album … or the "Last Import" album or the "All Imported" album. (These are the only albums from which you can delete photos on the iPad.)

4. Tap on the file icon at the top right of the screen to enter the "Select Photos" screen.

5. Select the images you want to delete.

6. Tap on the red "Delete" button. A second button will appear to ask if you want to delete selected photos.

7. Tap on this button to delete the images, or tap the "Cancel" button on the top right to cancel out of the deletion process.

8. When the images are deleted, they are gone. There is no "Undo."

When you're browsing through images in the Saved Photos, Last Import and All Imported albums, you will also be able to delete the current photo by tapping on the "Delete" icon at the top right. It looks like a little trashcan. Tapping it brings up a "Delete Photo" button. Tap this to delete the image, or tap anywhere else on the screen to cancel.

No New Albums

Here is something you can't do in the iPad Photos app, and I find it really annoying. In fact, it bothers me so much that I use a couple portfolio apps instead. (These are covered a little later in this chapter.)

There is no way to create albums on the iPad and no way to move images from one album to another. This means that if you import images to a certain album, they are stuck there.

For example, say I have an album of concert images on my iPad and I want to show someone only the images of the guitar player. To do this, I'd have to create another album in iPhoto on my Mac, and then sync the images over to my iPad in a new album using the USB cable. What a pain! It's a good thing there are apps to remedy this gross functional oversight by Apple.

Slide Show

The iPad has a built-in slide show. Yup, built right in … no app to buy. The problem is that it is a very simple slideshow without a lot of functionality or customizable options. But then again, it's free (minus the cost of the iPad of course) and tied to the Photos app.

The slide show options are located in the Settings app of the iPad. You'll see that there are only three options. You can control the length of time that each slide is visible; you can turn Repeat on and off; and you can turn Shuffle on and off.

The length of time that each slide is visible can be set for:

- 2 seconds
- 3 seconds
- 5 seconds
- 10 seconds
- 20 seconds

That's really about it. To play the slide show, just select an album or group of photos using one of the five options: Photos, Albums, Events, Faces or Places. Then, tap on the slideshow button, located at the top right of the screen.

Figure 10-14
The slide show options are located in the iPad's Settings app under Photos.

This opens a set of slide show controls that allows you to play music with your slideshow and pick the music to use. It is also where you can pick the transition between slides. There are five choices: Cube, Dissolve, Ripple, Wipe and Origami. There is also a "Start Slideshow" button. Just tap it and the images start to play. It doesn't matter if the iPad is in portrait or landscape orientation; the slide show works in either. And if you change orientation in the middle of the slideshow, the image display will adjust automatically. This is a solid feature on the iPad.

PORTFOLIO APPS

The Photos app on the iPad can be limiting, especially if you want to have a presentation portfolio on the device that looks professional. There are two different apps that do a great job creating portfolios on the iPad.

Portfolio App ($14.99)

Every portfolio needs a cover image—something to grab viewers' attention. And this app really excels at this. The Portfolio app can be used in landscape or portrait view, and it can even be used with an external television via component or composite cables … to allow you to present your images on a big screen.

Now the app is not free; at about $15, it actually costs quite a bit for an iPad app, but that's a drop in the bucket compared to creating a traditional printed portfolio.

With the Portfolio app, you can create special images to use in different circumstances. That is, you can pick three different images to set as the portfolio cover, and the app will pick one to use depending on the orientation of the iPad. I absolutely love this. It means that if I hand over my iPad to someone, (s)he can see my images and the cover image is always displayed correctly for whatever orientation it's in.

Another great feature is that you can lock the portfolio, so unless a person has the pass code, (s)he can't change any of the settings in the app. This means that a viewer can see what you want them to see … and nothing more.

After you open the Portfolio app, tap on "Configure" to manage galleries, change the front image or read the Help file. You can also lock the configure menu here by entering a four-digit pass code. Don't forget the code, because there is no way to get it back. If you lose the code, you will have to delete the app and start over.

When you tap "Manage Galleries," you can add galleries and add photos to each gallery. The really nice part of this gallery is that you can choose images for the gallery from the images on your iPad in the Photos app.

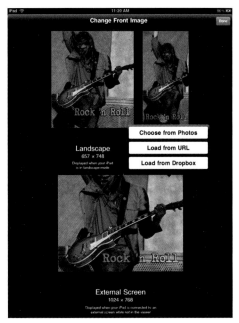

Figure 10-15

Here are the main cover image page of the Portfolio app (above) and the main gallery page (below).

You can also use Dropbox to get the images in your portfolio. You can even load images using a URL, so you can grab your images from the Internet and put them right into the portfolio. (There is more information on Dropbox in Chapter 15.)

149

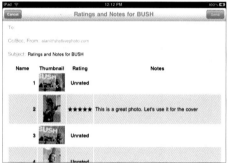

Figure 10-16

Rate a photo and send an e-mail from the rating in the Portfolio app.

Tap on any photo in the Portfolio app to set that image as the Gallery cover, edit the keywords associated with it, or rename the photo. This is all really rewarding stuff.

For the people who get to see your portfolio, there are some nice touches. The one that really stands out to me is the ability for viewers to leave notes on your images.

To leave a note on a photo you're looking at, tap the screen and then tap the file icon at the top of the screen next to the portfolio name. This opens a "Notes" window that allows you to leave a message and rate the image. Great stuff, especially if the person reviewing the photo is not with you.

The best part is that if you go back into the "Manage Galleries" section and click on a

gallery, you can "Clear Ratings and Notes" or "E-mail Ratings and Notes." The e-mail sends out a message with the name of the image(s), a thumbnail, its rating and any notes that viewers have left. The message is in either a PDF or a HTML5 file. Keep in mind that you can't edit the information at all; but getting feedback, even if it's negative, is good. At least it is in my book …

FolioBook ($7.99)

FolioBook is a slick app for showing your photos on the iPad. As I was working on this book, FolioBook released a new version that really improved the app and removed the two biggest complaints from previous versions. You can now have more than three galleries, and the app works great in both landscape and portrait view. So if you've been using this app and haven't updated to the latest version, I suggest you do.

The FolioBook app allows you to have a full-screen image for the main page of your portfolio, and the other portfolios are accessible from the front page. To access the menu, just place a finger on the screen and hold it there until the menu appears at the top of the screen.

There are two menus at the top of the screen. The first looks like an F and allows you to edit the structure of the portfolio. You can rename, enable or delete each gallery. You can also adjust your e-mail settings here, and the menu shows the current style of your portfolio cover.

The second menu has an icon that looks like a pencil, and it allows you to edit your style preferences. With these options, you can build a portfolio that you're proud to share. They are:

- **Background:** You can set the image for the cover. Choose between one of your images

Figure 10-17
This is the FolioBook interface; the main menu is showing. Just hold your finger on the screen to bring it up.

and a generic cover. With this app, even the generic covers are very cool, trying hard to look like traditional portfolios.

- **Logo:** Add a text logo to the cover of your portfolio here. You can also adjust the size of the text or just turn off the logo completely.

- **Colour and Alpha:** This allows you to change the color and the Alpha (transparency) of the cover text, including the gallery names.

- **Fonts:** Here, you can change the fonts used on the cover, and this gives you control over the look of your portfolio.

When you start to add images to your galleries, you can also change the way the images are displayed by tapping the "Preferences" button at the top of the page of individual images. Turn Autoplay on or off, change the transitions, adjust the picture duration and the transition duration, and even control the gallery sizing here. Your sizing options are "Exact," "Fit" and "Fill."

All this might seem like a lot, but once you have the gallery set up the way you

want it, the portfolio will really stand out, especially compared to one you'd get with the Apple Photos app.

IMAGE EDITING APPS

The standard app for photo editing on a computer is Adobe Photoshop, and fortunately Adobe believes there is a future in the iPad. The company seems committed to developing photo-editing software for the iPad platform. And Adobe is not alone; the photo-editing category for apps is growing with top-quality options.

Some of these apps are for serious photo editing, while others are for creating a special effect or two. But for $1.99 or so, they can be a lot of fun for anyone.

Photoshop Express

Adobe Photoshop Express allows you to edit and share your images from anywhere. It allows you to do basic edits like crop, straighten, rotate, flip and adjust the exposure. You can also change the colors, turn a color image to black and white, and add a variety of filters and borders.

The bonus: You get all of this for the very affordable price of FREE. That's right, Adobe gives away this software for free, but there is a catch (of course). This app is the companion to Photoshop.com, which is Adobe's online photo editing and sharing Web site. This means, to use the Photoshop Express app, you need to create an account at Photoshop.com. But this account is also free, so what's stopping you?

Go to Photoshop.com or download the app and create an account. All you need is an e-mail and a password. And this allows you to upload and download images directly from your photoshop.com account.

151

Figure 10-18
The PSE user interface is clean
and intuitive.

Sketch

Soft Focus

Sharpen

Figure 10-19
This PSE user interface shows the
Sketch, Soft Focus and Sharpen
menu choices.

The Photoshop Express app allows you to edit
your images very quickly and easily.

1. Open the Photoshop Express app.

2. Sign into your Photoshop account.

3. Tap "Edit" at the bottom of the screen.

4. Tap "Select a Photo," which brings up a list
   of albums saved on your iPad.

5. Navigate to the image you want to edit and
   tap on it.

6. Here, there are four options across
   the bottom of the screen that control
   your editing.

   ○ The "Crop" menu allows you to Crop,
     Straighten, Rotate and Flip.

   ○ The "Exposure" menu is where you
     adjust Exposure, Saturation, Tint, Black
     & White, and Contrast.

   ○ The "Effects 1" menu offers effects such
     as Sketch, Soft Focus and Sharpen.

   ○ The "Effects 2" menu gives you Effects
     and Borders.

7. Add whatever effects you like and, here
   is the fun part, just slide you finger up
   and down or left and right to increase or
   decrease the effect on the image you've
   selected.

8. When you're done, you can either tap
   "Save" or "Cancel," or you can upload the
   image directly to Photoshop.com or to
   Facebook, if you have an account.

9. If you click "Upload," then the upload page
   will open. The Photoshop icon and the
   Facebook icon will appear at the bottom of
   the screen.

10. Tapping on the Adobe icon allows you to
    select the destination for the image on the
    Photoshop Express Web site and offers
    you the opportunity to enter a caption.

11. Tapping on the Facebook icon will open
    a menu that allows you to log into Face-
    book with your e-mail address and pass-
    word. You then need to allow Photoshop
    Express to post to your Wall by tapping
    the "Allow" button. From there, just add a
    caption and tap "Upload."

This app works well and does a good job with basic editing and enhancement of images, but it has a lot of room to grow, especially when you compare the editing features to an app like Filterstorm 2.

Filterstorm 2

This is one slick image-editing app. It does a great job with basic editing and gives you enough controls that even advanced editing is possible.

When you open Filterstorm 2, you get lots of options right off the bat. The first thing to do is load an image that you want to edit. This can be done by either tapping the "Load Photo" button or, if you have copied an image into the iPad's memory, you can use "Paste Photo" to transfer it into the app.

The Filterstorm 2 app screen is divided into three parts. The adjustment controls are on the left; the menu is right down the middle; and the image that you're editing is on the right.

While this app works great in both portrait and landscape modes, I prefer to use the app in landscape mode, so the image is on the right and options are on the left.

Speaking of options, there are three categories of adjustments available on this app: Canvas, Filters and Metadata.

Canvas Adjustments are made to change the size and physical appearance of the canvas— not the actual image. Those changes are made in the Filters Adjustment menu. Here are available canvas adjustments:

- Crop: You can crop your images and even lock and unlock the ratio. Just tap on the "Crop" button to bring up the options. Then tap on the "Crop" button again to bring up an adjustable grid that can be manipulated with your fingers.

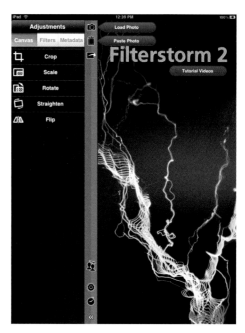

Figure 10-20
Take a look at the main Filterstorm page.

Figure 10-21
This is the crop overlay in Filterstorm 2.

- Scale: Want to make your image smaller? Just enter the width and/ or height you want to change, and tap "Scale."

- Rotate: This rotates the image to either the left or right.

- Straighten: A slider will adjust the photo to either the left or right. Once positioned the way you want, tap "Straighten" to fix your image.

- Flip: You can flip your images vertically or horizontally with the tap of a finger.

Filters Adjustments is what you use to adjust the way your image looks. The tools available here are really powerful and amazingly easy to use … with fingers and not a mouse or a graphics pen in sight.

- Luminance: This allows you to change the Brightness and Contrast of the image by using the sliders and / or the histogram view.

- Hue / Saturation: These sliders allow you to change the hues, and there is a saturation slider for overall image saturation.

- Temperature: Need to adjust the white temperature of your image? This is the place to adjust it. It can be adjusted with a slider, or you can move the temperature target over the area in the photo you want to use as the sample area.

- Black & White: There are many ways to adjust how your black and white photos look. You can even adjust the individual red, green and blue channels and paint the effect onto parts of your image.

- Soften/ Sharpen: This is a simple slider that makes the whole image either softer or sharper.

- Blur: You can add blur to your image or paint blur into selected parts of it right here.

- Text: Use this tool to add text to your images. This gives you tons of options and does a great job with image text.

- Tone Map: Give your images that really popular HDR look with just two sliders.

You can apply the effect to the whole photo or just paint it into selected areas.

- Reduce Noise: This reduces graininess in an image, which is especially useful for images shot at very high ISOs.

- De-Vignette: This helps to remove the dark edges that can appear on the edges of images when shot with certain lenses.

- Vignette: Use this to add the dark edges that you tried to get rid of in the last menu.

- Color: You can adjust the color of each part of your image. Use the target to select an area of the image and then adjust the color for that area.

- Posterize: Apply this effect to your images or just part of your image using this menu. This effect converts smooth tones to a series of areas of solid tones.

Metadata Adjustments help you to change the information associated with your image, like the name and date and description.

There is also a menu strip between the adjustment panel and the image. And this is where you can load an image from your albums, paste an image into the app from the clipboard, and export an image after you've

Figure 10-22
The Black & White adjustment menu in Filterstorm 2.

turned it from an average image into a great one. It is also where you can adjust the tool size, launch automations and even take a snapshot of your work.

The best advice I can give you about this app is to play with it. It's only $3.99—an amazingly low price for this application.

PRO APPLICATION INTEGRATION

Most pro and serious amateur photographers do their photo processing on computers and not directly on the iPad. If you are in these categories, then you too were probably very excited about what the iPad could offer and, at the same time, also quite disappointed at the lack of options available for display, organization and editing photos. Good news: You can use your pro photo-editing apps on the iPad to make your content look great.

Aperture

Aperture is the pro photographer's application from Apple. And since it's part of the Mac ecosystem, it integrates really well with iTunes and, therefore, with the iPad.

It's possible to create a great-looking portfolio using Aperture and then sync it into the iBooks app on the iPad. This takes advantage of iBooks' ability to show PDFs natively, and it also means that you can create different books for each subject or shoot.

To create a custom portfolio book in Aperture:

1. Collect all the images that you want to use in the book and then click on File>New>Book.

2. Name the new book.

3. Select "Custom" from the Book Type menu, and then click "New Theme" to enter the iPad dimensions.

Figure 10-23

Creating a custom book in Aperture lets you put multiple images on a page.

4. Name the new theme and enter the page size.

5. Because of the 4:3 aspect ratio, I used a width of 8 inches and a height of 6 inches.

6. Set the margins to zero since this book is not being printed.

7. This iPad-ready theme can now be used for other iPad books.

8. You can change the layout by clicking on the arrow next to the page and picking another page, or use the page tools to create your own pages.

9. Now it's time to add your photos.

10. Once the book looks just the way you want it to, it's time to print. But instead of printing on paper, you'll be creating a PDF. Remember to add a title, so that people seeing the book will know who made it.

11. You can print your book as a PDF and then import it into iTunes and sync it to the iPad. It is also possible to auto load the pages directly into iTunes.

155

Figure 10-24
The book will show up in the PDF section of iBooks.

12. Click on the PDF button at the bottom of the print dialog; and instead of saving as PDF, choose "Edit Menu" at the bottom of the menu.

13. Click on the (+) at the bottom of the menu and add iTunes. It now supports PDFs, thanks to iBooks.

14. Once you have added iTunes to the PDF menu, it will show up in the drop-down menu. So print your book to PDF > iTunes.

15. Open iTunes and click on "Books." There is your new Aperture Photo Book.

16. You can now customize your iBook by selecting it and pressing Command-I. Enter in all the info you want.

17. Go ahead and sync your book over to the iPad and it will be in the PDF menu on iBooks.

This is a great way to make a customized portfolio book. You can also export the images as a PDF and send it onto clients. They can then load the PDF onto their iPads and take the photos with them as custom iBooks. I'm sure all your photography clients have iPads right now, right?

Adobe Lightroom

Adobe created Lightroom for professional photographers ... or at least serious amateurs. It is a very powerful workflow program that

Figure 10-24
These Lightroom settings make the iPad presets.

can help photographers tag, sort and edit images. But what it can't do is create books like Aperture.

When it comes to creating images to be shown on the iPad with Adobe Lightroom, you can create an export preset so that the images will be sized properly. This is where that resolution stuff from the beginning of the chapter comes into play. Since we know the size and resolution of the iPad screen, we can create images to fit this device perfectly.

Actually, there are two different presets we can create for images on the iPad. One preset exports the biggest possible photo files that the iPad can deal with, which allows you to zoom in and see details in the images. The second preset creates an image that fits the iPad exactly ... without taking a ton of space on the device.

When using Lightroom, you can create presets so you don't have to invent the wheel over and over again. The key is the Image Sizing menu.

What you have to do is set the Long Edge to 2304 pixels. This will automatically keep the aspect ratio of your images correct while keeping the size as big as possible.

If you want to make the images just big enough for the iPad screen, then the Long Edge needs to be set at 1024. This works for both landscape and portrait images.

For both presets, the resolution is set to 132 Pixels Per Inch, the same resolution as the screen.

DIGITAL PHOTO FRAMES

Did you know that your iPad can serve as a digital frame with the push of a button? It can, but the button is usually passed right over, because it's on the screen ... right next to the "Slide to Unlock" area on the front page when the iPad is turned on. But if you tap the picture frame button, the iPad will to play the images that are selected in the Picture Frame menu.

So this draws the question: Where is the Picture Frame menu? It's located in the iPad Settings app menu. Just tap on the Settings app and select "Picture Frame" from the menu on the left side. This offers options on transition, zoom, shuffle mode and which photos to use.

The Picture Frame is pretty simple … with very few precise controls. And since the iPad

is on while Picture Frame is running, it will drain your battery. So I recommend that you only use this feature when your iPad is docked and/or plugged in.

Internet Content

E-Mail

The Skim

The size and portability of the iPad makes it easy to check, answer and write e-mails. This is especially true when a user is in landscape mode, where the split-screen view can show both the opened mailbox and the e-mail message at the same time. I use the iPad to check my e-mail regularly, because it is easier and faster than my iPhone, laptop and desktop computer.

The iPad has only one e-mail app. It's created by Apple and comes installed on the iPad. So while you don't have any choice when it comes to e-mail apps, it's okay. The app you get is pretty good. You can even have a variety of different e-mail accounts on the same iPad at the same time. Managing e-mail on the iPad will improve with the iOS4 upgrade, but more on that later.

Since the iPad is larger than a phone, the keyboard is larger as well, making it a breeze to type e-mail messages. It's easy to type in both landscape and portrait modes, and you can use the external Bluetooth® keyboard, if you have one, for times you want a little more space on the screen or a more traditional keyboard.

The e-mail app on the iPad displays messages in rich HTML format. This means that images and photos appear inside the e-mail messages and can be downloaded to the iPad photo library with a tap. The iPad

Figure 11-1
As one of the iPad's built-in apps, the Mail icon will stick around ... even if you never use it. You can't delete it.

e-mail app can view and zoom attachments, including PDFs and documents created by Microsoft Word, Excel, PowerPoint and the iWork suite.

The toughest thing about the iPad's e-mail program is setting the device to receive your e-mail. There are so many choices for e-mail now that it can be a little overwhelming. And many times there are no real instructions available.

Luckily, Apple took this into consideration when writing iOS, which runs the iPad (and the other iDevices), and the company made e-mail setup pretty easy. Nevertheless, we'll review the basic process and explore some of the problems that can arise. You'll also find out how to include images and attachments, which can cause problems when sending e-mails via your iPad.

SET UP YOUR E-MAIL

The first thing to do when setting up your e-mail is to figure out what e-mail provider you're using. This is usually pretty easy to figure out since it is part of your e-mail address; it's the part after the "@" symbol.

Some of the most common e-mail programs are:

○ **MobileMe from Apple:**
ipadfullyloaded@me.com

○ **Gmail from Google:**
ipadfullyloaded@gmail.com

Figure 11-2
The Mail settings panel here is showing the default account setting.

○ **Yahoo! mail:** ipadfullyloaded@yahoo.com

○ **AOL mail:** ipadfullyloaded@aol.com

Then there are the enterprise e-mail solutions that run on Microsoft's Exchange server along with e-mail accounts that run from a Web host. For example, the e-mail address **alan@ipadfullyloaded.com** is from my Web host and tied to the domain **www.ipadfullyloaded.com**.

Every one of these different e-mail types can be set up and used on the iPad. Let's take them in the order that they appear on the iPad.

Microsoft Exchange

When Apple added support for Microsoft Exchange servers for the iPhone, business users rejoiced because it meant that the iPhone could be used as an "enterprise" business phone. Well, that same Exchange support is present on the iPad, which allows the Mail app to be used for business e-mail.

Setting up the Mail program to work with Exchange servers is really easy, but you might need to get some information from your business IT office. To set up your iPad to access your Microsoft Exchange e-mail:

1. Tap "Settings."

2. Tap "Mail, Contacts, Calendars."

3. Tap "Microsoft Exchange."

4. Enter your full e-mail address.

5. You may now need to enter domain information. This can be a variety of things, but here are a few to try:

   ○ Leave it blank. The information is most likely going to be found by the program automatically.

   ○ Ask your IT department what the company domain is.

   ○ Try the Internet domain of your company's Web site—both with the ".com" part and without it. Your best bet is just to ask.

6. Enter your Exchange username, usually the first part of your e-mail address: the characters that come before the "@" symbol.

7. Enter your password. This is the same password you use at work to log in and check your e-mail.

8. Enter a description for your account. This is especially important if you plan on having multiple e-mail accounts on your iPad.

9. Tap "Next."

10. The iPad will then try to verify the account information. Be patient; this can take awhile.

11. If your Microsoft Exchange server does not allow for auto-discovery, you will get an error message and will need to enter the rest of the information manually.

12. If you need to add the server data manually, ask your IT department for the information and enter it in the Server field. If

the techs are confused by this request, just ask them for the information they would use to set up a Windows Mobile smart phone; it's the same info.

MobileMe

To set up a MobileMe e-mail account—an Apple program—you need to already have a MobileMe account, sign up for a free trial, or buy an account online at www.me.com. Once you have an account, you can set up access to your e-mail on the iPad by following these directions:

1. Tap on "Settings."

2. Tap "Mail, Contacts, Calendars."

3. Tap "MobileMe."

4. Enter your name.

5. Enter your full e-mail address.

6. Provide your MobileMe password.

7. Add a description of your account. This is especially important if you plan to have multiple e-mail accounts on one iPad.

8. Click "Save" to set up the account.

A person may have as many MobileMe e-mail addresses on the same iPad as (s)he wants—but not multiple contacts, calendars and bookmarks. More on that in Chapter 13.

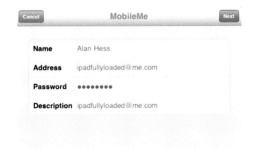

Figure 11-3
The MobileMe account set up screen.

Cancel	Gmail	Save
Name	Alan Hess	
Address	ipadfullyloaded	
Password	●●●●●●●●	
Description	Gmail account	

Figure 11-4
The Gmail account set up screen.

	Yahoo!	
Name	Alan Hess	✓
Address	ipadfullyloaded@yahoo.com	✓
Password	●●●●●●●●	✓
Description	Yahoo! Email	✓

Figure 11-5
After you tap "Save," the Yahoo! Mail account set up screen shows that all info is correct.

Gmail

Gmail, the Google e-mail solution—is free and widely used. It is a great solution for those who want a free e-mail account with lots of storage and a clean interface. To sign up for a Gmail account, just go to **gmail.com** and click "Create an account." To read your Gmail on the iPad, set up your e-mail as follows:

1. Tap "Settings."
2. Tap "Mail, Contacts, Calendars."
3. Tap "Add Account" if you already have a Gmail e-mail account set up.
4. Tap "Gmail."
5. Enter your name.
6. Enter your full e-mail address.
7. Enter your Gmail password.
8. Add a description for your account. This is especially important if you plan on having multiple e-mail accounts on your iPad.
9. Click "Save."
10. Enjoy!

Yahoo! Mail

Yahoo! Mail is a great solution for those who want a free e-mail account. To sign up for a Yahoo! Account, go to **www.mail.yahoo.com** and sign up. To set up access to your Yahoo! e-mail on the iPad:

1. Tap "Settings."
2. Tap "Mail, Contacts, Calendars."
3. Tap "Add Account" if you already have a Yahoo! e-mail account set up.
4. Tap "Yahoo! Mail."
5. Enter your name.
6. Enter your full e-mail address.
7. Enter your Yahoo! Mail password.
8. Add a description for your account.
9. Tap "Save" to finish setting up the account.

AOL Mail

AOL has been in the world of Internet and e-mail for a very long time. What used to be a

Figure 11-6
The AOL Mail settings panel.

Figure 11-7
The New Account settings panel is waiting for you to enter your information.

paid service is now free, and anyone can have an AOL e-mail account. Most people who started out with AOL as an Internet service provider began using e-mail with an AOL e-mail account. There are enough of these folks still using AOL that the company developed the basic setup to work with the iPad.

Make your AOL e-mail accessible on the iPad by following the steps below:

1. Tap "Settings."

2. Tap "Mail, Contacts, Calendars."

3. Tap "Add Account" if you have an AOL e-mail account.

4. Tap on "AOL."

5. Enter your name.

6. Enter your full e-mail address.

7. Type in your AOL password.

8. Add a description for the account.

9. Tap on "Save" to finish setting up AOL account access.

Other types of e-mail accounts

What if your e-mail service isn't provided by one of the preceding companies? Well, then you fall into the Other category. And honestly, while I use all of the e-mail types described, my main e-mail—the one I use every day—falls into the Other category.

These are usually e-mail accounts that you have from an ISP (Internet Service Provider), like the phone company (e.g., AT&T) or your cable company (e.g., Comcast, Cox), or as part of your own Web site (**www.ipadfullyloaded.com**).

Setting up these types of e-mail accounts to be delivered to your iPad requires that you do a little research. You'll want to make sure that you have the information you need to enter in to the e-mail set up menu.

The first thing you'll notice when you tap "Other" is that there are choices that have nothing to do with e-mail. Don't worry about these right now; we'll tackle them in Chapter 13. For now, tap "Add Mail Account" and let's get started.

The first thing you'll notice here is that the screen looks just like the menu for any of the other e-mail accounts. When we set up the other accounts, you tapped on "Save" and the account setup was done. Well, here you are presented with a second screen that asks for more detailed information about the e-mail account.

The first choice is IMAP and POP, and many people have no idea what IMAP and POP are. I know I was clueless the first time I heard these terms. So here's the skinny:

- **IMAP** stands for Internet Message Access Protocol, and this service format allows an e-mail client to access e-mail messages on a remote server. What this means is that the e-mail you see is not actually on the device you're using; instead, the device is looking at the e-mail on an external computer.

  Among the advantages of this is the automated syncing you can enjoy if you have multiple devices that can access your e-mail account. If you read an e-mail on one of them, the message gets marked as "Read" on the server, so every other device that accesses the account will show the accurate status of your messages and activity. On the downside, if you delete a message, then it is gone. Poof! Once you delete a message on the server, it is deleted on the devices as well.

- **POP** stands for Post Office Protocol. It's used by e-mail clients to get messages from an e-mail server. What usually happens is that the e-mail client goes out to the e-mail server and downloads the new messages directly to the device.

Once you read an e-mail on a certain device and delete it, the message is deleted from the e-mail client. But … an important distinction here … it survives on the server. This means that when you instruct another device to go get e-mails from the server, that message you deleted from the other device will be sitting there waiting to be read. So if you have an e-mail account on an iPad and a laptop … and an iPhone and a desktop computer … you'll get the same message four times with a POP setting. You'll have to delete, file or mark it on four separate devices.

Which one do I have?

Different e-mail hosting companies choose the service format they prefer. Some offer IMAP service and some offer POP service. The best bet is to contact the company and ask which type of service you're receiving.

Once you know which type of account service you have, you can move onto the questions related to your incoming mail server. You'll gather information about this from the e-mail hosting company, too. Typically, it will look something like: mail.(your domain.com), where "your domain.com" is replaced with the name of your domain. For example, since the domain for the e-mail address I am adding is **www.ipadfullyloaded.com**, the incoming mail server will be: **mail.ipadfullyloaded.com.**

The next thing is to enter the username for your account, which is usually the full e-mail address. If necessary, enter your password; but it should auto-fill based on your entry on the previous page.

The final step is to configure an outgoing e-mail server, because we not only want to get e-mail but to send it as well. Again, all the information on this screen is available from

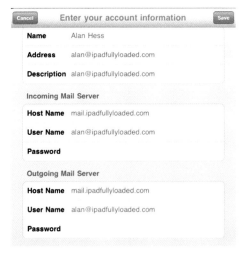

Figure 11-8

This screen shows where your info is entered for a domain-based e-mail account.

the company you use for your e-mail service. When you have entered your outgoing mail server and the username and password, it's time to tap "Save." That's when the iPad goes out to see if the e-mail account info you entered is correct.

After your e-mail is set up to send and receive, it's time to access the advanced features. Among these features is an ability to work with the Sent Mail, Drafts and Trash correctly. To access the advanced e-mail tab:

1. Tap the "Settings" icon.

2. Tap "Mail, Contacts and Calendars."

3. Tap on the e-mail account to edit.

4. Tap on the "Advanced" button, which is located at the bottom of the screen. Note: You might have to scroll down to access this button; sometimes the keyboard hides it.

5. You can now dictate where the mailboxes for Drafts, Sent messages and Trash will

reside. Your options depend on the type of hosting you're using for the account, so check with your e-mail hosting company for information.

E-MAIL SETTINGS

There are some general e-mail settings that are accessible in the Settings panel. They're all pretty standard, but one can make a big difference in how your e-mails are sent.

Halfway down the page is a Default Account setting. This establishes one of your e-mail accounts as the go-to when sending e-mail from other apps. You can also set the length of the preview in the Inbox (from none to five lines) as well as the maximum number of e-mails that the iPad will have in any one account at a time. You can show 25, 50, 75,100 or 200 recent e-mails. If you have more than 200 e-mail messages in an account, then only the first 200 are shown. Set these according to your personal preferences.

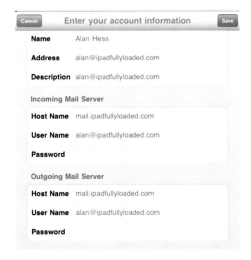

Figure 11-9

The Mail panel here is showing the default account setting.

167

GETTING YOUR E-MAIL: PUSH VS. FETCH

Now that you have your e-mail account(s) set up, it's time to instruct your iPad to go out and check for mail. If you tap on "Settings," and then "Mail, Contacts and Calendars," you'll see a button called "Fetch New Data" in the middle of the iPad on the right side. Tap on that to bring up the "Push and Fetch" menus.

These are the two methods the iPad uses to retrieve mail. The first is Push. This means that e-mails are pushed from the server to the device whenever there are new messages present. E-mails are on the iPad as soon as the e-mail server receives them. And this is great, but the real-time service comes with a price … in the form of battery life. Constantly monitoring your account to keep your mailbox current requires a lot of power.

To help users preserve battery life when enjoying push delivery, Apple provides an OFF switch. When you're running low on battery power or want to conserve your limited power, turn off push.

One thing to keep in mind is that not all e-mail servers are compatible with the push service. To see which of your e-mail accounts offer push service, make sure push is turned ON and then tap the "Advanced" button. This will bring up the list of e-mail accounts on your iPad, and it will show you which ones offer push and which do not. Watch for more on the Advanced menu a little later.

The other option for receiving e-mails on your iPad is to Fetch it. This is usually set up to happen in regular intervals—every 15 minutes, 30 minutes, hourly—or you can fetch your messages manually. The less often you check for new messages, the longer your iPad battery will last. So this really is a matter of priority. I usually have the iPad fetch new mail every 30 minutes.

THE ADVANCED BUTTON

There is one final way to get your e-mail and that is manually. If you change your setting from, say, a 30-minute fetch interval to manual retrieval, then the e-mail app won't go get new messages until you tell it to go out and fetch your e-mail. This setting is really useful when you're running on a low battery.

Tap the Advanced button to change the way each e-mail account checks for mail. Those who can use the push method can change from push to fetch or manual delivery here. Those who use the fetch method can change delivery between fetch and manual. To change your settings, just click on the account you want to change and pick the new method of e-mail retrieval.

To get your e-mail when the fetch is set to manual, you have to open the Mail program. When you open the program, it goes out to check for new mail. If the mail app is already open, then you need to tap on the "Update" button at the bottom of the accounts panel. It looks like a three-quarter circle made up by an arrow.

READING E-MAIL

Reading your e-mail on the iPad is as easy as tapping on the Mail app and picking an account. The first thing to note is that the e-mail information you see on your iPad will change depending on how you hold the device.

If you hold the iPad in portrait orientation, all you'll see is the currently selected message.

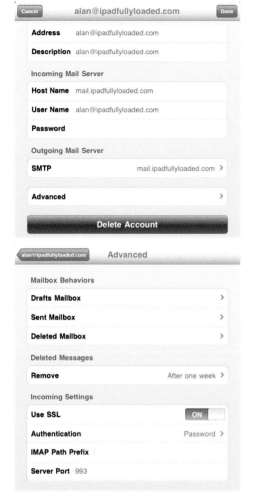

Figure 11-9
The Advanced Mail Settings panel is showing the settings available for each account.

But when you turn it "sideways" to landscape orientation, you'll see not only the currently selected message but also the Inbox showing the message list with a two-line preview. This is one of the reasons I like to read my e-mail in landscape orientation on my iPad. The more info the better, I say!

Figure 11-10
The Mail app on the iPad is showing where the main controls are.

If you have multiple e-mail accounts on your iPad, it's pretty easy to change which one you're accessing at any given time. On the top of the Inbox is a button that shows the currently selected account. It also shows you how many unread e-mails are in the account ... and offers an "Edit" button. Let's start from the right and work toward the left.

The "Edit" button allows you to delete or move multiple e-mails at a time. Just tap on "Edit," and then select the e-mails you want to delete or move by tapping the message in the list. You will know if you have selected an e-mail because a red circle with a white check mark will appear to the left of selected messages. You can then delete or move the selected e-mails by using the buttons at the bottom of the screen.

To change accounts, tap on the account name. This takes you out of the Inbox and into the account. You can then look at the folders in that account, or you can go back further to a list of accounts by tapping on the "Accounts" button at the top of the screen.

When you are actually reading an e-mail message, there are some helpful tools available to help you manage the mail. The most obvious is the Trashcan. By tapping the Trashcan, you send the e-mail to the trash. Tapping the folder icon saves the e-mail to that folder. Not all e-mail accounts have folders to which you can save e-mails, and there's more on that a little later. In the meantime, the last two options are to compose a new e-mail and to forward/ reply to the e-mail you're reading.

ACCESSING ATTACHMENTS

What really gets interesting is how the Mail app deals with attachments.

The iPad can display images—that are sent in the following common formats—inside an e-mail message: JPEG, GIF, PNG and TIFF. The iPad can also play audio attachments that are sent as MP3, AAC, WAV and AIFF files. These audio files will show up as attachments in the e-mail program, and once they finish downloading to your iPad, a single tap will play them.

Other attachments can be downloaded and viewed on the iPad. These include PDF, Rich Text (RTF), Pages, Keynote and Numbers documents as well as Microsoft Word, Excel and PowerPoint documents. If your e-mail doesn't open a file you've received as a mes-sage attachment, chances are the iPad doesn't support the file type.

A simple way to get content onto your iPad is to e-mail a file to yourself. But which files are supported by the Mail app, and which will just not open? The following file types are supported by the iPad Mail app and can be viewed there. And in many cases, these files can be downloaded to your iPad and opened. Some files types are even editable.

- **PDF** files are very common e-mail attach-ments, and the iPad Mail app makes these files visible as part of the e-mail message.

You can pinch to zoom; and if you hold your finger on the PDF part of the message, a menu pops ups to ask if you want to Quick Look at the PDF or if you would like to open it in any of the apps on the iPad that can read or edit PDFs. These apps include iBooks, GoodReader and CloudReaders.

- **DOC/ DOCX** files are Microsoft Word files. And since Microsoft Word is the most commonly used word processer (most of this book was written using Word), chances are, at some point, you will get a Word document as an e-mail attachment. Now there is no Microsoft Word for the iPad, but that doesn't mean you can't read Word documents! On the contrary, Apple has made it possible for iPad users to read Word files right in the Mail app. Just tap on the "Attachment" icon.

When you are viewing the attachment, you can also open it using a document reader (e.g., GoodReader and CloudReaders) app. If you have the Pages app on your iPad, you can even edit Word files. Just know that not all of the Word functions and formatting tools are available within the iPad apps.

- **HTM/ HTML** are Web files; and since they are actually in the same format as the e-mail program, they are easily readable there.

- **PPT/ PPTX** are PowerPoint files. And while they can be viewed in your e-mail and edited in the Keynote app, some of the formatting and controls that are available in PowerPoint will be missing in the Keynote app.

- **RTF/ TXT** are rich text files and regular text files. The Mail app handles these with ease, and both can be edited in the Pages app and read by numerous other applications.

- **XLS/ XLSX** files are based on the Excel program and are readable by the iPad Mail app. So if you want to check those spreadsheets or charts, it's easy. If you want to edit spreadsheets, then you have to wait to be back on a real computer. Or you can use the Numbers app. Just know that it doesn't support all the functions or formatting of Excel.

- **Numbers, Keynote** and **Pages** files are accessible through the Mail app. When you receive a Pages file, one tap will open it in a viewer or allow you to look at the file in one of the reader apps. However, since there is a Pages app for iPad, you can also open the file and edit it. The same is true for Keynote and Numbers files, but—and there is a big *but*—even though these files can be loaded and edited on the iPad versions of the software, some functions are missing. If you open a file created in the full version of Pages, Numbers or Keynote, and open the same file with the iPad versions of the software, you will get a warning that certain information will be changed. Find more on this topic in Chapters 15, 16 and 17.

IMAGE FILES

I love to send and receive photos by e-mail. Being a professional photographer, I do this all the time. And I'm not alone. One of the really nice features of the Mail app is that images show up in the e-mail message; and tapping on an attached image downloads it right to the image gallery of the iPad. It's so easy.

Many e-mail programs have a limit on the size of e-mails and e-mail attachments. Many times this limit makes it necessary to reduce the file sizes of images being sent by e-mail. Well, the iPad has a resolution of 1024 by 768

Figure 11-11

Tap on any image in your e-mail to save the image to your iPad.

pixels at 132 pixels per inch (ppi). This means if you're e-mailing images, you don't have to make them any bigger than that. There is a lot more on photographs in Chapter 10.

SENDING E-MAILS AND ATTACHMENTS

Sending e-mail is very straightforward when using the iPad, but adding attachments isn't so simple. Once you're ready to write an e-mail on the iPad, just follow these steps:

1. Tap on the Mail app.

2. On the top right side of the screen, tap the "New Message" icon to bring up a blank e-mail.

3. Enter the name of the recipient or tap the (+) to bring up your iPad Address Book.

4. Enter any CC or BCC recipients.

5. Enter the subject, and type your message.

6. When finished, tap "Send."

The process of adding attachments to an e-mail when using an iPad is a little different from the one used when working on a computer. This is because you need to send the attachment(s) from the original program. The browse and attach option is not available here. So images need to be sent from the Photos app. Pages documents are sent from the Pages app, and so forth. You get the idea. Here are the details:

Send photos

One of the easiest things to do is e-mail photos from your iPad. All you have to do is open the photos program, tap on a folder, and then tap on the image to open it. One more tap brings up the top menu bar. Tap on the icon that looks exactly like the New Message icon in the Mail app. This will cause a drop-down menu to appear that lets you choose "E-mail Photo" as one of your choices. Tap that choice and the e-mail app will open with the image embedded in the body of the message.

It's also possible to add an image to an e-mail message you've already started to write. Here's how:

1. Open Mail.

2. Start writing a new message.

Figure 11-12
Clicking on the icon at the top right of the image allows you to e-mail directly out of the Photos app.

3. Press the Home button.

4. Open photos.

5. Navigate to the photo you want to add to the message.

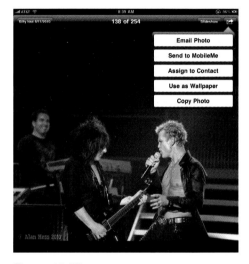

Figure 11-13
Copy the image you want to insert into an e-mail.

Figure 11-14
Paste the selected image into the e-mail.

6. Tap on the photo and then open the "New Message" menu at the top right.

7. Select "Copy Photo."

8. Press the Home button.

9. Open Mail. Your half-written message should be on the screen.

10. Press and hold where you want to insert the photo.

11. Remove your finger from the screen. The Select | Select All | Paste menu will appear.

12. Select "Paste"; the image that you copied will appear in your e-mail.

It is also possible to e-mail multiple images in the same message. To do this:

1. Tap on the Photos app.

2. Open a gallery by tapping on it.

3. Before opening an individual image, tap on the "New Message" icon in the top right corner.

4. The heading will change to *Select Photos*.

5. Tap on the images that you want to e-mail. They will be marked by a white checkmark on a blue background. (You can only e-mail five images at a time.)

6. Once you've selected the images you want to send, look at the top left of the iPad screen. This is where you'll see two buttons: "E-mail" and "Copy."

7. If the "E-mail" button is grayed out, it means you have selected too many images and need to unselect a few.

8. Tap on "E-mail" and the Mail program will open with all the images you selected. They will be embedded in your message.

9. Write out the e-mail message.

10. Tap "Send."

Figure 11-15
The Photos app shows your images from a gallery.

Figure 11-16
The Mail app showing multiple images in the same email.

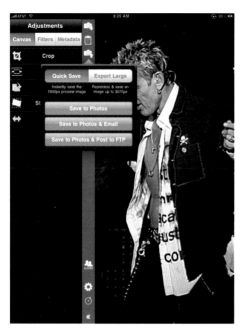

Figure 11-17
You can e-mail directly from apps. Here I am e-mailing an image of Billy Idol right from the Filterstorm app.

Many different apps will allow you to send content as an e-mail. Check with the specific app to see how it handles it. Find more on e-mailing documents in Chapters 13-15.

MAIL PROBLEMS (AND SOLUTIONS)

Not everything runs smoothly all the time. And while the Mail app works great most of the time, there are situations in which the Mail app doesn't work. At these times, you don't have to use the Mail app, there are alternatives.

Webmail

One way to check your e-mail on the iPad is to use the Safari Internet browser to access webmail. Most, if not all, e-mail providers

have a way for you to access your e-mail using an Internet browser. Just type in the correct URL and enter your info. Your e-mail should pop up in the window.

Since the iPad has a browser, this is a viable alternative, especially if you share an iPad and don't want your e-mail to be accessible to anyone who picks up your device.

Many providers also offer a special Mobile page that might be easier to use than Safari. Since the iPad version of Safari is based on the iPhone version, many Web sites recognize it as a mobile device and, by default, offer the mobile version of the site.

Dedicated E-Mail Apps

Some e-mail companies are also developing dedicated apps that will allow users to access e-mail much easier. So this, too, may be an option if you want to avoid the Mail app. For example, the MailPro app allows you to access your Hotmail and Windows Live e-mail accounts, and the E-mailPush app allows you to access your Gmail account.

THE IOS 4 DIFFERENCE

Apple has updated the iPad Operating System since it first shipped version 4. This brought some really great changes to the e-mail program.

The main improvement is the unified Inbox that is missing in iOS3.x. The upgrade makes it possible for you to see all the messages in all of your inboxes at the same time ... in one pane. And this saves a lot of tapping around if you have more than one e-mail account. And most of us do. In fact, if you don't have at least two different e-mail accounts, you should.

One other awesome feature in iOS4 is the ability to print to a Wi-Fi-enabled printer

WHY IT'S A GOOD IDEA TO HAVE MULTIPLE E-MAIL ACCOUNTS

I am a firm believer in multiple e-mail accounts. I think it's a good idea to have one for work and one for private (i.e., non-work-related) correspondence.

Among the many reasons for this is that when you start a job, your employer will typically assign you an e-mail account. Something like bob@companyXYZ.com becomes the main way for your colleagues to communicate business messages to you. But if you ever decide to leave the company, you lose that e-mail address; it stays with your company. So if you've been using it for personal e-mails, then those get lost to you as well. And your former employer retains access to those messages.

This also applies when dealing with a home e-mail. I am not a fan of getting my e-mail from an ISP (Internet Service Provider) for the simple reason that if I move hosting companies, I lose my e-mail. For example, say I use a cable company for my e-mail and then move to an area where that cable company doesn't provide service. I'd have to get a new ISP with a new e-mail account. Hassle!

So I recommend creating two (or more) separate e-mail accounts on a service like Gmail or Yahoo! Mail. These accounts go where you go, and it's usually possible to access the e-mail from any computer that's connected to the Internet. Devices like the iPad make it easy to check all your e-mail accounts in the same place. And with the unified Inbox, now it's even easier. Hurrah!

that is on the same network as the iPad. This means that you should be able to print e-mails directly from the Mail app. This helpful feature was missing when the iPad was originally released.

The Web

The Skim

When Steve Jobs announced the iPad, he made the claim that the iPad was the best Web browsing experience anywhere. Depending on which sites you visit on a regular basis, this may or may not be true.

Many Web sites still don't work perfectly on the device, especially for people who create or use Web sites that utilize Adobe Flash. This is because the iPad, like the iPhone and iPod Touch, doesn't support Adobe Flash natively. It's difficult to discuss the iPad's functionality with the Internet and its Web browsing capabilities without discussing the Flash situation. So you'll find more on the Flash debate a little later. (Here is a hint: The iPad doesn't support Flash and, most likely, it never will.)

On the upside, because of the size of the iPad, the days of squinting at the little display of your smart phone are gone … so is having to power up a laptop or Netbook to browse the Internet. The iPad is a perfect size to check out Web pages, and it's browsing speed is pretty impressive, too.

The really interesting part about using the Internet on the iPad isn't the Internet browsers; it's the specific apps that go out and get information from a Web site for you. More and more, I find myself using apps that bring me information from the Internet without ever making me visit an actual Web site. For example, I find it much easier to go to the Southwest Airlines app than to the Southwest Airlines site. And when it comes to

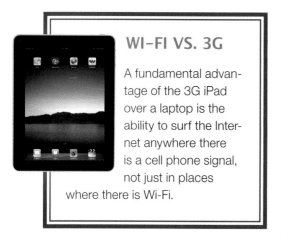

WI–FI VS. 3G

A fundamental advantage of the 3G iPad over a laptop is the ability to surf the Internet anywhere there is a cell phone signal, not just in places where there is Wi-Fi.

getting my news, I used to go to the news Web sites; now I just go to the media outlets' apps or, even better, the news aggregator apps. Find more on news and news aggregator apps in Chapter 8: News.

Here, let's start exploring iPad Web surfing with the traditional method: the Web browser.

SAFARI

The iPad comes preloaded with a version of the Apple-branded Internet browser, Safari. You can launch Safari by pressing the Safari app icon, which opens the touch-enabled version of Safari.

Most iPad users will start by using Safari to browse the Internet, simply because it's the browser that's there. And it does a pretty good job. If you are a MobileMe user, the bookmarks from your other devices can be synced to Safari on the iPad, which makes browsing that much easier.

The downside to the Safari browser on the iPad is that it acts like it's operating on an iPhone. So even though there's a lot more space available on the iPad screen, the browser doesn't support tabbed browsing or otherwise take advantage of the screen space.

Figure 12-1
Safari on the iPad is the same as Safari on the iPhone. The very simple menu bar leaves lots of space for actual Web content.

Dealing with Bookmarks

Adding bookmarks in Safari is easy. What's really cool is that you can add a bookmark to the home screen of the iPad. This means that a bookmarked Web page will look like an app on the home screen; but when you tap it, Safari launches and the Web site opens. This is really easy to set up; just follow these simple steps:

1. Open Safari by clicking on its icon.

2. Navigate to the page you want to bookmark.

3. Tap the (+) sign in the menu bar.

4. Choose "Add to Home Screen."

5. Name the icon and tap "Add" on the top right of the window.

Figure 12-2

Tapping on the (+) sign brings up the "Add Bookmarks" menu, which allows you to Add Bookmark, Add to Home Screen or Mail Link to this Page.

Figure 12-3

Tapping "Add to Home" allows you to turn the link into an icon on the home page of your iPad. You can even include a description.

This creates an icon that looks like an app on your iPad. One tap and you are right back to your selected Web site. As you might have noticed, you can also add a regular bookmark within Safari and send links in the body of an e-mail.

Adding bookmarks is one thing; deleting them is another. Many times, we tend to add and add … and, yes, add more … bookmarks, but we rarely get around to deleting the old ones. There are two ways to delete bookmarks on your iPad: one at a time or in batches.

THE IOS4 ADVANTAGE

The ability to create folders for apps on the iPad using iOS4 allows users to make folders of shortcuts on the main screen of the iPad. This means you can have a folder of your favorite personal shortcuts and a folder of business shortcuts. You can even mix shortcuts and apps in the same folder.

To delete bookmarks one at a time:

1. Open Safari.
2. Tap on the "Bookmarks" button.
3. Swipe your finger across the bookmark horizontally.
4. Tap on the red "Delete" button that appears next to the bookmark.
5. Poof. The bookmark is instantly gone.

Or you can delete bookmarks using the group-cuts approach:

1. Open Safari.
2. Tap on the "Bookmarks" button.
3. Tap the "Edit" button on the top right of the window (which turns into the "Done" button).
4. Each bookmark will sit next to a red circle with a line through it.
5. Tap on the red circle of the bookmark you want to delete.

179

Figure 12-4

This is the easy way to delete bookmarks. Tap on "Edit" and then mark and delete the bookmarks you no longer want.

THE SAFARI PREFERENCES

To access the Safari preferences, tap on the Settings icon. Once inside, look for the Safari tab on the left side of the screen. Tap the Safari icon to bring up the Safari settings. This is where you can choose the default search engine, set up auto fill, show the bookmark bar, and edit your security settings.

6. The word *Delete* will appear to the right of the bookmark.

7. Tap "Delete" to remove the bookmark.

8. Tap "Done" when you are finished deleting bookmarks.

Setting the default search engine

Google has been the default search engine for Safari since it was released on the iPad. But you don't have to use Google and you don't have to have Google as your default search engine. There are two other options: Yahoo! Search and Bing Search from Microsoft. So if you don't like Google and want another

Figure 12-5

Take a look at the Safari settings and the menu used to set the default search engine.

choice, you now have it. To change the default search engine used in Safari:

1. Tap on the Settings icon.

2. Tap "Safari" in the column on the left.

3. Tap "Search Engine."

4. Tap on whichever search engine you want as your default.

5. That's it!

Now, when you open Safari and use the built-in search function, it will use the search engine you chose.

OTHER BROWSER OPTIONS

Recently, Apple started to allow other companies to have Internet browsers on the iPad. These include apps from well-known browser companies as along with some that you've probably never heard of. All of the following browser apps work great and have features that Safari is missing.

Atomic Web Browser

When I started to look for alternatives to Safari, this Web browser came highly recommended. One thing about this browser that I absolutely love is that it can look like a full computer version of a Web browser. This means that it goes to real sites—not the mobile versions.

Here's how to set the Atomic Web Browser to look like a desktop browser (or a mobile browser if that's your goal):

Figure 12-7

These two screenshots show the same page. The only difference is how Flickr "saw" the Web browser.

Figure 12-6

The four browsers on my iPad are Safari, Atomic Web, Mercury and iCab Mobile.

TIP

Mobile versions of Web pages are usually scaled back versions of the full site. They're created for people who will look at the page on the small screen of a smart phone. The problem is that many of these sites see the Safari browser on the iPad the same way they see it on the iPhone. Therefore, the site responds to the iPad with the mobile version of the requested page.

Figure 12-8
The Atomic Web Browser can look like a variety of different browsers to the Web sites it visits.

1. Open the Atomic Web Browser.

2. Tap the gear icon. (It's right next to the (+) at the top of the screen.)

3. Tap the "Settings" button.

4. Tap "Identify Browser As" and set "Safari Desktop."

5. Tap "Settings" on the top left.

6. Tap "Close" on the top right.

That's it. The browser now appears to be the desktop version of Safari to every Web site it visits.

There is a whole lot more to the Atomic Web Browser. The app comes as a free "lite" version as well as a $0.99 full version. It's definitely worth a look.

Mercury

The Mercury Web browser is a viable alternative to Safari. In fact, it can be easier to use than Safari and much easier to navigate among different Web sites.

One of the very cool things about the Mercury browser app is that you can change your search engine right inside the app. It also gives you more choices than Safari in terms of which search engine to use. Mercury allows you to choose from Google, Yahoo!, Bing, Wikipedia and even eBay. To pick the search engine you want to use, just tap on the down arrow on the left side of the search box. Then tap on the search engine you want to use.

Figure 12-9
Your preferred search engine can be selected from inside the Mercury app.

The real plus with Mercury is that you can have multiple tabs on the main page. Well, you can have ten tabs if you want … and that's nine more than Safari. It's really easy to add a new tab; just tap on the (+) that's in the tabs bar, and a new tab opens to a blank page that's just waiting for you to enter a URL. If you want to close a tab, just tap on the little "x" on the right side of the tab, and the tab is instantly gone.

iCab Mobile

I find myself using this browser more frequently, mainly because of its nice simple layout and some cool built-in functions. This browser, at least to me, seems like a desktop, making it really easy to use.

One of the best features here is the opportunity to pick a search engine just by tapping in the search bar and choosing from the drop-down list. It's similar to the Mercury browser described above, but iCab Mobile adds the ability to easily add a new search engine or Web site. This means that in addition to the

traditional search engines, you can use sites like Amazon.com (or any other site you like) to search.

To add a new search engine or Web site, just navigate to the site and tap the (+) sign on the top of the page. This opens the "Add to Bookmarks" menu. Tap the "Add to Search Engines" button, and the current site will be added to the search engine menu choices in iCab Mobile.

For example, if I want to be able to search Amazon.com right from the search bar, I navigate to www.amazon.com then tap the (+) key and then "Add to Search Engine." From here, tap on the search bar and pick Amazon.com. The search bar will now search Amazon.com. Pretty cool, heh?

SYNCING BOOKMARKS

The key to a great Web browsing experience is being able to access your bookmarks, so you don't have to type in your favorite Web addresses over and over again. I have a lot of bookmarks on my computer. They're sorted and categorized, and I really don't want to enter them again by hand on the iPad. So this is one place that Apple Safari has a distinct advantage over the other browser options for the iPad. You can easily sync your bookmarks from your computer to the iPad as long as you're using Safari on the Mac and Internet Explorer or Safari on the PC … and Safari on the iPad. Syncing bookmarks is difficult if you use Google Chrome or Firefox.

The easiest way to synch bookmarks is in iTunes. Well, actually the easiest way is to do it automatically and wirelessly with a MobileMe account, but that's not for everyone; so let's look at the iTunes method first. I'll get to MobileMe in a minute.

Figure 12-10
Adding the current page to the list of search engines is as simple as tapping (+) and then the "Add to Search Engine" button.

To copy bookmarks from your computer to your iPad without a wireless method:

1. Turn on your computer and launch iTunes.

2. Use the USB cable to attach your iPad to the computer.

3. Select the iPad in the Device list on the left side of the iTunes window.

4. Select "Info" from the tabs across the top of the main window in iTunes.

5. Scroll down until you see "Other" and check the "Sync Safari bookmarks" (or Internet Explore on the PC) option.

6. Click "Sync."

This will keep the bookmarks on your computer and iPad synced. They will update every time you sync. This works great, but if you are a MobileMe user, there is an even easier way.

The Apple MobileMe service supports the wireless syncing of your bookmarks the same way it keeps your e-mail, calendars and contacts up to date. If you have MobileMe, then chances are that you already have this feature set up and working. To check:

1. Tap on "Settings."

2. Tap "Mail, Contacts, Calendars."

3. Tap on the MobileMe account.

Figure 12-11
Just click "Sync Safari bookmarks," and every time you sync, the bookmarks will be updated on the computer and iPad.

4. Check to make sure that the Bookmarks menu choice is turned on.

This will sync all the bookmarks on your iPad version of Safari with the other computers that are synced under the same MobileMe account. Apple has a great Help document on setting up your MobileMe on a Mac (**http://www.apple.com/mobileme/setup/mac.html**) and on a PC (**http://www.apple.com/mobileme/setup/pc.html**). Check it out.

There is a utility called xMarks that does a great job of keeping your bookmarks synced across various devices and browsers. It can be accessed by a free iPhone / iPad app. The problem with the xMarks service is that it might not be in existence anymore. Among the hazards of writing a book about technology is that it changes all the time and your information becomes outdated quickly. But right now, the xMarks service is the best way, actually the only way, to sync all your bookmarks over all the different Web browsers you use.

ADOBE FLASH

If you've ever watched a video on the Internet, you were likely watching it using the Adobe Flash plugin architecture. Many of the videos on the Internet were encoded using Flash, and many Web sites started to incorporate Flash into their design … and even in the navigation controls.

A great deal of attention has been put on the lack of support for Adobe Flash on Apple devices, starting with the iPhone and including the iPad. The feud between the pro Flash (Adobe) crowd and the anti-Flash (Apple) became all too public when Steve Jobs released an open letter describing why Flash was not on the iOS devices and would likely never be there. You can read this letter at

Figure 12-12
Some Web sites still use Adobe Flash for key elements. I like to keep track of what's going on every Sunday in the NFL, but NFL.com uses Flash to update the scores. So instead of updates, I get error messages. Not as fun …

Figure 12-13
Good thing there are apps that allow me to get the same information directly on my iPad. The really good CBS Sports app gives me the information I want without requiring a browser.

http://www.apple.com/hotnews/thoughts-on-flash/ and decide whether you agree or disagree with Steve. Either way, it's probably safe to forget about Flash ever being supported on the iPad.

All that said, there is a new format that's starting to replace Flash. It's called HTML5, and Steve has bet that HTML5 will replace Flash entirely. I don't know if he is right or wrong;

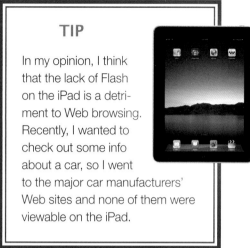

TIP

In my opinion, I think that the lack of Flash on the iPad is a detriment to Web browsing. Recently, I wanted to check out some info about a car, so I went to the major car manufacturers' Web sites and none of them were viewable on the iPad.

we'll need to wait a few years for the verdict. There will either be a wide acceptance of HTML5, or Apple will capitulate and finally allow Flash.

There are apps out there that allow you to use your iPad as a mirrored monitor to your desktop. Theoretically, these apps allow you to view Flash content on your iPad, because the device is just looking at what's playing on your computer. I wanted to be able to talk about one of those apps here, but they were so buggy and slow that they turned the very cool, very fast, really enjoyable iPad experience into a nightmare of slow, sluggish performance. On top of that, the apps really messed with the desktop settings on my computer.

So right now, the best advice I can give you when it comes to wanting Flash on a portable device is to look at the Android phones. I've been told they support Flash, but I haven't actually seen it. Of course I use an iPhone, and it doesn't support Flash.

Office Content

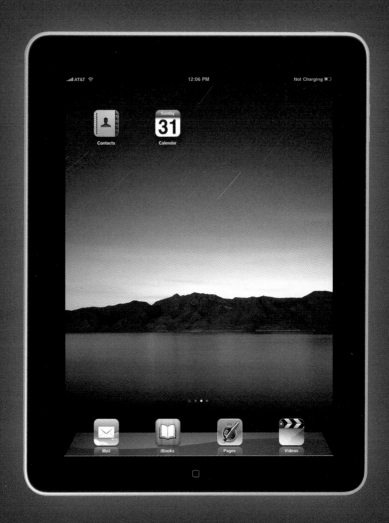

13

Calendars and Contacts

The Skim

Among the most useful things in the digital age are tools available to keep different calendars and contact lists on multiple devices. That said, I'm not always sure this is a good thing; and if not set up correctly, reliance on these tools can cause more grief than almost any other part of the new digital lifestyle.

I get lots and lots of e-mails from friends and clients asking why their contacts lists and calendars aren't working properly. And for all the time spent addressing these issues, sometimes I really think we may have been better off before we tried to keep multiple address books and multiple calendars all tied together. The fact is: your digital system is going to mess up at some point. So unless you also keep the information on paper, you'll probably lose an important date or phone number.

Don't blame me… When that happens at my house, I just go back to the old-school address book my wife keeps next to the phone. And while you have to update that the old way (using a pen), it never seems to lose a phone number due to a syncing problem.

The iPad has two built-in applications for managing your contacts and calendars. Both are really useful. If you use Outlook on the PC or the iCal and Address book applications on the Mac, then this is really simple stuff. If you are a MobileMe subscriber or use Microsoft Exchange serv-

 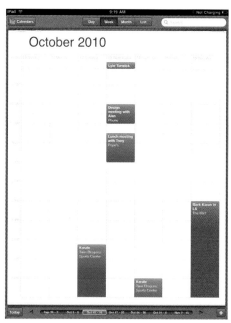

Figure 13-1
The four calendar views.

ers, then the syncing is really simple, too. For people out there who don't use these programs, life gets a little more complicated, so we'll get to that in awhile. Let's start with the simpler stuff and work our way to the more complicated, non-standard stuff.

CALENDARS

The iPad's Calendar app can be really powerful. But before we start syncing and setting up multiple calendars, let's cover some of the basics.

The first thing to know is that there are four views for your calendar: Day, Week, Month and List. Each of the views offers the same information but in a different format. This versatility makes it easy to get an overview or detailed information about what's on your calendar.

The **Day** view shows you the whole day by hour at a glance.

The **Week** view shows your events scheduled for the week.

The **Month** view offers information for the whole month on a single page.

The **List** view is a line-by-line display of events on the left side and a detailed day view of events on the right.

The Calendar app allows you to organize your events by type through the creation of multiple calendars. For example, say I have a work calendar, a home calendar, a birthday calendar and even a calendar of my wife's work schedule. I can create separate calendars for these types of events and decide which of them to display.

The thing is: You can see the different calendars on your iPad and pick the one to display, but you can't create a new calendar there.

190

That can only be done on the computer. So if, for some reason, you don't have a calendar on your computer and you don't plan to have one on your computer … and the only calendar you have is on your iPad, then you're out of luck and stuck with the one calendar. That's the deal for now anyway. There's a good chance that Apple could change this in the future. I hope they do.

Create an event.

Calendars are only helpful if you can enter information on them. Here's how to enter an event onto your iPad calendar.

1. Open the Calendar app on the iPad by tapping on the icon.

2. Tap the (+) button on the bottom right of the screen to open the "Add Event" window.

3. Enter a title for the event.

4. If you want, add a location in the location field or use this space as a secondary field for event info.

5. Tap the "Starts/Ends" area to open the date controls.

6. Adjust the day, hour, minute and AM/PM wheels to set the start time of the event.

7. Adjust the day, hour, minute and AM/PM wheels to set the end time of the event.

8. Or, if the event lasts all day, like a birthday, turn on the "All Day" switch.

9. Tap "Done" to finish entering the start and end times.

10. You can now set the repeat options for recurring events.

11. First, pick the frequency of the event. (Leave it as "None" if the event doesn't repeat.)

12. Choose "Every Day," "Every Week," "Every 2 Weeks," "Every Month" or "Every Year."

13. You can now set an alert so you have a better chance of remembering your event.

191

Figure 13-2
The edit window for an event

Alerts can be set for five minutes before the event's start time to two days before.

14. If you set an alert, you can set a Second Alert. (Never miss an anniversary again!)

15. Then click "Done."

16. You can now enter any notes you have for your event.

17. Tap "Done" to complete the entry.

Once an event has been entered, it will show up in your calendar and can be edited or deleted as needed.

There are lots of things that the iPad calendar *doesn't* do. Some of them are a mystery to me. For example, it's not possible to invite another person to an event from the iPad. Moreover, you can't even add people to an event on the iPad. This really does limit the calendar's

capabilities and usefulness; and again, let's hope that Apple will keep improving these apps as the company moves forward with the iPad development.

CONTACTS

When I first got a smart phone, the real thrill was being able to transfer all my contacts' information onto the phone. This meant I could call or text message or even e-mail anyone … without having to re-enter all that information onto the phone. While the iPad doesn't have a phone or a built-in text messaging system, it does have e-mail, and it's nice to be able to use the device as a great big address book.

Add a Contact

Adding a contact to your iPad address book is pretty easy. Just turn on the iPad, tap on the built-in Contacts app and follow these steps:

1. Tap on the (+) located at the bottom of the screen.

2. Enter the contact's first name, last name and company info.

Figure 13-3
In the Contacts interface, the list of contacts is on the left and the details are on the right.

3. Add a photo. Tap the "Add Photo" button in the Contacts app. This will enable you to pick a photo for this contact. Choose from the images that are loaded on your iPad.

4. Tap on the word "Mobile" and pick your type of phone from the pop-up menu.

5. Enter the contact's phone number.

6. Choose the phone type (e.g., home, work, mobile) in the field below the entry. Enter as many different phone numbers for a contact as necessary. As you start to type a new number, a new number box will appear below the existing one(s).

7. Next is e-mail. Tap on the type of e-mail (e.g., home or work) and then enter the e-mail address.

8. After you enter the first e-mail, you will be able to enter a second, third, forth and so on in the same manner you did with the phone numbers.

9. You can also enter a contact's Web site (or two, three, four or more of them).

10. Next, enter a mailing address.

11. You can then add a second address or even a third, fourth or fifth address, if needed.

12. Add any notes you want associated with this contact.

13. If needed, add custom fields, including a prefix, the phonetic spelling of the first and/ or last name, middle name, suffix, nickname, job title, department, instant message information, birthday and/ or a date.

14. When all the contact's information has been entered, tap "Done" on the top right.

Once a contact is in your Contacts app, you can use the information to send e-mails from your iPad. Just open the Contacts app and

Figure 13-4
Add a Contact page.

find the person you want to e-mail. Tap on his/ her name, and then tap on the e-mail address. The Mail program will automatically open with that recipient already entered in the "To:" field.

SYNCING CALENDARS AND CONTACTS

The real fun of calendars and contacts is the syncing the occurs among different devices, which puts your important info on your phone, desktop, laptop, iPad, etc. Syncing all the devices together means the information remains constant and correct on all of them. The idea is great, but it never seems to work exactly as advertised. And when syncing problems occur—and they will—it is possible to lose your information.

iTunes

A very simple way to sync your iPad and computer calendars is to use iTunes. The operative word here is *simple* … and, unfortunately, that means limited in this case.

In Chapter 2, we covered the process of attaching your iPad to your computer with the included USB cable and running iTunes. Well, when the iPad is attached to your computer, you can select it from the devices in the left column. From here, click on the "Info" tab at the top of the screen. Two of the options on this screen are "Sync Contacts" and "Sync Calendars." Click these, and every time the iPad syncs the data from the computer, information is compared and updated.

A potential problem you may have with this is that you can only sync the calendars and contacts when your iPad is attached to your computer. And you can only sync your iPad with the computer you regularly use for this process. This can be a problem if you have more than one computer.

So let's say you have a computer at home with all your music, movies and other media on it, and that's the computer you use to sync your

Figure 13-5
This iTunes interface shows where you can sync your contacts and calendars on your computer and iPad.

iPad. And you also have a computer at work with all your calendars and contacts on it. This is a crappy situation for you in terms of your iPad world, because you can't sync your iPad to your work computer without losing the information that's on your iPad from your home computer. Your iPad can only have a syncing relationship with one computer.

MobileMe

Apple really wants you to use MobileMe. According to Apple, it's the best solution for e-mail, calendars and contacts. And when it comes to keeping your information synced, MobileMe does a great job. It keeps the information in your contacts and calendars (along with e-mails and Internet bookmarks) synced among all your computers, iPad, the MobileMe Web site and your iPhone. Plus, it does so in the background; and if your hardware is new enough and running the latest OS, it does it automatically.

For full disclosure here, I have a MobileMe account, and have been using it since it was called a .mac account. I keep my calendars synced on a laptop, a desktop, the iPad and an iPhone. I also have an older PC; my address book and calendars are synced there, too.

MobileMe is a service made by Apple, and it's meant to be used on Apple products. If you use a PC, this is not the product for you, and you're probably using the Microsoft Exchange server. There is, of course, a good third-party alternative to MobileMe, and that's from Google, which makes applications for managing your calendar and contacts. And the data on the Google apps can be wirelessly synced.

But if you have MobileMe, here is a quick rundown on getting your iPad to play nice with your MobileMe calendars and contacts. More on the Google solution in a minute.

Figure 13-6
I set my MobileMe account to sync not only my e-mail but my contacts and calendars as well.

1. Turn on your iPad.

2. Tap on "Settings."

3. Tap "Mail, Contacts, Calendars."

4. Tap "Add Account" and choose "MobileMe."

5. Enter your MobileMe account information.

6. Tap "Next."

7. Turn on Mail, Contacts, Calendars and Bookmarks.

8. If it asks, tap on "Merge with MobileMe." This tries to make sure that the contacts, calendars and bookmarks already on your device sync with MobileMe and are not duplicated.

9. On the main Settings screen, tap "Mail, Contacts, Calendars" and tap "Fetch New Data."

10. Make sure that "Push" is set to wirelessly

and automatically get data from the server, so your MobileMe contacts and calendars will be automatically updated whenever a change is made.

Now, when I make a change to the address for a contact on my iPad, it updates my iPhone and computers, too. The same is true in the other direction. When you update an e-mail address on the computer, for example, the iPad receives the new information.

Microsoft Exchange
If you have a Microsoft Exchange calendar set up, you can sync it with your iPad. Do this the same way you would set up the iPad to access a Microsoft Exchange server for your e-mail.

1. Turn on your iPad.

2. Tap on "Settings."

3. Tap "Mail, Contacts, Calendars."

4. Tap "Add Account" and choose "Microsoft Exchange."

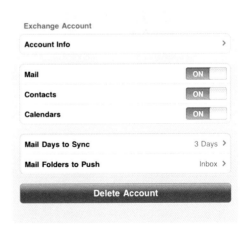

Figure 13-7
The Exchange account menu lets you turn on Contact and Calendar syncing.

195

5. Enter your Exchange Server account information.

6. Tap "Next."

7. Enter the server information.

8. Tap "Next."

9. Turn on Mail, Contacts, Calendars.

10. Your Exchange Server accounts are now being synced wirelessly and automatically to your iPad, including the contacts and calendars.

Google Sync

It seems that Google is everywhere these days. And it's not only searching the Internet. It's also providing maps and directions, Web site traffic data, and even price checks for a range of consumer goods. And Google does really good job with Google Sync.

Google Sync, of course, syncs your calendars and contacts on all your devices, including the iPad. I know there are folks out there who don't like the idea of all their information sitting on the servers of a single company; but for those who don't mind, the Google calendar and address book are great options. Plus, they're free.

To set up your iPad with Google Sync:

1. Turn on the iPad.

2. Open the Settings app.

3. Tap on "Mail, Contacts, Calendars."

4. Select Microsoft Exchange. (If you already have a Microsoft Exchange account set up, then skip to the next section.)

5. In the e-mail field, enter your full Google account e-mail address.

6. Leave the Domain field blank.

7. Enter your full Google account e-mail address as the username.

8. Enter your Google account password in the Password field.

9. Tap "Next" on the top of the screen. If you get the "Unable to verify certificate" warning, tap "Cancel."

10. In the New Server field, enter **m.google.com**.

11. Tap "Next" on the top of the screen.

12. You can now select the "Mail, Calendar and Contacts" to sync.

If you have a Microsoft Exchange server set up, you can still use Google sync, but you need to set up the e-mail as described in Chapter 11. Then you can set up a CalDav to sync the calendars. Apple has you covered here as well.

1. Turn on the iPad.

2. Open the Settings app.

3. Tap on "Mail, Contacts, Calendars."

4. Select "Other."

5. Select "Add CalDav Account."

6. Enter the following:

    ◦ In the Server field, enter google.com.

    ◦ In the Username field, enter your full Google Account or Google Apps e-mail address.

    ◦ In the Password field, enter your Google Account or Google Apps password.

    ◦ Enter a description of the account, like "Google Calendars."

7. Tap "Next" on the top of the screen.

8. You are done.

9. Open the Calendar app, and your Google calendar will begin to sync wirelessly.

To get the Google contacts and calendars on your computer, go to **http://www.google.com/sync/index.html** and follow the directions for your computer.

LDAP ADDRESS BOOK

If you have a LDAP (Lightweight Directory Access Protocol) address book and you know your account information, then you can access that address book from the iPad as well. (If you do not know your account information, you can get it from your System Administrator / IT person.) Just follow these steps:

1. Turn on the iPad.

2. Open the Settings app.

3. Tap on "Mail, Contacts, Calendars."

4. Select "Other."

5. Select "Add LDAP Account."

6. Enter the following:

   o The LDAP server

   o The user name (It's optional.)

   o The password (Again, it's optional.)

   o Description

7. Tap "Next" on the top of the screen.

8. That's it; you're done.

vCARDS

The default file format for address book data is called a *vCard*. This format is basically an electronic business card and can contain a contact's name, phone number, e-mail and address information; and you can actually keep a profile photo in the vCard format.

vCards can be sent in e-mails, too. (A little later on, I'll show you how the iPad deals with sharing contacts.) vCards can also be exchanged over the Internet or even on a disc or jump drive.

Since the iPad doesn't have a drive or a USB port, the only good way to get a vCard in to the iPad Contacts app is by e-mail. vCards that are sent as e-mail attachments can be instantly loaded into the iPad's Contacts.

SHARING CONTACTS

Here is something that Apple definitely did right when it comes to the address book on the iPad. They made it really easy for you to share your contacts with others. You can share any of the contacts in your address book with a simple click.

1. Open the Contacts app on the iPad.

2. Tap on the contact you want to share.

3. On the bottom of the screen, tap "Share."

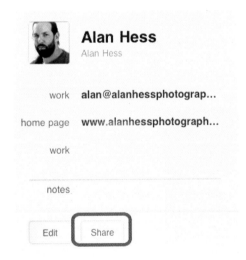

Figure 13-8

It's as easy as tapping a single button to share a contact by e-mail.

Accessing notes in Evernote is easy, too. They are posted right on the front page. Depending on the orientation you're using to look at your screen, the notes will be either on top (portrait orientation) or on the right side of the screen (landscape orientation).

You can also change the order that the notes are displayed by tapping on "View options." This opens a drop-down menu that allows the following sort orders:

- Date updated
- Date created
- Title
- Notebook
- City
- Country

And you can change the view from "Details" to a thumbnails view by tapping on your preference.

Tap on the note description or thumbnail and it immediately opens in a window that shows up below the list of notes (portrait orientation) or to the right of the list (landscape).

A nice feature here is Notebooks. These are for those who want to go that extra step and keep notes in different notebooks. To set up Notebooks, you need to use a computer or Web site. At this time, you can't use the iPad app to create different Notebooks. But once you've created a second (or third, fourth, etc.) Notebook, it will show up in the iPad app as soon as you synchronize your account.

If you are a very heavy note taker, you'll soon realize that the basic (read: free) Evernote package has some limitations. The free account has a monthly usage limit of 40MB. And this is fine for basic note takers, but perhaps not for the highly industrious. For these

folks, there is a Premium Evernote service that currently costs $4.99 a month or $44.99 a year (which gives you two months free). The premium account offers 500MB of monthly uploads and allows a user to sync all types of files, including Microsoft Office documents.

The premium package is also good for users who want to give others the ability to read and edit their notes. You can even search within PDFs with this service. Sign up for the premium service right from inside the app on the iPad; it couldn't be easier. When you tap the "Synchronize" button, an option to "Go Premium" appears. Just tap on this to access the sign up page for the upgrade.

LISTS

Who doesn't like making lists? I mean, they keep us on track and remind us of all the stuff we have—and have not—done. I love making lists. The problem is that I usually forget where I leave them, and I often don't bother to look at my lists after I write them. I have lots of lists that are AWOL … all the time.

The iPad is a great place to make and keep lists, and the number of apps available to help you with this is growing all the time. It would be impossible to cover all the list-creation apps available, but there are a few that do a great job.

Zenbe Lists

If I made a list of the best list-making tools, this would be at the top; because it does one thing … and does it really well. Zenbe Lists offers listmaking options and then syncs a user's lists among devices. With this app, you can also share lists and collaborate on lists. Plus, the interface is clean and easy-to-use.

So while this app doesn't have all the customizations of the other list-making apps, like

Figure 14-5
You can easily set due dates and priori-
ties for individual items on a list.

Figure 14-4
The Zenbe Lists layout is really clean
and efficient.

Todo (described below), it is the easiest and,
in my opinion, the fastest to use.

The key to the syncing and collaboration
functions is signing up for a free account on
Zenbe Lists. Do this on the Internet at **LISTS.
ZENBE.COM** or from inside the app. After
you sign up for an account, any of your Zenbe
lists can be synced to the account. Each item
can have its own note and priority assigned,
and the lists can be sorted manually, by due
date, by priority or alphabetically.

What I find really handy is sharing lists with
other people. And they can edit your list without having an account! To do this on the iPad:

1. Select a list.

2. Tap on "Share with contacts."

3. Your e-mail app opens and a link to the list
   is inserted into the message field.

4. Enter recipients who will view and edit
   the list.

5. If a recipient receives your e-mail on an
   iPad or iPhone, the list can be added to
   that device as well.

These recipients can now see and edit your
list. They can add items to it and mark items
off the list … and here is the best part: it
remains just one list.

What I'm saying is that your recipients'
changes do not create a copy or a separate
version of your list. Any changes made by
others are incorporated into the same list
you're creating. The minute you sync with
Zenbe (which is done automatically on start
up or by tapping the "Sync" button), your
list is updated and any changes automatically appear. That means that you don't have
to keep track of multiple versions or try to
figure out which list is the most current or
which version of the list people are seeing.
It's easy peasy.

This ability to share your list with multiple people is well worth the $3.99 app cost. The fact that others can edit and collaborate on a list makes it worth so much more. Of all the list-creating apps that I've tried and have loaded on my iPad, I still find myself using this one most of all.

Todo

This app is really slick-looking. I think it has one of the best looking interfaces for the iPad. It looks like an old-fashioned day planner, and you can customize everything from the color and texture of the paper to the metal rings that create the binder look. You can even purchase different looks from inside the app.

The real plus here is that Todo allows you to not only make normal lists but also project lists and check lists, which gives you more control over the sorting and organization of your lists. Todo also offers five built-in tasks to make list-building easier, and all these options are in the same place: the task menu.

To make a list or add a task to a list on Todo:

1. Open Todo on your iPad by tapping on its icon.

2. Tap the (+) in the top right corner to create a new task.

3. Tap on a list type:

   ○ **Normal** to make a normal list

   ○ **Project** to make sub-lists that are grouped together as a project

   ○ **Checklist** to create a list that allows you to easily mark off items that you've addressed

   ○ **Call a Contact** to search your Address Book for a contact, enter a new contact or enter a phone number

   ○ **Email a Contact** to search your Address

Figure 14-6
In-app purchases of new stationary allow you to really customize the look of the Todo app.

Book for a contact, enter a new contact or enter an e-mail address.

○ **SMS a Contact** to search your Address Book for a contact, enter a new contact or enter a mobile phone number.

○ **Visit a Location** to search your Address Book for a contact, enter a new contact, or enter an address manually or use your current location

○ **Visit a Web Site** to enter a URL of a Web site you want to visit

4. Once you've made your choice, you can continue to enter information for the current list.

Todo also offers an online service that will sync your Todo lists with other devices. This

Figure 14-7
The look and feel of the Todo app
is very reassuring to those moving
to electronic lists from a traditional
day planner.

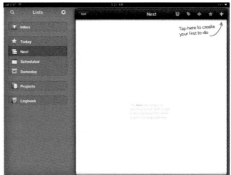

Figure 14-8
The Things for iPad app has a really
clean interface and offers nice hints on
getting started.

service costs an additional $19.99 per year. If
you want an app that allows you to organize
your lists, then Todo is a good choice.

Things for iPad

This is a beautiful list-making app, and it
works really well on the iPad. It can even
sync to a desktop as long as you are working
on a Mac.

So let's get the bad news out of the way first.
This app costs $19.99, which is a lot in the app
marketplace. Plus, if you want the app to sync
to your desktop, you need the "Things for
Mac" program which costs another $49.95. So
this is an expensive program; but for the cost,
you get a really polished app that looks fantastic and does a great job.

The layout of this app is very clean; it's beautiful,
especially if you're a fan of simple design. There
are two different views of the app, depending
on which way you hold the iPad. In landscape
view (my favorite), the screen is divided into
two parts. On the left is the sorting and selection
view; on the right is the actual list.

The app offers five different areas for saving a
list. When the iPad is held in portrait orientation, you need to tap on the "Lists" button
(located on the top left) to get the sorting and
selection choices:

- **Inbox** is where you put lists that don't have
a due date or don't fit neatly into a specific
category. I try to keep this empty, because
if an item's in here it means that I haven't
dealt with it at all yet.

- **Today** holds items from your lists that are
due today. These need immediate action.

- **Next** is where items are in queue and due
next, but not today. When you complete all
the items in your "Today" box, move on to
those in the "Next" box.

- **Scheduled** will show you items that are
scheduled for a certain day.

- **Someday** lists items that you can't or don't
want to deal with now but that you don't
want to forget about.

All of these categories are set up when you
create a to do list in the Things for iPad app,

and items can be moved from one box to another at any point.

Creating a new to do list in this app is really easy. Just tap on the (+) in the top right corner and enter information into the series of menus.

- **The New To Do Menu:** Enter a title for the task or item.

- **Tags:** Add a tag that sorts your item by either "Work," "Home" or "Errand." You can also add a "New Tag" or "Manage Tags." Tap "Save" when done.

- **Notes:** Add a note to an item or task. (This field is really useful when an address and other pertinent info needs to be associated with an item.) Tap "Save" when done.

- **Due Date:** Add a due date for the item and set when the item will appear on the Today list. This can give you a day or two lead time for items that require it. These items will be shown in the Today box before they are actually due. When done, tap "Save."

- **Create In:** This field allows you to identify where the item will be shown in the sorting system on the left side. Choices include (as described above): Today, Next, Scheduled and Someday. This menu makes it easy for you to organize your items in a logical way that makes sense to you when you look at your to do lists.

The Things for iPad app also allows you to create projects and logbooks. Just tap on the respective boxes on the front page and then tap the (+) sign in the top corner.

What stands out for me on this app is the way the lists are presented. I like that when I tap on "Today," I get a manageable list of items I need to do today—not a monster list of all the

Figure 14-9

The Things for iPad app offers menu choices when you enter a new item or task to your to do list.

things I need to do at some point. This can really make a big difference.

For me, it's easy to get overwhelmed when a ton of tasks are in my face. I much prefer to see a smaller list of urgent items. On the downside of that, this app will not allow you to view all your lists in a single place.

If you have the money and really like the way this app looks, then go for it. It's been great for me.

PRODUCTIVITY TOOLS APPS

The way a person uses lists and notes can be very personal. The apps that work for me might not be the best ones for your work-flow, but don't worry. There are tons of apps out there for you to choose from. Just look through the productivity category in the App Store. Chances are, you'll find the tools that meet your organizational needs very well.

Word Processing

The Skim

Pages ∘ Transfer Files ∘ Dropbox ∘ GoodReader ∘ Printing

A question that comes up time and time again is "Can the iPad be used as a laptop replacement, especially for work?" Obviously, it would be great if we could do all our mobile work computing on this device, but is that just a dream?

The answer goes both ways. While you can read and write on the iPad, the reading part is way more advanced than the writing part. And while apps like Dropbox (described below) make it easy to read, synchronize and access files via the Internet on your iPad, there is no *really* easy solution to getting the files off the iPad unless you count e-mail—and in this day and age, I don't consider this an Apple solution. But don't worry; we'll cover all your options for transferring files on and off the iPad, including e-mail, in this chapter.

Word processing is a primary function of computers in the business world. We tend to spend our days typing away. That's true for me anyway, since I spend a lot of time writing and editing books. So I put myself on a mission to find out if I could use the iPad to seriously write—not just take a note or two, but to actually write. This chapter was written using the Pages app on the iPad. At least the first draft was.

When it comes to word processing and managing word processing content on the iPad, the main concern is being able to read Microsoft Word documents as well as edit and share them. They are by far the most common

Figure 15-1
The Pages, Numbers and Keynote apps are shown here. Find more on Numbers and Keynote in the next couple of chapters.

type of word processing document, and the iPad does not have a Microsoft Word app. So the best bet (actually the only bet right now for editing on the iPad) is the Apple app called *Pages*.

PAGES OVERVIEW

The Pages app is a cut-down version of the iWork Pages word processing program. It was announced at the same time as the iPad. The app was meant to give users the capability to do real work on the iPad. And yes, it works!

Pages is not a free app, and it doesn't come pre loaded on your iPad. If you want the tools offered by this app, then you need to purchase it for $9.99, which is actually on the high end of app prices. If you also purchase Numbers and Keynote at $9.99 each, the cost can quickly add up ... to $29.97 to be exact. The full versions for the computer cost $79.

The first time you run Pages, you'll see that there is already a document present. This "getting started" document is your user manual and, as with all things Apple, it seems a little sparse. Just remember that this is a cut-down version of a more robust program.

CREATE A NEW PAGES DOCUMENT

The Pages app is an abbreviated version of the iWork Pages program that's available for

Figure 15-2
Open the document template viewer by tapping on "New Document" or the (+), which is located at the bottom of the screen.

Apple computers. Despite not being a "full version," this app packs a lot into a small package. It comes standard with a blank document template and 15 other templates that cover everything from letters and resumes to term papers, posters and flyers.

To pick a template:

1. Open Pages on the iPad.

2. Make sure you are in the My Documents view.

3. Tap on "New Document" on the top left of the screen, or tap on the (+) at the bottom of the screen and then tap "New Document."

4. Scroll up and down to find the template you want to use.

5. Tap the template to open a new document.

6. Begin writing.

After you've picked a template, a new document will immediately open with the chosen format loaded. It takes a little time to get used to navigating with your fingers, so don't get

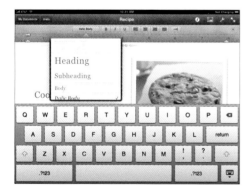

Figure 15-3
The recipe template can get a little crowded, especially when using the keyboard in landscape mode.

discouraged. Tap on various areas to edit, and be prepared: the keyboard will take up half the screen. Stick with it; it can be enjoyable to work this way. Well, maybe not *enjoyable*, but you can get work done.

One important thing to know is that these files are saved as you edit on the iPad. There is no "Save" button. So if you press the Home button or tap on "My Documents," the current file will close, and all your changes will be saved with it. This can be good and bad. No lost work, but you'll need to be careful with changes.

Similarly, there is no "Save As" button to retain a former version. The file you opened will be the one that all changes are saved to. If you want to edit a document and keep the original as a separate file, you need to plan that from the start. But all you need to do is duplicate the document before you edit, and then edit the duplicate.

To duplicate your document, go to the My Documents view and have the document you want in the middle of the page. Tap on the (+) button at the bottom. You will be offered a choice: either create a "New Document" or "Duplicate Document." Tap on "Duplicate Document" to get a new version of the selected document, and then edit away.

The new document will have the Word copy attached to the document name, so each time you duplicate it, a number will be added. To illustrate, the first time you revise a file, the name will end with "copy." The next time, it will end with "copy 1" and then "copy 2" and so on.

EDIT WORD DOCUMENTS

As I'm writing this, there isn't a Microsoft Word app for the iPad. Microsoft might release a Word app, but it really doesn't matter. Pages can import and export Word files.

Figure 15-4

When you open a Word file in Pages, there are certain formatting elements and fonts that do not translate. Pages automatically adjusts for these and lets you know what it changed.

That isn't to say that the import works every time without problems, but the problems are typically related to fonts, formatting and other non-standard (in Apple's opinion) data that's in your document.

I have imported and exported a wide variety of Word documents with lots of special formatting and non-standard fonts and, while some of the fonts needed to be changed, the documents still looked pretty close to the original (Word) versions.

But if you are just making one or two corrections to a document and want to format it in a certain way, it is a lot of work to change all the fonts back to the original ones when going back to using Microsoft Word on a computer. Just something to think about…

Right now there is no way to add fonts to the iPad, and I believe that is Apple's way of making sure there is enough space for apps and data. Fonts require space, and the iPad doesn't have much to spare.

STORE, TRANSFER AND SHARE PAGES DOCS

Storing, transferring and sharing documents are important functions for word processing. There are five methods of sending out your files from inside of Pages. When in the My Documents view of Pages, tapping on the file icon (it's the little box with the arrow coming out of it on the bottom left) brings up your choices. You can send a file as an e-mail, share it via iWork, send it to iTunes, copy to iDisk or copy to WebDav.

Using iTunes for transferring files is great when you are sitting at your desk, but some of the alternatives are easier and more efficient, especially when you're out and about.

E-Mail

We've already covered the types of documents that can be sent using e-mail (Chapter 11 : E-Mail), but it's worth repeating here. The Mail app on the iPad can send Microsoft Word, Pages and PDF files with no problems. These files can be viewed in Mail and opened in Pages from Mail.

To send a Word, Pages or PDF document from Pages by e-mail:

1. Open Pages.

2. In the My Documents view, navigate so that the document you want to send out is in the middle of the screen.

3. Tap the "File" button.

4. Tap "Send via Mail."

5. Pick the format for your document (e.g., PDF, Microsoft Word or Pages).

6. An e-mail message will appear with your file as an attachment. Complete the rest of the fields and tap "Send."

To open a file you received in an e-mail message:

1. Open Mail on the iPad.

2. Open the message that has the attached Word or Pages file.

3. Tap and hold on the icon of the attached file in the e-mail. (If you just tap on it, but don't hold, you'll get a "Quick Look" version of the file.)

4. Tap "Open in Pages." If the attachment can be opened in any other app, first tap "Open in" and then tap "Pages."

5. Mail will close and Pages will open.

6. When the document is finished downloading, it will open in Pages.

7. You are now ready to edit.

Figure 15-5
Sending out a Word document in an e-mail from Pages is easy.

Figure 15-6
A Microsoft Word document can be opened directly in Pages from an e-mail.

215

This method of sharing documents is nothing new. In fact, it used to be my method of choice for transferring documents among different computers. But the problem with this process is that you end up with a lot of different copies of the same document floating around.

To help manage this, and increase your confidence in knowing that you're dealing with the correct and most current version of a particular document, take a few extra steps to name the file. I like using -01, -02 or RevA, RevB at the end of the file name to keep track of my different versions.

iWork

There is a part of the iWork suite that is still in Beta according to Apple, but I have been using it without a problem since I got the first iPad. It's called iWork.com, and it allows users to share documents using a dedicated Web site to avoid having to attach the iPad to a computer. But this only works if you have Internet access, either through Wi-Fi or 3G. Users can use iWork.com to transfer not only Pages documents but Word documents and PDFs as well.

To send a document to iWork.com from your iPad:

1. Open the Pages app.

2. Scroll to the document you want to upload. The menu is in the center of the screen in the My Documents view.

3. Tap on the "File" button.

4. Tap "Share via iWork.com."

5. If you are not signed in, sign in using your Apple ID or tap "Create a new Apple ID."

6. You can now add the e-mail address of anyone you want to receive the document and attach a message if needed. If you don't want to share the document with anyone else, then leave this field blank.

7. Tap on the (i) button on the right side of the screen to open the Sharing Options menu. Here, you can:
   - Change the name of the file
   - Password-protect the file
   - Allow readers to leave comments

8. Tap "Share."

9. You can now view the document via Safari at iWork.com.

To download a file from iWork.com and open it in Pages:

1. Open Safari on your iPad.

2. Navigate to iWork.com and sign in.

3. Tap on the download arrow next to the document you want to edit in the list of shared documents.

4. A preview of the document will open. Tap "Open in Pages." If the document can be opened in any other app, you will instead tap "Open in" and pick Pages from the menu choices.

5. Safari will automatically close, and Pages will open. The selected document will download to Pages, and it will appear as the first document in the "My Documents" view.

When you're done editing the document, you can re-save it to iWork.com.

There are other options as well. These include the use of iTunes, iDisk and WebDav. Let's look at these tools.

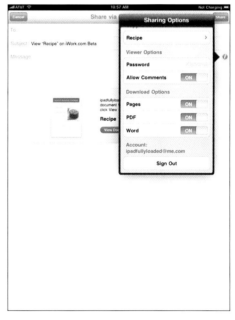

Figure 15-7

The four basic steps involved with sharing a file with iWork.com are to pick iWork from the export menu, sign in with your Apple account e-mail, set your sharing options, and tap "Share." Easy.

iTunes

It is possible to use iTunes to facilitate the transfer of files from your computer to your iPad and from your iPad to your computer. You can import documents created in Pages '09 and Microsoft Word from your computer to the iPad and edit those files in the Pages app. You can also send those files back to the computer when you're done. It's a pretty simple process.

Import a file: To import a document to your iPad for editing on the iPad:

1. Connect your iPad to a computer and start iTunes.

2. In iTunes, click on your iPad and then select "Apps."

3. Scroll to the bottom of the Apps window until you see the File Sharing part of the page.

4. Tap "Pages."

5. Tap "Add" and then navigate to the file's location in the "Choose a File: iTunes" window.

6. Select the file you want to import and tap "Choose."

Figure 15-8
The File Sharing window shows which files are in the My Documents section of the Pages app.

7. The file is immediately transferred to the iPad.

8. Open Pages on the iPad and from the My Documents view, tap on "Import." (The icon looks like a tray with an arrow pointing into it.)

9. Tap "Copy from iTunes."

10. Pick the document you want to import. (It should be the same document that you placed there in the previous steps.)

11. The file will be placed on the iPad and opened in Pages automatically.

When I did this for the first time, it took me awhile to actually find the document on my iPad. Files do not go to the "My Documents" section of the Pages app right away; you need to import it.

To do this, click on the folder in the top right corner of the "My Documents" screen. This will reveal a list of available files, which will pop up in the middle of the screen. Click on the document you want to open, and Pages will import it.

Export a file: To export a file from Pages and transfer it to your computer using iTunes:

1. Connect your iPad to the computer and launch iTunes.

2. Open the Pages app and make sure all the documents are closed.

3. Scroll until you see the document you want to export in the My Documents view.

4. Tap the button with the square and arrow, and then tap "Send to iTunes."

5. Choose the document format you want for the export: Pages, PDF or Word.

6. The file will be sent to the computer immediately.

Figure 15-9

The File Transfer window shows which files are in the My Documents section of the Pages app.

7. Select the iPad in the Devices area of iTunes, and then click "Apps."

8. Scroll down to the File Sharing section of the window.

9. Select Pages in the apps list of the file sharing section.

10. From the list on the right, select the document you just tranferred.

11. Click "Save To."

12. A window will open that allows you to navigate to a location to store the file.

13. Click "Open" to save the file from the iPad anywhere on the computer.

iDisk

iDisk is paid service from Apple that is part of a MobileMe account. It allows you to save documents and other files on the Internet in your own special place. To use iDisk as a place to send your files:

1. Open the Pages app and make sure all the documents are closed.

2. Scroll until you see the document you want to export in the My Documents view.

3. Tap the button with the square and arrow, and then tap "Copy to iDisk."

4. Sign into iDisk with your MobileMe user-name and password.

5. Choose the document format you want for the export: Pages, PDF or Word.

6. Select the folder in which you want to save your file on your iDisk. Then, select the document and tap "Copy," located on the right.

7. The file is now copied to your iDisk.

You can see your document by opening your iDisk on the computer and navigating to the folder that contains your copied file.

You can also copy a file from iDisk by tapping the "Import" icon (which looks like a tray with an arrow pointing into it). Once you've tapped on the icon, you can pick from "Copy from iTunes" (covered above), "Copy from iDisk" (covered here) and "Copy from Web-Dav" (covered next).

1. Open the Pages app and make sure all the documents are closed.

2. Tap the button with the tray and arrow pointing into it and then tap "Copy from iDisk."

3. Sign into iDisk with your MobileMe user name and password (unless you are already logged in).

4. Pick the folder on your iDisk that you want to open, and then click on the file you want to open in Pages on the iPad. If a document is grayed out, then you can't select it because it is unreadable by Pages.

5. Tap on the file. It will be copied to the iPad.

6. The file will automatically open in Pages.

WebDav

WebDav stands for Web-based Distributed Authoring and Versioning, and it's just a way to edit and deal with files that exist on a remote computer (called a server). If you have access to a WebDav server, you can send a copy of your files to it. If you tap on the "File" button on Pages and choose "Copy to WebDav," a menu will appear that asks for the server address, username and password. Enter this information and send a copy of your file to the server.

To import a file using WebDav:

1. Open the Pages app and make sure all the documents are closed.

2. Tap the button with the tray and arrow pointing into it, and then tap "Copy from WebDav."

3. Sign in with a server address, username and password.

4. Pick the folder that you want to open, and then click on the file you want to open in Pages on the iPad. If a document is grayed out, it means you can't select it because it is unreadable by Pages.

5. Tap on the file. It will be copied to the iPad and automatically opened in Pages.

Dropbox

Dropbox is a web-based service that offers a suite of applications for your computer and iPad. The service allows you to access, store and transfer files easily. Dropbox can be accessed on any device with a Web browser, and it's free! Well, you get 2GB of storage for free, and you can buy more if you need it.

Figure 15-10
The Dropbox sign-in screen

Use this service to sync files of any size; it makes no difference what computer you're using. A single Dropbox account will store an entire library of documents.

When you set up a Dropbox account for the first time, you will find two folders and two PDF files already present. The two folders are titled "Photos" and "Public."

The Photos folder has a sample album and an .rtf file with instructions on how to use this folder. For more information on the photography-related capabilities of Dropbox, check out the Photography Chapter (Chapter 10).

The Public folder is the default way to share single files. And, boy, this is easy! To transfer a file from a computer to your iPad, just drop the file into the Public folder on the computer and it'll show up on the iPad … as long as both devices are connected to the Internet.

Since this chapter is about word processing, let's look at how Dropbox deals with Word documents, Pages files and PDFs.

Turns out it handles them seamlessly. To access files in Dropbox, simply click on the

Figure 15-10

This is the default view when you log into Dropbox. Your files and folders are on the left with a preview of a highlighted document on the right. If the file in the preview window can be opened with another application, just tap the "Open in" menu and pick the app you want to use.

folder that contains the file you want to read or edit. You'll find a list of documents that are present in your Dropbox account.

Clicking on any of the documents in your Dropbox will give you an in-app preview of that document. If you like what you see, tap in the upper right corner of the screen on the "Open in" icon to open the file in any of the installed apps that can read it, including Pages.

At this time, you cannot export files that you edit on the iPad back into Dropbox. Don't ask me why … All I know is that this means it's easy to use this service to get your files onto the iPad, but you can't use it to get your files off it. For that you need to use one of the methods (described earlier in this chapter) for exporting from Pages.

GOODREADER

Before Apple updated iBooks to enable it to read PDFs natively, I used GoodReader. I actually still use GoodReader; it's my go-to app when I want to read documents on my

iPad, because it lives up to its name. It really is good for reading.

In fact, GoodReader is one of the most versatile document readers available. While it isn't free, as of this writing, GoodReader is still only $0.99 in the United States iTunes Store.

Right off the bat, it is important to know that GoodReader is not an editor but a reader app.

Figure 15-11

This GoodReader interface shows the Preview option turned on and the "Open In …" submenu opened.

It natively supports the following platforms:

- Microsoft Office
- Pages
- PDF
- PowerPoint
- Keynote
- Excel
- Numbers
- HTML
- Safari Web archives
- image files
- audio files
- video files

This means that whatever file you want to read on the iPad, chances are that GoodReader can do it. Now, since the app is dependent on the underlying iOS, some file types are not supported that might make a difference to some users (see list below). That said, in my practical use of the app, I've found GoodReader to work great, and I haven't come across any files it failed to show. Since the iOS and the app are being updated all time, I expect even more file types to be supported in the future.

Figure 15-12
The GoodReader interface when reading a file.

As I write this, the following files and file types are not supported by GoodReader.

- DRM-protected PDFs are not supported, but password-protected regular PDFs are.
- PDF annotations are not supported.
- PDF portfolios must be extracted into separate PDF files in order to be viewed via GoodReader.
- Microsoft Office files that are password-protected are not supported.
- PDFs with 3D, audio, and/ or video content are not supported.

The GoodReader interface is really intuitive and easy to navigate. The first view divides the screen into two sections. My Documents is on the left and a series of menus are on the right. These menus include:

- **The Preview** section makes it easy to see what file is selected. Especially when a file name is misleading, this feature enables you to see if a certain file is what you want to open. There's also an option to open the file in another app on the iPad. So if you have downloaded a PDF to check out, you can choose to open the file in iBooks instead of GoodReader.
- **Find Files** allows you to search the files in your My Documents area.
- **Manage Files** is jam packed with options that range from choosing where new files are added to creating new folders. It also allows you to compress and decompress files.
- **Use Web Downloads** to browse the Internet for files. It shows downloads in progress as well as recently downloaded files.

Figure 15-13
The GoodReader interface here shows
the Manage Files menu.

Figure 15-14
A new text document can be created
inside GoodReader.

○ **Connect to Servers** shows the list of servers
you have set up to access, and it allows you
to add more servers by tapping the "Add"
button. You can also edit the list of servers
you have set up.

There is a group of icons positioned across the
bottom of your screen. They are listed below
with a description of the tools they offer:

○ Use the camera to import images from the
photo albums on your iPad.

○ The Wi-Fi transfer window enables you to
transfer files over Wi-Fi.

○ The Settings menu records your preferences
for GoodReader.

○ Find help with GoodReader through the
GoodReader Help Menu.

○ You can use an external display with
GoodReader, and the external display menu
will control those options.

So why did I include this document reader
in a chapter on word processing? Well it's
because you can actually create new text
documents right inside of GoodReader. In the
Manage Files menu, just tap on the "New File"

button. A new text file will appear in the My
Documents folder … or whatever subfolder
you happen to be in.

And that's not all …

One of the real advantages of using
GoodReader is that there are a variety of
ways to transfer files into and out of the
GoodReader app. This alone makes it a viable
choice for reading documents online. Some of
these options are described below.

USB Connection

To move files from a computer to your iPad
using the USB connection:

1. Open iTunes on your computer and
connect your iPad to the computer via
USB cable.

2. Click on your iPad in the Devices list on
the left side of the iTunes window.

3. Select the "Apps" tab.

4. Scroll down until you see the "File Sharing" section.

5. Select "GoodReader" in the list of apps.

6. See the GoodReader Documents window

Figure 15-15
The documents saved in the My Documents folder of GoodReader are viewable in iTunes on any computer the iPad is attached to via USB cable.

and the files stored in the My Documents folder of GoodReader.

7. Add files to this folder by using the "Add" button (located at the bottom of the screen) or by dragging and dropping your files to this window.

8. With either of the methods in Step 7, files will be transferred immediately to GoodReader.

9. You cannot drop folders, but you can drop zipped folders that appear as a single file. The files can be unzipped inside GoodReader on the iPad.

Remove files from the GoodReader app the same way you added them … when the iPad is connected to iTunes via USB cable. In fact, this is still the fastest way to move files onto and off of the iPad. All the files you move into GoodReader in this manner will show up in the default My Documents folders and can be sorted and moved into sub-folders inside GoodReader on the iPad at a later date.

One item to note is that GoodReader will only allow you access to the root file system of the app. So if you have a PDF in a folder and

you want to transfer it, you will have to save the whole folder to your computer. You cannot navigate through folders in this iTunes window.

Wi-Fi

GoodReader has the capability to transfer files from a computer to the iPad using Wi-Fi. This is more complicated than the USB method and a lot more complicated than simply using Dropbox. But to use the Wi-Fi transfer, you first need to secure access to a Wi-Fi network, and then make sure that the computer and iPad are on the same network. With that all settled, follow the steps below for each transfer.

1. Start the GoodReader app on the iPad.

2. Open the Wi-Fi transfer page (via the little icon on the bottom of the page that looks like a piece of pie). Keep this page open during the file transfer.

3. The transfer window will indicate whether or not you are connected to a Wi-Fi network, and it provides you an IP address.

4. Make a note of the IP address. You will need it in a later step. (See how much more complicated this method is than just using Dropbox?!)

5. On your computer, open any Web browser and type in the IP address from the previous step. (It should look something like 192.168.1.16:8080.)

6. Finally, select the file you want to transfer and follow directions on the screen.

The IP address can and will change for each file transfer, so you need to check it each and every time. This is a very useful method if you need to get a file from a computer that you don't use all the time. For example, if a

Figure 15-16

The Wi-Fi transfer window of GoodReader must stay open during file transfers.

co-worker needs to send you a single file from his/ her computer, then this is a great method to consider.

Web Download

GoodReader also allows you to download files directly from the Internet—either by typing in the exact URL or by using the simple built-in browser.

∘ If you know the URL address of the file you want to download, tap the "Enter URL" button on the Web Downloads menu.

∘ If you don't know the URL address of the file, tap the "Browse the Web" button on the Web Downloads menu.

∘ Each time you tap on a link in the browser, GoodReader will ask if you want to follow the link or download the linked file. Pick "Follow the Link" until you arrive at the file you want. At that point, pick "Download Linked File."

∘ Be aware that several different downloads can run at the same time.

∘ The downloaded files are placed in the main My Documents folder. If there is already a file there with the same name, a number will be added automatically to the new file's name to differentiate it from the other. You can rename it if that's more convenient for you.

This is a useful process when someone has left a document out on the Internet for you to access (e.g., class notes or a publicly shared file).

Server Direct

GoodReader enables you to get your files directly from a variety of servers. This includes E-mail Servers, WebDav servers, Google Docs, Dropbox servers and FTP serv-

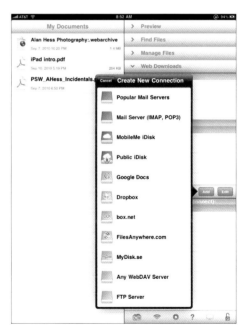

Figure 15-17

The list of server and server types are available in GoodReader.

ers. All of these servers are set up the same way, and GoodReader has done the heavy lifting in the background to make it easy for users. All you need are the passwords and addresses.

The first step here is to open GoodReader on the iPad. From there, tap "Connect to Servers." Tap the "Add" button to view a list of servers available. This list will include the options that are described below.

E-Mail Server

Back in the e-mail chapter, we talked about opening files with apps on your iPad. We also covered how to open documents with GoodReader that you receive by e-mail—straight from the Mail app. But you can also

Figure 15-18
The built-in e-mail servers available inside of GoodReader cover the most popular options used today.

use GoodReader to access online IMAP and POP mail servers.

The first thing to know is that the IMAP protocol is much more advanced than POP, and it works much faster. So if you have a choice (and sometimes you don't), pick IMAP.

The list of e-mail servers built-in to GoodReader includes the popular ones: Gmail, Yahoo! (paid account), Me.com, Hotmail and AOL. To access any of these, just fill in the user information as requested. The server will show up in the "Connect to Server" list. GoodReader can then access the Inbox of the e-mail account without ever having to go to the Mail program.

WebDav Server

Web-based Distributed and Versioning (a.k.a., WebDav) is a standard way of dealing with documents on the Internet. Examples of WebDav servers include MobileMe iDisk,

Figure 15-19
I added a WebDav server to the list of locations that GoodReader can access in order to point to my friends' public iDisk. So, with one tap, I can open the public folder and browse for file uploads for me.

Public iDisk, Box.net, MyDisk.se and File-sAnywhere.com. Luckily, all these services are built right into GoodReader.

To access these servers, tap the "Add" button in the "Connect to Servers" menu and pick the one you want to use. Then just add a description, a password (if needed) and you are ready to go. Couldn't be easier …

Dropbox

The Dropbox App (described above) works with GoodReader really well. And while you can access GoodReader from Dropbox with the "Open in" command, it is also possible to access your Dropbox from inside GoodReader.

Tap the "Add" button in "Connect to Servers" and pick "Dropbox." Then just enter your title, username and password, and you're done. The

Dropbox will show up in the list of servers.

By the way, nothing is stopping you from having more than one Dropbox at the same time. So if you have an account for work and an account for home, you can access them both here.

Google Docs

GoodReader gives you server-style access to Google Docs. It not only allows you to browse your Google Docs account as if you were on simple file server; but you can also download, upload and delete files and folders with ease.

Tap the "Add" button in "Connect to Servers" and pick Google Docs. Then, just add your title, e-mail address and password … and you're done.

When you connect to your Google Docs account and tap on a file, GoodReader will

Figure 15-20
Just sign into your Dropbox and all your files are suddenly available in GoodReader.

give you a choice of formats: PDF, TXT, DOC, HTML, PNG, RTF, ZIP (with HTML and images).

GoodReader can also upload files and folders to Google Docs. This is because Google Docs allows you to store unmodified files, of any type, without converting them to Google's format. The type of files you can upload from the iPad will depend on the type of Google Doc account you have. If you're using the free account, you're limited to file types that Google recognizes. But if you have a Google Docs Premier account, you can upload any file regardless of type.

Figure 15-21
Signing into an FTP server is slightly more complicated than the other server options, because you need to have the URL address available. But, as you can see, the rest is taken care of for you.

FTP Server

Many folks still use FTP (File Transfer Protocol) accounts to move and store files on the Internet. All the files that went into making this book were transferred using FTP protocols.

GoodReader allows you to access FTP servers just as easily. Tap the "Add" button in "Connect to Servers" and pick "FTP Server." Enter your title, full URL address, username and password. Done.

You can now browse folders, download, upload and delete files, but you can't work with any of the security-protected FTP protocols like FTPS and SFTP.

PRINTING

The iOS that shipped with the original iPad did not support printing. I know that sounds really odd since Apple had also released a word processor for the iPad at the same time, but it is true. On the original iPad, you can create a document, but you can't print it from the iPad ... and there are no really good third-party apps.

This has been remedied with iOS4. This upgrade allows printing from the iPad (called AirPrint), and you can use printers on the Wi-Fi network or those shared by computers on the same Wi-Fi network. This makes it much easier to do to real work on the iPad.

So you can use Pages to type up a quick invoice while using GoodReader to check your receipts stored in Dropbox. Then you can just print the document without ever having to use a laptop. Indeed, things are looking up for the iPad's world domination …

16

Number Crunching

The Skim

No one has ever called me a *number cruncher*. And rightfully so. I tend to run away—far away, fast and screaming—from spreadsheets. But in this day and age, most of us need at least the ability and courage to work a simple spreadsheet—or even a fairly complicated one in some cases.

Well, Apple created Numbers, a spreadsheet application for all of us who aren't data nerds … uh, I mean *whizzes* … and it's part of the iWork suite. Numbers is a powerful spreadsheet program with a very friendly interface.

For number crunching on the iPad, Apple has released a scaled-down version of Numbers. It isn't free. In fact, at $9.99 it's on the high-end pricewise of iPad apps. But I have to say, you do get a lot for your money in this case.

When I think of spreadsheets, I tend to envision very serious business people working with long columns of numbers, trying to work out some atrociously complicated math or accounting problem. But that just isn't the case anymore, and Numbers goes out of its way to prove it.

While you can use Numbers to do traditional (i.e., complicated) spreadsheet calculations, you can also use it for tracking and dealing with data in your personal life.

NUMBERS

The Apple app Numbers was designed specifically for the iPad, and it was released at the same time as the iPad launch. This app was supposed to appease the iPad's business users and prove that the device can be used for serious work as well as fun.

Numbers works well. And if you don't think you need spreadsheets or want to deal with them in any way, you may want to check out the built-in template section. I think you'll be surprised at what Numbers offers.

FILE TYPES FOR NUMBERS

The most popular spreadsheet software is Microsoft Excel. Good news: The Numbers app reads and edits Excel files as well as CSV

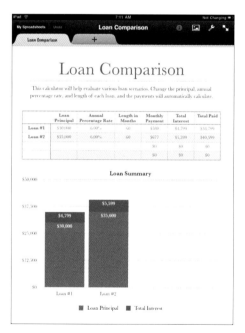

Figure 16-1

The Numbers app can handle simple spreadsheets along with more complicated graphs and text.

files. It also reads Numbers 09 documents and can export files as Excel, Numbers 09 files and PDF documents.

Excel and CSV

The Comma Separated Value, or CSV, file format is used in older versions of Microsoft Excel. It was a standard in other older spreadsheet applications, too. CSV files have now become dated and aren't used as much anymore, but Numbers will still import these file types. That's right: Numbers will import CSV files, but it won't export them.

The new Microsoft Excel file type is .xls or .xlsx. These file types are readable and editable in Numbers. I haven't personally checked every type of Excel file, but the ones I've worked with on my iPad have opened in the Numbers app just fine.

The thing is, when the Numbers app first came out for the iPad, it could only export spreadsheets as Numbers files or PDFs. But Apple recently updated the app to version 1.2, which finally allows Numbers files to be exported as a Microsoft Excel (.xls) file. This makes the app much more useful in the real world, where Microsoft Excel is the norm. As mentioned above, you can now export a file you created or edited on the iPad as a Numbers file, a PDF or an Excel file.

Numbers 09

Life in the spreadsheet world would be so much simpler if the Numbers app could just read all the Numbers file types. But, of course, that's not how it is. The iPad Numbers app does not support Numbers files created prior to the Numbers 09 version. But if you really want spreadsheets on your iPad and Mac, think about buying iWork 09. It's only $79 at Apple. You can also try before you buy with a free 30-day trial. Visit www.apple.com/iwork/ for more information on the full version of iWork.

IMPORTING FILES

By far the easiest way to get files into Numbers is by e-mail, but you can also use iTunes and one of my favorites … the Dropbox app. It's also possible to use an iDisk or WebDav server.

E-mail

When you receive an e-mail with a spreadsheet file attached, just hold your finger on the attachment until the "Open in" menu opens. This will give you the option to get a "Quick Look," "Open in Numbers" or "Open In…"

Tapping on "Quick Look" opens the file right in the Mail program. You can look at the spreadsheet, but you're not able to edit it here. This is fine if you aren't sure what the file is and you don't want to go through the trouble of opening a file through the right app just to find out it's not what you need.

And if you're looking at a file in Quick Look, you can open it for editing in an app by tapping the "Open In…" button at the top of the preview window. Quick tip here: The button sometimes disappears. When it does, just tap the screen and the button will appear on the top of the screen.

When you tap "Open in Numbers," the file will be transferred into the Numbers app, and the app will launch. If there are any elements in your spreadsheet that are not compatible with the iPad Numbers app, like fonts or permissions, Numbers will take care of it.

And if you tap on "Open In…," a list of apps installed on your iPad that can read the spreadsheet will pop up, and you can use any of them. More on that later…

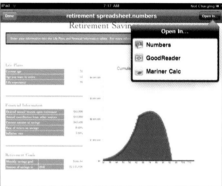

Figure 16-2

The Numbers app can handle simple spreadsheets as well as more complicated graphs and text.

iTunes

Transfer files to the Numbers app on your iPad with iTunes and the USB cable. Plug the iPad into your computer and launch iTunes. Select the iPad from the Device list and go to the "Apps" window. Scroll down to the "File Sharing" window and click on "Numbers." Click "Find" and then select the file you want to put on the iPad. Click "Choose" on the Mac or "Open" on the PC.

The file will load onto your iPad. But be forewarned that when you open Numbers, you won't see your file. You still have to import it. To do this, tap the "Import" button and then "Copy from iTunes." Now, a list of available files will appear. Tap the one you want to import, and the Numbers app will import and open it.

iDisk and WebDav

These two import options work the same way. To use them to import a file to your iPad, tap the "Import" button in the Numbers app and then hit "Copy from iDisk" or "Copy from WebDav." Enter your account information, navigate to the document you want to import, and select it. Numbers will download the document to the iPad and open it.

Dropbox

I cover Dropbox in the last chapter, and it really is a great application. Along with all the other ways it can make your life easier, Dropbox can also be used to transfer spreadsheets (or almost any other file type) from your desktop to your iPad. All you have to do is drop the spreadsheet into the Dropbox program on the computer and then open the Dropbox app on your iPad and locate the file.

Tap on the file to open it in your Dropbox

Figure 16-3

A spreadsheet transferred to your iPad by Dropbox can be previewed and then sent to whichever app you want to use to edit it.

app, and then tap the "Export" button. This opens a lineup of apps that can read the spreadsheet. Tap on "Numbers" and your spreadsheet will open in the Numbers app.

EXPORTING FILES

Once you've finished editing, creating or reading your spreadsheet, you might want to get it off your iPad. And lucky days, there are five built-in methods for getting a file out of your iPad's Numbers app. These options are easily accessed by tapping on the "Export" button, located at the bottom of the page in the "My Spreadsheets" view.

E-mail it.

The e-mail option is the simplest and most convenient method for moving a spreadsheet from an iPad to a computer. Tapping this option opens a menu that asks what type of file you want to export: a Numbers file, a PDF or an Excel file. Once you tap on the file type, Numbers opens the Mail program and attaches the file. Fill in the rest of the info and tap "Send."

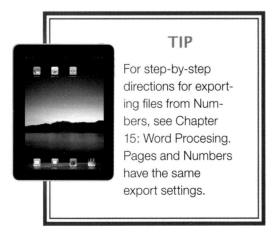

TIP

For step-by-step directions for exporting files from Numbers, see Chapter 15: Word Procesing. Pages and Numbers have the same export settings.

Share it via iWork.com.
This method works with the Apple **iWork. com** Web site. You can sign in with your Apple ID, which is the same username and password that you use in the Apple Store to get content. If you want to use a different Apple ID or create a new Apple ID, you can do that here as well.

To export your file with iWork.com, tap on "Export" and then tap "Share via iWork.com." Enter your Apple ID and password.

After entering your Apple ID, tap "Sign in." The file will be uploaded to iWork.com and an e-mail will be generated with a link to where iWork stores your Numbers file. In the e-mail message, enter your recipient e-mail addresses. If you just want to move the file(s) off your iPad and not share it with another person, leave the "To" field blank.

Tap the "Share" button on the top right. You will receive an e-mail stating that the file can now be viewed on iWork.com. And when you log into iWork.com, you can view and edit the file right on the Web site.

What you'll notice about this method is that you don't get to choose the file format for your shared file. But you can pick the format when you download the file from iWork.com. Your options are Numbers 09, PDF and Excel.

Send to iTunes.
This is the way to send your file(s) to a computer that is attached to your iPad by a USB cable. This works best if you actually attach the iPad to the computer and launch iTunes first. For step-by-step instructions on how to move content to and from iTunes, see Chapter 1: Content.

The only difference between this and the transfer of Pages documents (covered in

TIP

To create a new Apple ID, tap on "Create a new Apple ID" at the bottom of the page.

Chapter 15) and Keynote documents (covered in Chapter 17) is the file format. When you send a Numbers file, your file format options are Numbers 09, PDF and Excel.

Copy to iDisk.
If you have a MobileMe account, then here is another great use for your iDisk. Transfer files from the iPad anywhere you have an Internet connection. Tap on the "Copy to iDisk" option, sign into your MobileMe account, and pick the format you want to use: Numbers, PDF or Excel. And then tap "Copy." This is a great way to use your MobileMe account and the iDisk service to its full potential.

Copy to WebDav.
If you use a WebDav server, you can copy your Numbers file to this server. All you have to do is tap "Copy to WebDav" and enter the server address along with your username and password. After you sign in, navigate to where you want to place the file and tap "Copy."

TEMPLATES

Numbers has fifteen built-in templates along with a blank spreadsheet. There are templates for budgets, loan comparisons, weight loss tracking and even a running log. There's even a travel planner.

This is where the Numbers app really shines. It makes using a spreadsheet easy and practical for everyday life. So instead of turning to spreadsheets only when calculating monthly sales data for work, think about using them to keep track of your family's schedule, an upcoming dinner party or even your kitchen remodeling project.

The templates aren't groundbreaking. They've been part of the Numbers application on the Mac since it was released. The full version of Numbers has thirty templates, including the blank template. But these templates make the spreadsheet format useful for everyone, not just the number crunching types.

To use one of the built-in templates:

1. Tap "Numbers."
2. Tap "New Spreadsheet."

Figure 16-4

Check out the template chooser in the Numbers app.

3. Select a template.
4. Enter your information.

That's it… Simple.

THE BASICS OF NUMBERS

Using Numbers is intuitive … even for a non-numbers guy like me. To get started, just tap on the Numbers app. It opens on your iPad in either the portrait or landscape mode.

I'm always impressed with the speed at which the iPad opens apps, by the way. Since apps are small and need to run on what is basically a mobile device with limited memory, they tend to be lean pieces of code that run fast. I just think it's cool. But back to Numbers…

The first page of the Numbers app is the "My Spreadsheets" area. All of the spreadsheets that are loaded onto your iPad are here. You can navigate through the files by swiping your finger left or right. When the spreadsheet you want is in the middle of the screen, tap on it to open it.

My Spreadsheets is also where you'll find the "New Spreadsheet" button, which gives you access to all those cool templates (covered later). You can export and import documents from here as well as duplicate a spreadsheet or delete it.

With a spreadsheet open, there is one really important feature … that you won't find. There is no "Save" button. Instead, the document is saved constantly. So if you want to save an earlier version, you have to think ahead. That is, once you've entered the basic information for whatever spreadsheet you're creating, tap the "My Spreadsheets" button on the top of the screen. Then tap the (+) sign at the bottom of the screen and create a "Duplicate Spreadsheet."

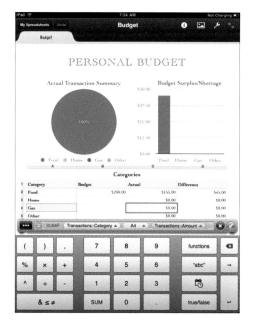

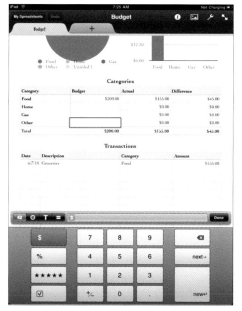

Figure 16-5

Here is the basic Numbers app interface. Depending on what cell is selected, the input area adjusts so that the best tools are presented.

From here, you can add different data to the file while retaining a previous version. You'll want to rename the different versions to differentiate them.

To rename a document in Numbers, tap your finger on the document name in the "My Spreadsheet" view. This will allow you to edit the file name. When you're done, just tap "Done" in the top right corner.

ALTERNATIVES TO NUMBERS

Apple really has this category wrapped up, but if you are determined to try some other options out there, search around the App Store. There is one alternative I've found that works very well. It's called Mariner Calc, and it has some cool features.

Mariner Calc

The interface of this app is not as friendly as Numbers, but many users who work with traditional spreadsheets really like it. Validating the $5.99 price tag, in my opinion, is the app's ability to transfer files over the Internet directly into and out of the app.

But that's not all that Mariner Calc can do. You can also save a spreadsheet while you're working on it. The app has ten built-in templates with spreadsheet types ranging from a class schedule to home inventory. And it can handle really big spreadsheets—32,000 rows by 256-columns. That's a lot of spreadsheet.

To transfer files to the Mariner Calc app over a Wi-Fi network from your computer:

1. Open the Mariner Calc app.

2. Tap the "File" button on the Mariner Calc toolbar.

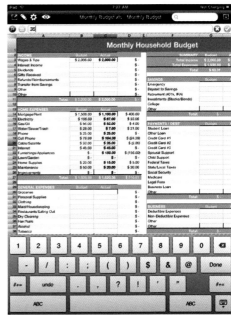

Figure 16-6

The interface for Mariner Calc looks more like the traditional spreadsheet application. It's not as slick as Numbers, but it can get the job done at half the price ($5.99).

3. Tap the "Sharing" button; it's in the lower left corner.

4. The Sharing screen opens and the IP address is shown.

5. On your computer, open a Web browser.

6. Enter the IP address that is shown on iPad in the address field and press "Enter."

7. An image of an iPad appears in the Web browser with a list of files accessible to Mariner Calc.

8. To upload a file from your computer to the iPad, choose the file from your computer and click "Choose."

9. Click on the "Upload" button.

10. The file will now be accessible on your iPad in Mariner Calc.

Getting files from your iPad to a computer wirelessly is the same as the getting files onto the iPad. Just follow steps 1-6 in the previous section. And when the list of files on the iPad appear, just click on the file you want to transfer to the computer, and it will download immediately.

TIP

The iPad and computer need to be on the same Wi-Fi network for the Mariner Calc transfer process to work.

If you find the Numbers app too limiting and not powerful enough to meet your needs, then I suggest you give Mariner Calc a try. There are versions for the iPhone and a free lite version in addition to the iPad version, so you can take your spreadsheets with you wherever you go.

GoodReader

GoodReader can also read spreadsheet files. Yes it can. As I've said again and again, GoodReader is a great app for reading files. It works well with Word documents and it works great with spreadsheets, too.

Keep in mind that GoodReader is not an editor; it is a reader. So while you can look at your spreadsheets here, you cannot edit them in the app. What you can do is open a spreadsheet in GoodReader and then open it in an app that can edit that type of file. This allows you to get the files onto the iPad using the GoodReader file transfer. These processes are covered in detail in Chapter 15.

Once the files are in the GoodReader app, a single tap on the document shows you a preview. One more single tap on the "Open In…" button reveals a menu that lists the apps that can open the file.

The cool part about all of this is that you can load all the different types of files into GoodReader and then use the app to pick the file you want to use to edit it … and open that app from GoodReader. What a deal.

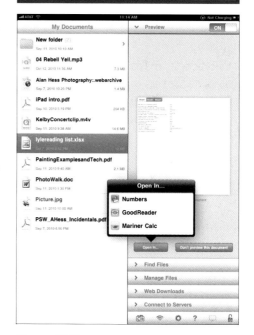

> **TIP**
>
> The Mariner Calc app can read and edit Excel documents, but it cannot edit Numbers documents. So if you want to edit a spreadsheet created in the Numbers app or the Numbers desktop application, you first need to export that file as an Excel spreadsheet and then import it to Mariner Calc.

Figure 16-7

This GoodReader interface is showing the list of apps that can open the selected spreadsheet.

Presentations

The Skim

I was never a big user of Keynote or PowerPoint until last year. That's when I started to give more presentations, and I realized how much I needed a program like these. Now, I use Keynote on a regular basis and absolutely love the way this app works on the iPad. It's great for presentations, and it's a lot of fun to play with.

KEYNOTE APP

The first thing you'll notice about Keynote is that you have to use it in landscape mode. This means you can't use it with the combination keyboard/ dock accessory from Apple or with the regular Apple dock, because both products keep the iPad in portrait mode.

IMPORT FILES

The Keynote app is great for building presentations from scratch. But if you have a few slides already done and want to get them onto your iPad, here are your options for importing them:

E-mail

It's easy to send an e-mail with a presentation attached. So send your slides to yourself, open the message on your iPad and access the file with the Keynote app. The thing is, presentations can be really big files. The last presentation I gave was on Low Light Photography, and the Keynote

Figure 17-1
The Keynote window has the individual slides on the left and the slide-editing window covering the rest of the screen.

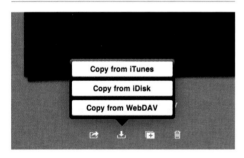

Figure 17-2
The import menu in the Keynote app is easy to navigate.

file weighed in at 194.5 MB—way too big to e-mail. Thus, for large presentation decks, the other options for moving the file to your iPad may be more practical than e-mail.

Copy from iTunes

This is my go-to method for importing presentations to my iPad. It's a fast way to transfer big files, and presentations can get really big. To use this method:

1. Open iTunes on the computer.

2. Connect your iPad and computer with the USB cable.

3. Select "iPad" from the Devices list on the left side of the iTunes window.

4. Click on the Apps window and scroll down until you see the File Sharing window.

5. Select Keynote and then add the file you want to send to the iPad by clicking "Choose" (Mac) or "Open" (PC).

6. On the iPad, open Keynote.

7. Tap "Import" and choose "Copy from iTunes."

8. Tap on the file you want to import into Keynote.

9. Keynote will now download the presentation and check it for compatibility. Depending on size of the file, this could take awhile.

Copy from iDisk and WebDav

This is the easiest way to get files onto the iPad without having to connect to a computer. I have these two programs grouped together, because they work the same way. Just:

1. Tap the "Import" button.

2. Pick the method.

3. Enter the account information.

4. Find the file to download.

EXPORT FILES

Once you've created or edited your presentation, you can either export it from your iPad or use the iPad as a presentation controller. To export the file, you have five options and all are available from the My Presentations view. Tap the "Export" button to access the menu of export options.

E-mail

Attach your presentation to an outgoing e-mail. Tap on the "E-mail Presentation" but-

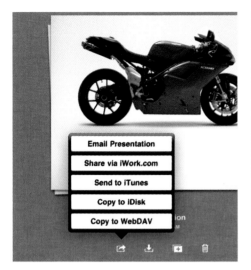

Figure 17-3
This is the export menu in Keynote.

Figure 17-4
If you try to send a file that's too large for your e-mail provider, the Mail app will give you a warning.

ton and Keynote will ask what type of file you want to send: a Keynote file, PDF or Power-Point (.ppt) file. Choose a file and the Mail program opens; type in the recipient's address and hit "Send."

Be careful when using e-mail to send a large presentation. The e-mail program will warn you if the file is too large. When it does, pay attention. If you continue with the e-mail option, it's likely no one will receive it. The warning will suggest that you share the file using iWork.com instead.

Tap "Cancel" to back out of the e-mail process and begin the process of sharing the file with iWork.com. Alternatively, if you tap "Continue," the attachment will be added to an e-mail message and you can try to send it. (Chances are it won't work.) So let's look at iWork.com.

iWork.com
iWork.com might have the same name as the suite of applications that Apple created to com-

pete with Microsoft Office, but this is actually a free Web-based service that allows you to share documents. It facilitates the sharing of documents created in any of the iWork applications—those created on the computer in the full version of iWork as well as those created using the iPad app versions.

Right now, iWork.com is free. It's not bundled or a part of the iWork suite, but Apple has reserved the right to charge for future versions.

Sharing files using iWork.com is easy. All you need to do is:

1. Open Keynote on the iPad.

2. In the "My Presentations" view, make sure the document you want to export is in the middle of the screen (selected).

3. Tap "Export."

4. Tap "Share via iWork.com."

243

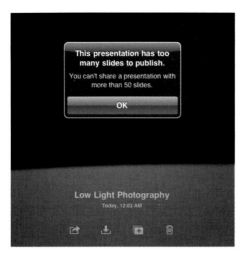

Figure 17-5
If you try to export a Keynote file with more than 50 slides to iWork.com, the iPad will give you this error message.

Figure 17-6
Copying a large presentation to iDisk can take awhile.

5. Sign in with your iWork.com username and password. (This is your Apple ID from the iTunes Store or your MobileMe account. Or, you can create a new Apple ID right from this screen if needed.)

6. A "Share via iWork.com" screen appears. Here, you must enter at least one recipient name. (Enter your own if you don't want to share with others and only want to remove the presentation from your iPad.)

7. Tap "Share" to send the file or "Cancel" to stop the process.

You can share a presentation on iWork.com if the file contains less than 50 slides. If you try to send a presentation with more than 50 slides, you'll get an error. If this happens, your best bet is to use one of the remaining three options.

○ **iTunes**

This is my favorite method for removing big presentations from my iPad. It's the

fastest and it doesn't have the size limitation of the previous methods. To use iTunes to export a Keynote file, just attach your iPad to the computer with the USB cable, open iTunes on the computer, select the iPad from the Device list, and click on "Apps" at the top of the window. Then, on the iPad, tap "Export," send to iTunes and pick a format. The file will be visible in the File Sharing window when Keynote is selected from the list of apps on the left. No file size problems and no slide count issues.

○ **Copy to iDisk / Copy to WebDav**

Both of the last two options copy your file to a Web location using either the MobileMe iDisk or a WebDav server. I lump the two methods together because they are very similar. Just tap the "Export" window, sign into your iDisk or WebDav account, pick the file type you want to export, and select a location. The presentation will be copied to the new location. This works really well, but it can take awhile to transfer depending on the file's size.

PRESENT

The difference between Keynote and the other iWork apps—and most all other presentation apps actually—is that Keynote needs to be output to a screen for it to be really useful. That is, when I stand in front of a group of people, I need my presentation to be visible on a bigger screen, so I need to project the file from my iPad to a television monitor or pull-down screen. Of course, Apple knows this and has taken it into account.

Projection Gear

While most of this book is about getting content onto the iPad, this section is how to get it off. And I have some bad news: It's going to cost you. There's just no way to attach the iPad to a projector or monitor without some extra gear. Here are your options:

- **Apple iPad Dock Connector to VGA Adapter ($29.00):**

  This accessory from Apple allows you to connect your iPad to a TV with a VGA connection. You can also connect to a computer monitor, a projector or any other type of LCD display that uses a VGA connector. The output is available only in landscape orientation, but that's perfect for presentations … and Keynote only works in landscape orientation anyhow. This accessory from Apple doesn't have great reviews, but if you're going to give presentations from your iPad, it's the only way to get VGA output from the device.

- **Apple Composite AV Cable ($19.00)/ Apple Component AV Cable ($49.00):**

  These cables allow you to connect your iPad to the Composite or Component inputs on a television or any other audio-visual device that accepts these types of connections (e.g., older VCRs). The

Figure 17-7

This is the presentation screen on the iPad when it is playing a Keynote file on an external device.

Composite kit connects to the iPad via the dock connector and to your TV through the composite video and red/white analog audio ports. The Component kit connects to the iPad via the dock connector and to your TV/ home theater receiver through the component (Y, Pb, and Pr) video and red/white analog audio ports. These cables also have a USB connector, so you can keep the iPad powered by plugging it into a USB port if one is on the display or the device to which you are connecting. You can also use the included USB Power Adaptor.

Presentation Controls

When the iPad is plugged into a projector or display device using one of the aforementioned devices, the iPad becomes your presentation controller. When the Keynote presentation is in edit mode, nothing will appear on the external display. When you press "Play" and the presentation begins on the external display, the iPad goes into controller mode.

The controls are simple—basic buttons to move forward and backward through your presen-

245

tation. There are two other features as well, and one of them makes this a presenter's dream.

° Thumbnails: Displaying thumbnails of your slides on the left side of the screen helps you jump to any slide instantly. Once you've picked a new slide, the thumbnails disappear. I wish they didn't, but they do.

° Pointer: The iPad's built-in laser pointer is probably one of the coolest things about presenting using the iPad. That's right, you can make a red dot appear on the screen, and you can control it with your finger! It's so very simple to use, like most of the things on the iPad. So when you're running a presentation on the iPad, just hold your finger on the screen until a laser dot appears on the display. You can move it around by moving your finger around. Take your finger off the screen and the dot disappears. I love this…

Keynote Interface

The Keynote programmers did great job of streamlining the interface. The collection of slides are on the left and the main slide covers the rest of the page. The controls are spread across the top with the exception of the "New Slide" button (a plus sign), which is on the bottom left of the screen.

By giving the control buttons different tasks depending on what element was selected on the screen, the Keynote developers made this app very easy to use. The most important button on the page is the "Info" button; it's the one with the "I" in the middle. This button opens the editing function for whatever element is selected on the slide. Tap on a piece of text to edit it; tap on an image to adjust.

Figure 17-8
The Keynote interface: Tap on a photo and then on the "I" to get image controls.

Figure 17-9
The Keynote interface: Tap on some text and then on the "I" to access text controls.

Figure 17-10
Need to add another slide? Use the (+) key on the bottom left.

ALTERNATIVE PRESENTATION FORMATS

There are ways to present your PowerPoint presentations on the iPad without spending a dime. It's true; you can show off your presentations with an iPad without using the Keynote app. You won't get the great transitions or the laser dot, but you also won't have to spend any money or do any difficult re-formatting. The key is to use the built-in export tools from PowerPoint along with the built-in tools on the iPad.

There are also some very promising Web sites/ applications, like MightyMeeting, which is currently in beta testing. Options like this appear to solve some very difficult presentation problems by storing the files needed on a Web site and not on the iPad itself. It means you're no longer limited by the iPad software.

MightyMeeting stores presentation files online, so a presenter can access it with any Internet-connected device. The app basically functions as a PowerPoint streaming service. I know a lot of presenters who would love to keep copies of their presentations online, just in case something goes wrong while on the road. I know I like this security.

But I digress. Here are some ways to get your presentation onto your iPad from a computer without using the Keynote app.

Presentation as Photos

The iPad has a great photo viewer built-in, and it allows you to arrange your photos in a particular order. This becomes a presentation option, because PowerPoint allows you to export your slides as photos.

To do this:

1. Open your presentation in PowerPoint.

2. Click on File > Save As.

3. Select "Save as Type."

4. Choose ".jpg."

5. Choose "Every Slide" when PowerPoint asks if you want to export all the slides.

6. When all the slides have been exported, transfer them onto the iPad using any of the methods described in Chapter 10: Photography.

The slides can then be viewed in the photo viewer of the iPad. Just swipe your finger to go to the next side or back to the previous one. It's great as long as you don't include video in your presentation. Also, there are no transition effects or audio with this method.

PDF Presentation

It seems like PDFs can do anything. And when it comes to presentations, it only reinforces that feeling. The advantages of having your presentation as a PDF file is that there are multiple apps on the iPad that can show the PDF, including the iBooks app. It is also really easy to get PDFs onto the iPad. Just e-mail them; they're relatively small files.

There are many ways to create PDFs from PowerPoint files, but they have some drawbacks. Basically, the transitions will go away … along with all the audio and video from your PowerPoint deck. I did a quick Internet search and there are numerous utilities available that will convert your .ppt files to PDFs, but the easiest way is to just save the file as a PDF.

To do this from PowerPoint, click File>Save As and then scroll through the file types and select "PDF." Just keep in mind, as I mentioned earlier, the PDF file will not contain your slide transitions, audio or embedded videos.

Video Presentation

A third option is to view your presentation as a video on the iPad. This has the advantage of including transitions and audio, but you can't really control the timing of your show, and this could be an issue if you're talking through the presentation.

The movie can be paused and restarted, but that isn't as smooth or as professional as using an actual presentation software package (like Keynote). You can save your PowerPoint as a video in PowerPoint by going to File>Save as Movie. You can now set the size and quality of the movie-style presentation.

There are many other options for converting a PowerPoint (.ppt) file to a video file; just make sure that the one you use creates a video file that is compatible with the iPad. (Your best bets are .m4v, .mp4 and .mov.)

Obviously, some of these choices can cost more than free, and some can actually cost more than the Keynote app. But knowing your options can be quite useful if you've already created a long presentation with fonts, transitions and features that are not available in the Keynote app.

Databases

The Skim

Bento • FileMaker Pro • HanDBase

Databases are used to keep track of large compilations of data types, and they've become integral to how most of us keep track of the information we use daily. For instance, every time you use the Contacts app or the Calendar app on your iPad, you're using a database. They're very handy.

Take the Contacts app for example. It stores a person's name and phone number and e-mail address … and it could store a whole lot more. The best part is that this database is searchable, so the information you need to find is easily accessible on demand.

Many years ago, when I was in college, I was a database programmer. Back then I worked on programming forms that were used to enter data into a student database. The system was developed for the school to check student information when they came to register for classes. So when I think of people creating their own databases for the iPad and using them to keep track of their personal stuff, I start to have flashbacks … and not the fun kind … to those old programming days. Fortunately, things have changed dramatically since then. Creating and using databases on the iPad is easy, and the programs are really quite powerful.

There are two standout choices for database apps on the iPad. Both are made by FileMaker, which is a subsidiary of Apple. FileMaker offers two lines of products, each aimed at a different type of user.

- Bento is a personal database suite for use on the Mac. A Bento app is available for use on the iPad. The Bento app can be used alone on the iPad or in conjunction with the Bento application for the Mac.

- FileMaker Pro is a full database solution and offers a FileMaker Go iPad app for both PC and Mac users.

BENTO

The Bento app for the iPad brings the power of databases to your mobile device. The app costs $4.99 and is worth every penny. The Bento app is even more useful when paired with the Bento desktop software, but it's only available for Mac.

This database program not only gives you a way to store your information, but Bento allows you to search and look at your data in different ways. For example, the Bento app takes your information from the Contacts and Calendars apps on your iPad and presents them in a different view. It also allows you to enter new information without actually opening your Contacts or Calendar app. Bento can access the information directly and update those databases without going through the regular apps to do it.

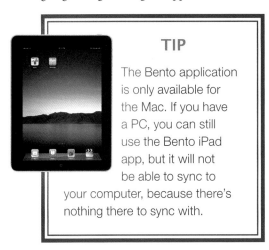

TIP

The Bento application is only available for the Mac. If you have a PC, you can still use the Bento iPad app, but it will not be able to sync to your computer, because there's nothing there to sync with.

Figure 18-1

The Bento app comes with databases installed, including recipes.

After you've downloaded and installed the Bento app, you can start to use it immediately. If you have the Bento application running on your Mac, you can set up the iPad Bento app to sync the information between the two machines wirelessly. For this to work, the iPad and computer need to be on the same Wi-Fi network.

Syncing Bento ... Mac Only

If you are syncing Bento for the first time, follow these simple steps:

1. Open the Bento app on the iPad.

2. Tap the "Setup" icon in the top right corner of the screen; it looks like a little gear.

3. Tap "Sync with a New Computer." A four-digit passcode will appear.

4. Turn on your Mac and launch the Bento application.

5. Choose "Set up Sync with Device."

6. Select the iPad and click "Continue."

7. In the Connect pane on your computer, type in the four-digit passcode that's on your iPad.

Figure 18-2
The desktop Bento application for the Mac.

Figure 18-3
The Bento app produces a passcode that is needed to sync the iPad Bento app with the desktop Bento application.

8. Click "Done."

9. Now you can select the libraries to be synced.

If you've already set up the first-time sync, then a new button will appear when you tap the gear icon on the top right of the screen: "Sync Now." Tap this button, and the iPad Bento app will sync with the computer's Bento software … as long as they are both running and on the same network.

So, this means if you make changes to any of the databases on your iPad while it is not on the same network as your computer, or when you are connected only by 3G, the sync will not happen. You will have to make sure you sync manually when you get back on the same network.

For those who haven't used a database before, using Bento is pretty simple. So simple, in fact, that unlike other business apps, there is not a lot of importing and exporting capability. Instead, the data is kept on the iPad and accessed in various views, so you can get the info you want easily.

When the Bento app first launches, there are four choices:

- Start using Bento

- Guided Tour

- Learn about Bento for Mac

- Help

I strongly suggest that you read the Guided Tour; it will cover everything you need to know about Bento to get started. Now, if you're like me, then you probably just tapped on the "Start using Bento" button and dove right in. That's fine too.

The key to working with Bento is the libraries. In the Bento world, databases are called *libraries*. Bento comes preloaded with example libraries that are filled with data, and it makes it easy to add your own.

Figure 18-4

The window that allows you to pick a template is in a CoverFlow-style interface.

Figure 18-5

The Bento Template Exchange Web site is a forum for trading templates.

Built-In Templates

The Bento app makes it really easy to create your own databases, because it comes with a ton of great templates. Each of the templates can be customized to make your database exactly what you want.

If you have the Bento application on your Mac, then you have access to even more templates. And, dare I say: There is something even cooler. It's a Bento Template Exchange, where you can access templates that other users have posted to share. Find the Bento Template Exchange at **http://solutions.file-maker.com/database-templates/index.jsp.**

To use any of these templates on the iPad, you must first download the file to the Bento

BENTO TEMPLATES

- Blank
- Projects
- Contacts
- To Do Items
- Recipes
- Diet Log
- Events
- Files
- Inventory

- Event Planning
- Time Billing
- Home Inventory
- Expenses
- Exercise Log
- Vehicle Maintenance
- Classes
- Digital Media
- Student List

- Membership List
- Products for Sale
- Equipment
- Issue Tracking
- Items Sold
- Customers
- Donations
- Notes

Figure 18-6
Customize the library screen by tapping the pencil icon.

application on your Mac and sync it to the iPad. For example, I liked the idea of a Book Inventory database, so I downloaded it from the exchange, added a record and then synced it over to the iPad where it showed up perfectly.

To create a new library:

1. Open the Bento app on your iPad.

2. Tap on "Libraries" at the top left of the screen.

3. Tap on the (+) sign to bring up the template chooser.

4. Scroll through the templates until you see the one you want.

5. Tap "Create Library" when you have selected the correct template.

6. The new library will open.

You can now start to enter information into your new database, or you can edit the template by tapping on the pencil icon that's located at the top right of the screen. This icon brings up the "Customize" screen, which

Figure 18-7
When you indicate that you want to delete a field on your form, Bento will double check that it's what you want to do; because once a field is deleted, all the entered data for that field is deleted, too.

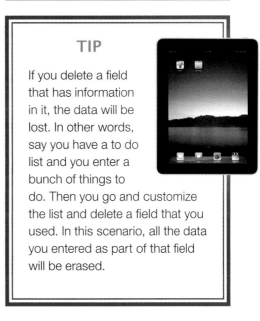

TIP

If you delete a field that has information in it, the data will be lost. In other words, say you have a to do list and you enter a bunch of things to do. Then you go and customize the list and delete a field that you used. In this scenario, all the data you entered as part of that field will be erased.

is where you can rearrange the fields, add new fields or delete those already there. As you'll see, each of the current fields has a small red and white "X" on the left and two icons on the right: a black and white "I" and a black and white ball.

Tapping on the red "X" will delete the field … but not until you confirm that you want to proceed with the deletion.

255

Tap on the "I" icon to rename a field. And remember that each field in a library needs to have unique name. Tapping on the ball icon will remove the field from the form, but it won't delete it. Instead, the field becomes hidden and unable to accept new data. If you choose to use it at a later time, just bring it back into the form. Hidden fields are listed across the top of your screen, right next to the "New Field" button.

Tap the "New Field" button to create a new field for your form and library. Pick a field type from the following options: Text, Number, Choice, Checkbox, Media, Time, Date, Duration, Currency, Rating, Address, Phone Number, E-mail Address, URL and IM Account. All these choices give you lots of options in creating the exact type of field you want in your form. For example, a phone number field will only accept numbers, not letters, allowing a uniform collection of data. This is key in the creation of a database, since it is uniform data that allows for easy searches and fast retrieval of information.

You can also change the order of your fields by holding your finger on the field and sliding it up and down into the position you prefer. And when you have the form formatted the way you want it, tap "Done." From here, you're ready to begin entering data.

FILEMAKER PRO / FILEMAKER GO

The FileMaker Go app for the iPad allows you to access your FileMaker Pro information on your iPad. The main downside to this app is the price. FileMaker Pro costs $299 and the FileMaker Go app costs $39.99. That's right, $39.99 … for an iPad app! This is the most expensive app I've encountered.

Now, if you have FileMaker Pro, then this is the app for you. FileMaker Go allows you to connect to databases that are hosted on FileMaker servers or on FileMaker Pro using a Wi-Fi network and over the Internet using 3G. This means you get remote access to the database from just about everywhere, and it does a great job … a really professional-level job.

The iPad app allows you to find, add, edit and delete records and to even switch layouts. It's very cool … and convenient.

HANDBASE DATABASE MANAGER

There is one more database option that I really like for the iPad, and that's DDH Software's HanDBase for the iPad.

TIP

Bento is one app that I tend to use in landscape mode … not because I have to but because it shows more information that way.

TIP

To create or modify databases with FileMaker Go for the iPad, you must have FileMaker Pro or FileMaker Pro Advanced on your computer. So don't buy this app unless you have these computer programs or plan to get them.

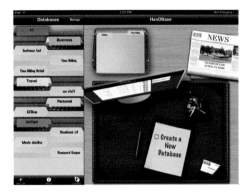

Figure 18-7

I wish my desk was this clean. Here is the opening screen of the HanDBase app.

The thing about this app that stands out right away is the cool interface. I love that it looks like my desk. Actually it looks like my desk if I ever cleaned my desk. Instead, I have a ton of papers everywhere; my workspace never looks this neat. But I digress.

This application allows you to create and manage databases right on your iPad and it, too, has templates. Boy, does it have templates! The cool thing is that the templates are stored on the Internet, so the app doesn't take up that much space on the iPad.

To create a new database in HanDBase:

1. Tap the sheet on your desktop that says "Create New Database."

2. A pop-up menu appears that presents options to "Download a Template," "Use Existing Template" or "Create from Scratch."

3. Tap "Download a Template."

4. A Web site opens with a list of template categories.

5. Tap on a category to access the templates.

6. Tap on the one you want, and there it is … right on your iPad.

This database app works with both Mac and PC. So if you want to synchronize your data with your Mac or Windows computer, you have to have the HanDBase program on the computer. You also need to purchase one of the following add-on programs:

- Plus Add-On

- Professional Add-On

- Enterprise Add-On for the PC

- HanDBase Plus for the Mac

Each of these allows you to sync databases to your computer with the iPad.

FINAL THOUGHTS ON DATABASES

The key to making databases worth the work is entering data that can be used efficiently. That is, the information you enter needs to be retrieved in a quick and easy way. (This is why Bento works so well.)

It's great to think of the iPad as something more than a really big iPod, but it really isn't. So trying to create and manage extra-large databases that live on your iPad is an exercise in futility.

The two products from FileMaker really shine because both can be used on a computer (although Bento only operates on a Mac), so the tedious process of data entry is easier. But if you plan to do a lot of data entry with your iPad, I suggest that you invest in the Apple Wireless keyboard; it will make your life a lot easier.

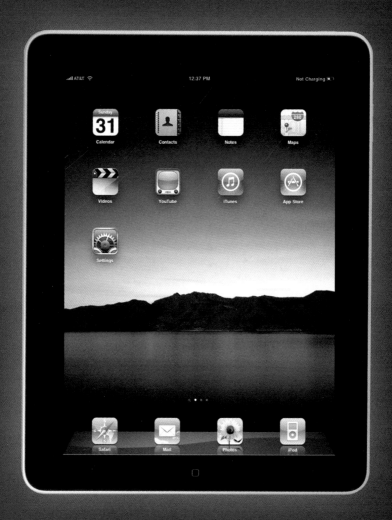

APPENDIX
I

Accessories

I love new gadgets. And nearly as much as I enjoy new gadgets, I love new gadget *accessories*!

When I bought an iPad, I also made sure to get a case and a stand and the Camera Connection Kit and … well, you get the idea. There are a lot of different accessories out there for the iPad, and I can only assume that there will be more as time goes on.

As expected, some of these are purely for looks and protection, but others are actually very useful and can really increase your device's productivity. For instance, a great keyboard is just no-nonsense necessary—for me anyway.

Other accessories might come to mind, but many times it just isn't worth the bother. There is no mouse for the iPad—not even the Apple Magic Mouse that seems to be a perfect fit. There are also a slew of screen protectors for the iPad, but Apple doesn't support them, recommend them or even sell them.

A stylus for the iPad, perhaps? Nope, Apple doesn't think you need it. Instead, the company believes you should be able to do everything on the iPad with your finger. So, there are no styluses in the Apple Store.

And while there are car chargers for the iPad, please don't use one while driving; that's just dangerous.

Stick to the basics; put your money into apps; and enjoy this terrific device. The following accessories can help you with that.

KEYBOARDS

The iPad has a pretty good onscreen keyboard. It pops up when you need to use it and hides when you don't. But Apple has a couple external keyboard options that are worth exploring if you type a lot. They are the iPad Keyboard Dock and the Apple Wireless Bluetooth Keyboard. Let's take a look.

Keyboard Dock

This is exactly what it sounds like: a combination dock and keyboard. And this device is meant for those who plan on doing a lot of typing on the iPad and want to be plugged in all the time (to avoid running out of juice).

Sounds great, except for a few small things. The most detrimental downside is that the iPad can't fit into the dock if it's in a case … yeah, even a case designed by Apple. So every time you want to use the keyboard dock with your iPad, you have to take the iPad out of its case. This can drive a person crazy. And it really makes you wonder what was happening over at Apple when these accessories were being developed. Did someone miss a

meeting? Were the designer and manufacturer having a fight that week? How did the left hand not know what the right was doing? Anyway …

The second thing that can be a hindrance to this theoretically great accessory is that the iPad has to be in portrait mode to use it. And thirdly, because of the placement of the connector and because the iPad is connected to the keyboard, you also need to make sure you're using the Keyboard Dock on a proper surface.

But if you get over these three things, there are some real plusses to using this combo. Primarily, the iPad can be charging while being used, because there's a rear dock connector port that allows you to plug in the USB cable.

Wireless Bluetooth® Keyboard

The Apple wireless keyboard uses Bluetooth, which makes it compatible with the iPad. Ahhh …

As much as I *don't* like the keyboard with the built-in dock, I really do like the wireless keyboard. I've had one for awhile and I use it with my laptop and iPad.

To use the Bluetooth keyboard with the iPad:

1. Turn on the iPad.
2. Tap "Settings."
3. Tap "General."
4. Tap "Bluetooth."
5. Slide the Bluetooth switch to ON.
6. Turn on the Bluetooth keyboard.
7. Wait until the iPad Bluetooth finds the Apple Keyboard.
8. Once the Keyboard is listed, tap to select.
9. Enter the code shown on the iPad using the keyboard to pair it.

TIP

Bluetooth devices need to "pair" with a host device, and the iPad is no exception. But if your keyboard is already paired to a different device, like a Macbook or iMac, it's a good idea to un-pair it before you try to pair it with the wireless Bluetooth keyboard.

Now you're all set. Just position the iPad up close to the keyboard and use it to enter info on the iPad. This makes it much easier to use Pages and Numbers.

The wireless keyboard costs $69.00 and can be used with other Apple computers if they have Bluetooth capability. Just keep in mind that having the Bluetooth on uses more power and will drain the battery of your iPad rather quickly.

STANDS

Apple doesn't make an iPad stand; instead, it sells the iPad Dock. Now I like to have the iPad on my desk, but I like the versatility of using both the portrait and landscape orientation. I also want a stand that allows the iPad to be plugged into a computer or charger, and I don't want to take it out of the case. The Compass stand from TwelveSouth is my solution. (Find it at **http://twelvesouth.com/ products/compass/**.)

I'm not saying this is the perfect stand for you or even the best stand on the market, but I love it. It accommodates the iPad in portrait and landscape orientation … inside the Apple case and with the USB cord plugged in. The stand also folds up really flat, making it easy for travel. The only problem I have is that the stand looks a little like a weapon, especially when folded, so I'm a little afraid I'll have it confiscated by airport security one day.

THE APPLE IPAD CASE

I need to make a confession here: I buy cases for my electronics, because I'm a bit clumsy. When I saw Steve Jobs present the iPad, I knew immediately that I would need a case for it. Luckily, Apple has me covered with the Apple iPad Case.

I ordered the case along with the iPad; and, honestly, I was a little disappointed when it arrived. It seemed to be rather thin and the edges were slightly uncomfortable. But after using it for a few weeks … and then a few months … I can't mentally envision any changes to it I'd want to make.

The case does exactly what it should. It stays out of the way when I'm using the iPad and, when closed, it protects the screen. I've seen some of the newer third-party covers and, while they all do a great job of protecting the device, they all add bulk that in my opinion diminishes the style of the iPad.

THE IPAD DOCK

All of the Apple iPods, iPhones and iPads have docks, and these docks allow the devices to be plugged in and remain upright. The iPad dock is no different. Here is the problem though: If you have an iPad case on your device, then the iPad won't fit into the dock. If you're planning to use the iPad as a digital picture frame, then you'll want to keep it plugged in and will need the dock … or a really good stand. And you'll need to forego the case.

THE POWER ADAPTER

When you got your iPad, it came with a 10W USB power adapter. This is necessary because the iPad needs a little more juice to recharge its battery. Go ahead and plug the iPad into your computer and chances are you'll see "Not Charging" on the top of the screen next to the battery symbol.

This is because older Macs and most PCs use a standard USB port, which doesn't supply enough power to run and recharge the iPad at the same time. You can get your iPad to

Tips from Apple on Extending Battery Life

- **Turn off Wi-Fi:** Tap on Settings > Wi-Fi and set Wi-Fi to "Off."

- **Turn off 3G:** Tap on Settings > Cellular and set Cellular Data to "Off."

- **Check fewer e-mail accounts:** Save power by checking fewer e-mail accounts. You can do this by turning off certain e-mail accounts or by deleting them. Tap on Settings > Mail, Contacts, Calendars. Pick an e-mail account, and set Account to "Off." To delete an account, tap Settings > Mail, Contacts, Calendars; pick an e-mail account; and tap "Delete Account."

- **Turn off push notifications:** To turn off push notifications, tap Settings > Notifications and set Notifications to "Off."

- **Fetch new data less frequently:** Mail can be set to fetch data at timed intervals. The more often that e-mail or other data is fetched, the faster your battery may drain. Tap Settings > Mail, Contacts, Calendars > Fetch New Data, and tap "Manually" to get the data only when you request it. Tap Settings > Mail, Contacts, Calendars > Fetch New Data and then tap a different (longer) time period if you want to continue getting the mail automatically. The longer the time period you set, the longer your battery life will be.

- **Turn off push mail:** Turn off push by tapping Settings > Mail, Contacts, Calendars > Fetch New Data. Set Push to "Off." E-mail will now be received only when you request it manually or during the timed-fetch commands.

- **Adjust screen brightness:** Your best bet here is to use auto brightness. The brightness commands are in Settings > Brightness & Wallpaper. This setting adjusts the screen's brightness according to the ambient light of the room it's in.

- **Minimize use of location services:** Certain applications use the iPad's location services, and this feature may reduce battery life. Tap Settings > General > Location Services to disable all location services.

- **Turn off push notifications:** Applications that use Push notifications can reduce battery life. To disable push notifications, tap Settings > Notifications and set Notifications to "Off."

One more note about getting the best life from your iPad battery: Apple suggests that you remove your iPad from any case when charging, especially if the iPad seems to get hot. You should also go through one complete charge cycle each month. What is a charge cycle? It's when you charge the iPad up to a full 100% and then run it down to zero … or close to it. One more thing: When the iPad isn't in use, put it to sleep by pressing the Sleep/ Wake button.

charge when attached to these computers by putting the iPad to sleep and making sure the computer is awake. This will charge the iPad, but it will do so about three times slower than when you do it with a direct power connection to the 10w power brick.

The best way to charge the iPad is with the supplied 10W charger; and if you take the iPad from home to work often, it's nice to have an extra charger. This optional charger accessory comes with a six-foot-long cord, so it's perfect for use in outlets that may be a little further away than your home outlets. I have one of these in my office, so I can plug in the iPad and charge it while I work.

SPEAKERS

The iPad uses a standard headphone jack, so there are tons of speaker options out there. My friend Scott turned me onto the iHome portable rechargeable iHM79BC speakers while we were working in Florida earlier this year. They are a tiny set of speakers that have some really great sound. They do not come with batteries, so they need to be recharged once in awhile through a USB cord. But turns out, they work great on a laptop and iPod as well.

One of the newer developments in iPad speakers is Apple's AirPlay. This technology is going to make it a snap to send the audio output from iTunes and the iPad to speakers on the same Wi-Fi network. So look for a whole slew of AirPlay-enabled speakers out there.

HEADPHONES

The headphone market is huge. New headsets are coming out every week … or is it every day? Either way, Apple has a couple of basic headphones that do a good job, but nothing special.

The real key to the Apple headphones is the remote control that's built into the cord. This gives you control over the iPod app on the iPad. But there are hundreds of headphones available, and dozens with the same on-cord functionality. Just pick a set that you like that's in your budget range.

For example, on the high end there are Sennheiser PXC 450 Travel headphones for $449.95 and the Bose® QuietComfort® Acoustic Noise Cancelling® headphones for $349.95. In the middle range are the Bose® Mobile in-ear headset for $116.95 and Scosche IDR305md Increased Dynamic Range Earphones with Remote and Microphone for $39.95 on the low end.

Headphones are especially useful if you plan to use your iPad on a plane or when you want to hear what's playing on your iPad, but the people around you don't.

THE CAMERA CONNECTION KIT

This is one of the more useful accessories for the iPad, especially if you take photos on a regular basis. These two little plastic pieces give you two ways to import your images to your iPad. You can import images directly from a SD card or use your camera's USB cable to your import images from the camera. The Camera Connection Kit is covered in Chapter 10.

IPAD DOCK CONNECTOR TO VGA ADAPTER

If you're going to give presentations from the iPad and need to attach it to a projector, then get this; otherwise don't. It will not mirror the iPad on the projector. Rather, it projects output from apps that allow it.

APPLE COMPOSITE CABLES & APPLE COMPONENT CABLES

These two sets of cables are great. They provide a way to project output from your iPad on a television. Now you can't get the TV to mirror your iPad, so if that's the goal, you're out of luck. But you can output certain things right to the TV, including the video content of your iPad and Netflix. I've tried this with HuluPlus and it doesn't work right now. It does work with Netflix though.

I have the Apple composite cables and I take them with me on the road. It's much more likely that the television in a hotel room will have external composite inputs than component inputs. So I can plug the cables in and watch whatever movies I have loaded on my iPad on the room television. As a bonus feature, the cables have a plug and a charger that allows me to charge the iPad with the same cables. That's a win-win as far as I'm concerned.

APPLE TV

I know that the Apple TV isn't technically an iPad accessory, but hear me out. You might think of it in a new way.

There are two reasons that the Apple TV and iPad go together so well. The first is that the iPad is the best remote control for the Apple TV ever. It's actually the best remote for your iTunes ever, too. The free remote app from Apple allows you to control all aspects of the Apple TV. You can rent movies and TV shows, control playback and use the keyboard instead of the supplied Apple TV remote.

You can also control your iTunes library and output the music to the built-in Apple TV speakers.

The other … and better … reason to have the Apple TV listed here is that with AirPlay, the content from your iPad can be streamed to play on the Apple TV. So if you have the iPad, I just gave you a great reason to go out and pick up the $99 Apple TV. Now if only I could get a kickback from Apple…

One word of warning, the Apple TV requires a TV or receiver with HDMI inputs. Older TVs without HDMI will not work with the Apple TV.

APPENDIX II

iOS: The iPad
Operating System

The iPad, like all the portable devices that Apple makes, runs on a special Operating System (OS) called iOS. When the iPad shipped, it was running a version of iOS3. This book was written using iPads that were running iOS3.2.2; yet things will be changing soon, because Apple has released iOS4.2.

The new upgrade adds functionality to the iPad that has been available for the iPhone 4 since its initial release. The new features will make it even easier to use the iPad.

When iOS4.2 is released, it will mark the first time that all of the iOS devices will be on the same operating system. This means that the iPad, iPhone and iPod Touch will all be at the same place—technology-wise—at the same time … for the first time.

But it's important to keep in mind that these changes don't actually mean much when it comes to getting most types of content on the iPad. And many of the changes don't technically affect the way that content is used on the iPad. But there are some really fun changes.

MULTITASKING … SORT OF

The idea behind multitasking is run multiple programs at the same time. And, more importantly, switch between programs that are running without fully exiting any of them.

There are definite advantages to multitasking. Among them are listening to audio while you do other tasks and printing while enjoying other programs on your iPad.

Switching between apps on iOS4.2 and later is easy. Just double click on the Home button to bring up the recently launched apps. From there, just tap on the app you want to open, and it instantly reloads right from where you left off.

So, in practical terms, you can be reading a book in iBooks and then quickly double click on the Home button, open the Mail app, and check the new unified inbox in iOS 4.2 Mail. Then, just double click the Home button, tap on iBooks again and you're right where you left off. It's just a lot of tapping.

The downside to multitasking is that the more apps that are running, the quicker your battery will drain. Apple has taken this into account and only allows certain apps to multitask. Only those that have been developed specifically to take advantage of the limited multitasking can do it.

For example, Pandora can run in the background and still receive and play music while you check your e-mail or read a book. Other apps are fully suspended in a sleep mode and don't actually continue running when you switch to a different app. These sleeping apps don't use the battery any more than they do when turned off.

AIRPRINT

With the release of iOS4, the iPad is now able to print wirelessly. This is a great advantage for those of us who do actual work on the iPad, because now we can edit a document and print it without having to get the file onto a regular computer first.

There are some limitations though. The most critical is that the printer needs to be on the same Wi-Fi network as your iPad, for obvious reasons.

I use a wireless printer in my home office. It works great, and the best part is that I can print from any of my computers no matter where they are in the house. It doesn't need any wires. The same thing will be true when working with the iPad. iOS4 will allow me to select a range of pages to print and pick single or double-sided printing if the printer supports it.

The AirPrint capabilities are tied to the multitasking capability of the iOS and the iDevice. The Print Center is available by tapping the Home button twice. AirPrint runs in the background (hence the need for the multitasking), and there is just one Print Center that controls all the printing from all the apps on the iPad. Doesn't matter if you are printing an e-mail message or a Word document from Pages, the single Print Center deals with all the printing from the iPad.

Apple has announced that the iPad and AirPrint will be supported on a number of HP printers that support ePrint technology … without needing any additional software. We'll see.

One thing I'm sure of: The longer that AirPrint is available, the more printers that support it will be available.

IPAD E-MAIL

One of the biggest improvements to the iPad with iOS4.2 is the new and improved Mail program. This is especially true if you have more than one account.

The new unified inbox feature allows a user to see all the incoming messages in one place no matter what e-mail account (s)he uses. I have a lot of mail accounts, and this single feature alone will save me a ton of time.

Another new e-mail feature is that messages can be organized in threads so it will be much easier to follow e-mail conversations.

FOLDERS

The ability to group apps into folders is something so simple, but makes a HUGE difference in the way I'll use my iPad. I have approximately 140 apps on my iPad, and they are spread out over nine pages. Many times it takes me longer to find an app than it does for me to do the task on it. There are just so many of them.

Folders will allow you to group apps together. So, instead of nine pages, I'll have everything on two pages. With a 20-app capacity per folder, you can have a News folder that contains all your news apps and a Games folder … or two.

And you can name the folders anything you want and move them around, so your folders are sorted and identifiable in a way that helps you use you iPad.

Another benefit to this is that although there has never been a limit per se to the amount of apps you could install on your iPad, previous to iOS 4.x, you could only display 180 of them over the multiple screens. With iOS 4.x, you are almost unlimited in the number of displayable apps—assuming that 2,160 apps can be considered "unlimited." For most, it should be more capacity than you'll ever actually need, so I think *unlimited* is a safe word choice.

AIRPLAY

The AirPlay feature of iOS4.2 is definitely one of the coolest things I have ever seen. It allows you to stream the audio and video content of your iPad to devices like the new Apple TV and other AirPlay-enabled devices. If you are playing a movie or TV show on the iPad, just tapping the AirPlay button allows you to stream the movie to the big screen through the Apple TV.

JAIL BREAKING THE IPAD

When covering any of the iProducts… iPhone, iPad, iPod, etc … we need to talk about jail breaking. There are a lot of people out there who believe that Apple shouldn't be allowed to control the iPad the way it does. They love the concept of jail breaking, because it interrupts that control.

If you jail break your iPad, you can download apps that do not go through the Apple approval process, and you can do things Apple doesn't allow. Those who used the jail breaking process on their iPads were able to multitask before Apple released iOS 4.2. They can also access non-Apple apps.

Sounds great, right? Well, there's a downside. It's this: Since the non-Apple apps don't go through the Apple approval process, they can harm your iPad. And while it might not happen, it's possible these apps will brick your iPad—that is, cause it to not work at all.

Also, by jail breaking your iPad, you void the Apple warrantee. So if something goes wrong, Apple won't fix it. You also block your own access to any software updates Apple may release for your device.

So let me be clear: I do not suggest that you jail break your iPad. Why would you want to? I looked … and I couldn't find one thing that a jail broken iPad could do that the regular iPad couldn't. So what's the deal? Just enjoy this amazing device as it is.

APPS LIST

I try to keep the number of apps on my iPad down to a reasonable number, but it's really difficult. The apps covered in this book were all purchased by me; I received none of the apps for free, except for those that are free for everyone. Here is a list of apps covered in this book along with the price I paid for them.

ABC Player	ABC Digital	Free
ABC News	ABC Digital	Free
Airfoil speaker	Rouge Amoeba Software LLC	Free
App store	Apple	Free (preloaded)
AP News	The Associated Press	Free
Atomic Web	Richard Trautvetter	$0.99
Audiogalaxy	AG Entertainment	Free
BBC news	BBC Worldwide LTD	Free
Bento	Filemaker	$4.99
Boom!	comiXology	Free (Price for comic issues varies.)
Calendars	Apple	Free (preloaded)
CloudReaders	Satoshi Nakajima	Free
CNN	CNN Interactive Group	$1.99
Contacts	Apple	Free (preloaded)
Comic Strips	Reilly Watson	$0.99
Comic Zeal	Bitolithic Pty Ltd	$7.99
Comics	comiXology	Free (Price for comic issues varies.)
Comics+	iVerse Media	Free (Price for comic issues varies.)
DC	DC Comics	Free (Price for comic issues varies.)
Dropbox	Dropbox	Free
Early Edition	Glasshouse Apps Pty Ltd.	$0.99
Evernote	Evernote	Free
EyeTV	Elgato Systems	$4.99 – requires EyeTV device

FileMaker Go	Filemaker	$39.99
Filterstorm 2	Tai Shimizu	$3.99
Flipboard	Flipboard Inc	Free
Foliobook	Paul R W Freeman	$7.99
GoodReader	Good.iWare Ltd.	$1.99
HanDBase	DDH Software Inc.	$9.99
Hulu Plus	Hulu LLC	Free app

(requires $9.99/ monthly subscription)

iBooks	Apple	Free
iCab	Alexander Clauss	$1.99
Instapaper	Macro Arment	$4.99
iPod	Apple	Free (preloaded)
iTunes	Apple	Free (preloaded)
Keynote	Apple	$9.99
Kindle	Amazon	Free
Last.fm	Last.fm	Free
Mail	Apple	Free (preloaded)
Mariner Calc	Mariner Software Inc.	$5.99
Marvel	Marvel Entertainment	Free (Price for comic issues varies.)
Mercury	iLegendSoft Inc.	$0.99
Netflix	Netflix Inc.	Free (requires Netflix subscription)
Nook	Barnes & Noble	Free
Notes	Apple	Free (preloaded)
Numbers	Apple	$9.99
Pages	Apple	$9.99
Pandora	Pandora Media	Free
Photos	Apple	Free (preloaded)
Photo transfer	ERCLab	$2.99
Photoshop Express	Adobe Systems	Free
Popular Science	Bonnier Corporation	$4.99 with current issue

$2.99 for back issues

Portfolio	Britton Photography	$14.99
Pulse	Alphonso Labs Inc.	$1.99
Safari	Apple	Free (preloaded)
Slingbox	Sling Media	$29.99 (requires Slingbox)
Sports Illustrated	Time Inc.	Free app - $4.99 or $5.99/ issue
Stanza	Lexcycle	Free
Things	Cultured Code	$19.99
Time	Time Inc.	Free app - $4.99/ issue
Todo	Appigo Inc.	$4.99
USA Today	USA Today	Free
Video	Apple	Free (preloaded)
Wired	Condé Nast Digital	Free app - $3.99/ issue
Zenbe Lists	Zenbe Inc.	$3.99
Zinio	Zinio LLC..	Free

(Pricing varies for different titles.)

273

INDEX